Webb Society Deep-Sky Observer's Handbook

Volume 4
Galaxies

Compiled by the Webb Society
Edited by Kenneth Glyn Jones, F.R.A.S.
Written and Illustrated by Edmund S. Barker, F.R.A.S.

With a foreword by Professor Halton Arp
(Mount Wilson and Las Campanas Observatories)

Enslow Publishers
Hillside, New Jersey 07205

Lutterworth Press
Guildford and London

1981

Library of Congress Cataloging in Publication Data:

Webb Society deep-sky observer's handbook.

First published under title: The Webb Society
observers handbook.
Includes—Bibliographies.
Contents: v. 1. Double stars—v. 2. Planetary, and
gaseous nebulae—v. 3. Open and Globular Clusters.
—v.4. Galaxies.
1. Astronomy—Observers' manuals. I. Jones,
Kenneth Glyn. II. Webb Society.

QB64.W36 1979   522   77-359099
In the U.S.A. ISBN 0-89490-050-1 (vol.4)
In the U.K.   ISBN 7188 2527 6 (vol.4)

Manufactured in the United States of America

10 9 8 7 6 5 4 3 2 1

To Professor Halton Arp,
unrivaled explorer of galaxies,
with gratitude and respect.

CONTENTS

List of Illustrations   ix
Foreword   xi
General Preface to the Handbook   xiii
Preface to Volume 4: Galaxies   xv

            PART ONE: Properties of Galaxies
Introduction and Historical Review   1
1. Classification of Galaxies   7
2. Distribution of Galaxies   21
3. Formation and Evolution of Galaxies   25
4. Gaseous and Stellar Content of Galaxies   31
5. Nuclei of Galaxies   35
6. Seyferts, QSO's and Related Objects   37
7. Interacting and Peculiar Galaxies   43
8. Catalogues of Galaxies   51
9. Observation of Galaxies   53

    PART TWO
A Catalogue of Galaxies   67
Drawings of 156 Galaxy Fields   158

    PART THREE
List of Additional Objects   197
    Interacting and Peculiar Galaxies   198
    Seyfert Galaxies   203
    Variable Extragalactic Sources   207

    APPENDICES
1. Emission Regions in M33   215
2. Emission Regions in NGC 6822   217
3. The Distances of Galaxies   219
4. Non-Velocity Redshifts   221
5. Examples of Arp's Peculiar Galaxies   223
6. Further Drawings of Galaxies   225
7. Faint Systems near NGC Galaxies   231
8. Photographic Sources   233
9. Bibliography   235

List of Illustrations

Wolf's Classification of Galaxies   8

Hubble's Tuning-Fork Diagram   9

Sandage's Box Diagram   11

Two Examples of Van den Bergh's Luminosity Classification   14

Four Examples of Vorontsov-Velyaminov's Classification   15

Arrangement of Arp's Peculiar Galaxies   20

Distribution of Galaxies with m_{pg} 15.0 - 15.7   24

Star Distribution in M33   27

Two Examples of Smooth-Arm Galaxies   30

21-cm Radio Emission in NGC 6822   32

Boundaries of Radio Emission in NGC 5128   38

Synchrotron Radiation   39

NGC 5128 in Ultraviolet Light   44

Composite Photograph of M51   46

Model of the Tidal Encounter in M51   47

NGC 4038-9   48

The Ring Galaxy A0035   49

Model of the Formation of Ring Galaxies   50

Intensity Gradients of Edge-on and Face-on Galaxies   55

Surface Brightness Measures in NGC 1569   56

Surface Brightness Measures in A1009   56

Emission Regions in NGC 2403   61

Six Examples of Zwicky Compact Galaxies   63

Finding Charts for Mkn 335, NGC 262, Mkn 352
            NGC 449, Mkn 372, Mkn 3   204

Finding Charts for IC 450, Mkn 374, Mkn 10
            Mkn 382, NGC 2691, Mkn 315   205

Finding Chart for 3C 390.3   206

Finding Chart for BW Tau (3C I20)   208

Finding Chart for OJ 287   209

Finding Chart for W Com   210

Finding Chart for X Com   211

Finding Chart for AP Lib   212

Finding Chart for 3C 371   213

Finding Chart for BL Lac   214

NGC, IC and Other Emission Regions in M33   215

Four Brightest Emission Regions in NGC 6822   217

Spectrum of 3C 273   220

Non-equilibrium No. 3   222

NGC 523 (Arp 158), NGC 2608 (Arp 12), NGC 2782 (Arp 215)
NGC 3432 (Arp 206), NGC 3445 (Arp 24), NGC 3718 (Arp 214)   223

NGC 4618 (Arp 23), NGC 4676 (Arp 242), NGC 5665 (Arp 49)
NGC 5929-30 (Arp 90), NGC 7603 (Arp 92), NGC 7678 (Arp 28)   224

FOREWORD

We are all aware that galaxies are the fundamental building
blocks of the universe – the material particles that fill the
volume of the universe. But unlike electrons and protons, which
will form a gas of all identical particles, each galaxy is
different from all other galaxies. Naturally there are broadly
different types of galaxies, but even the reasons why spiral
galaxies are spiral and elliptical galaxies are elliptical are
still not well understood. In actual fact an enormous range of
filaments, jets, explosions, deformation, multiplicities,
dispersions, concentrations, colours, contents and various other
differences go into characterizing this class of object we call
galaxies. To me, one fundamental mystery is why do galaxies show
such an enormous range of characteristics.

At first it was hoped that by simple starting assumptions, a
hot primeval medium of all identical protons and electrons, one
could condense the galaxies into the different forms we see. It
was investigated whether different-sized lumps, spinning with
different amounts of angular momentum, would condense and evolve
into the various kinds of giants, dwarfs, spherical and flat
galaxies we observe. It was really an excercise in extending the
terrestrial physics we know out to understanding the universe.
But basic questions such as why are some galaxies presently
forming stars and others not forming stars, have proved difficult.
Perhaps the greatest difficulty has arisen from the evidence of
internal activity in galaxies. In the 1940's radio astronomy
showed for the first time that many galaxies ejected excited
gases from their nuclei. In 1957 it was realised that luminous
matter was ejected from galaxies. From the 1960's onward it
became evident that there were enormously compact concentrations
of radiant energy called quasars in the universe, and that they
had some relation to another kind of galaxy which has a very
concentrated, active nucleus.

In the search for a unifying physical principle from which a
natural explanation for various galaxy forms will flow, a certain
tension has been set up between various researchers and schools
of thought. The competition between these different interpret-
ations of observations is healthy, in that all conclusions are
tested and challenged and new observations and new concepts
are stimulated.

Difference and cross-differences exist on many levels, but the
broadest division of opinion which I see in the interpretation of
galaxies is the following: Many astronomers wish to start from a
galaxy which condenses out of the primeval medium and using only
the known laws of gravitation, nucleosynthesis and radiation,
build all the forms and phenomena we see in galaxies. They use
processes like stellar birth and death, recycling of interstellar

medium, black holes and galaxy collisions to build models of
all the phenomena we observe. A smaller group of astronomers
wonder if galaxies are giving us evidence of new laws and
processes in the universe. Are there such things as white
holes, creation of matter, non-velocity redshifts and origin
of galaxies from compact bodies? As an illustration of how various
researchers view things differently we might discuss "peculiar"
galaxies for a moment. An astronomer of the majority school
would view a perturbed or distorted galaxy as a galaxy in
collision with another, as an opportunity to construct models
of gravitationally-entrained stellar structures and gravitationally induced excited gas. An astronomer of the second kind would
view all this as possible evidence for an internal explosion, a
recent internal fissioning or the ejection of material in little-
known states.

Now I think all sides will admit that some galaxies are undergoing collision and normal gravitational mechanics will explain
their contorted forms. Most astronomers, on the other hand, will
also well admit that some other galaxies are showing enormous
internal activity, ejecting material and exhibiting puzzling
expansions.

The fact that examples of both kinds of galaxy activity are
abundant and that they cannot be explained wholly by one approach
or the other, does not mean that the basic tension between the
two schools is resolved. The basic question still remains
unanswered: Can the observed phenomena in galaxies be totally
explained with conventional physical mechanisms? If there is
even one galaxy which can incontovertibly demonstrate the
operation of a new, or as yet unknown, physical law, then
astronomy would have led human beings to a deeper and fuller
understanding of the universe than physics has been able to.
This perhaps illuminates the reason why some astronomers work so
diligently on the observation and analysis of various exotic
objects in the panoply of galaxy forms. It must also explain why
many a non-specialist looks at the enormously varied forms of
galaxies and thinks to himself - "I wonder what is really going
on there?"

Halton Arp

General Preface

Named after the Rev. T.W. Webb (1807-1885), an eminent amateur astronomer and author of the classic Celestial Objects for Common Telescopes, the Webb Society exists to encourage the study of double stars and deep-sky objects. It has members in almost every country where amateur astronomy flourishes. It has a number of sections, each under a director with wide experience in the particular field, the main ones being double stars, nebulae and clusters, minor planets, supernova watch and astrophotography. Publications include a Quarterly Journal containing articles and special features, book reviews and section reports that cover the society's activities. Membership is open to anyone whose interests are compatible. Application forms and answers to queries are available from Dr. G.S. Whiston, Secretary, Webb Society, C.E.R.L., Kelvin Avenue, Leatherhead, Surrey, England.

Webb's Celestial Objects for Common Telescopes, first published in 1859, must have been among the most popular books of its kind ever written. Running through six editions by 1917, it is still in print although the text is of more historical than practical interest to the amateur of today. Not only has knowledge of the universe been transformed by modern developments, but the present generation of amateur astronomers has telescopes and other equipment that even the professional of Webb's day would have envied.

The aim of the new Webb Society Deep-Sky Observer's Handbook is to provide a series of observer's manuals that do justice to the equipment that is available today and to cover fields that have not been adequately covered by other organisations of amateurs. We have tried to make these guides the best of their kind: they are written by experts, some of them professional astronomers, who have had considerable practical experience with the pleasures and problems of the amateur astronomer. The manuals can be used profitably by beginners, who will find much to stimulate their enthusiasm and imagination. However, they are designed primarily for the more experienced amateur who seeks greater scope for the exercise of his skills.

Each handbook is complete with regard to its subject. The reader is given an adequate historical and theoretical basis for a modern understanding of the physical role of the objects covered in the wider context of the universe. He is provided with a thorough exposition of observing methods, including the construction and operation of ancillary equipment such as micrometers and simple spectroscopes. Each volume contains a detailed and comprehensive catalogue of objects for the amateur to locate and to observe with an eye made more perceptive by the knowledge he has gained.

We hope that these volumes will enable the reader to extend his abilities, to exploit his telescope to its limit, and to tackle the challenging difficulties of new fields of observation with confidence of success.

Editor's Preface
Volume 4: Galaxies

This volume really takes us into the realms of deep-sky objects: extra-galactic observation, by definition, extends one's vision to the widest horizons of space, and at the same time transports us, like time travellers, millions of years into the past. That the amateur astronomer can observe so many distant and diverse forms of galaxies – the elemental 'building blocks' of the universe at large – is both challenging and encouraging.

In many fields of astronomy we are on the threshold of new discoveries of the greatest significance. Most of this lies in the domain of high technology: – observations made by orbiting observatories, by large-aperture optical and radio telescopes, and by sophisticated (and expensive) methods of detecting gravity-waves or neutrino particles. For the amateur with a modest aperture telescope, however, the galaxies are still accessible, and with the practical and theoretical knowledge which modern professional astronomy has made available, he can observe them with an eye much more informed than ever before.

It is the purpose of this volume to make the observation of galaxies by the amateur astronomer as profitable and enjoyable as possible. The reader is provided with a comprehensive and up-to-date text covering the classification, distribution and evolution of galaxies, together with appropriate information on their physical condition. In addition, some of the more esoteric systems such as 'peculiar' and 'interacting' galaxies, radio-galaxies and quasars are described. Finally, a thoroughly practical guide to the observation of all types of galaxies is given for the amateur to follow.

All this detailed text serves to introduce the comprehensive catalogue of somw 275 selected objects, itself supplanted by 156 telescope drawings made by members of the Webb Society during the last 12 years. This form of presentation follows the well-tried method used in previous volumes of this series, and has been favourably commented upon both by reviewers and experienced amateur observers. We hope that this volume will be similarly well-received, since it represents the combined efforts of a number of skilled and dedicated observing members of the Society, to whom the Editor unhesitatingly pays the highest tribute.

The collation and presentation of all this diverse material has once again been undertaken by the Director of the Nebulae and Clusters Section, Edmund Barker, FRAS, who has written all of the text, barring the historical reviews, compiled the catalogues and lists and supplied the numerous illustrations. His has been an immense labour, but it has been a labour of love, for he is an amateur astronomer both in the literal meaning of

the term and in keeping with its highest tradition. Amateur
astronomy in general, and the Webb Society in particular, have
reason to appreciate his experience, skill and devotion: the
Editor's debt is no less, and is gratefully acknowledged.

As before, our Publications Officer, Eddie Moore, has maintained
a watchful eye in proof-reading and vetting, especially in the
final stages of production, and our thanks are due for his
invaluable help at all times.

We are pleased to acknowledge, also, the encouraging support
and expertise of Ridley M. Enslow, Jr., President of Enslow
Publishers, who has contributed so greatly to the success of this
series.

Finally, we wish to express our warmest appreciation to
Professor H.C. Arp for doing us the signal honour of accepting the
dedication of this volume, and for compounding this by generously
contributing a Foreword. In the realm of galaxies, Professor Arp
can claim much territory that is peculiarly his own (if the pun
may be condoned) and the kind appreciation of our modest efforts
by one so eminent in the field commands our deepest respect.

Author's Acknowedgements.

The author is grateful to the Editor, Kenneth Glyn Jones, for
applying his knowledge of the history of astronomy to the
historical review. Dr. Alar Toomre of the Massachusetts Institute
of Technology proved a stimulating correspondent, while Robert
Argyle and other staff members of the Royal Greenwich Observatory
generously applied themselves to supplying data and processing
photographs. Thanks are also due to the numerous astronomers who
allowed reproductions of their work to be used and submitted
relevant photographs. Much of the research for this volume was
undertaken at the Royal Greenwich Observatory, the Royal
Astronomical Society and University College London. The author
expresses his thanks to the Leverhulme Research Awards Committee
for a research grant to aid in the compilation of this volume.

PART ONE: Properties of Galaxies

INTRODUCTION AND HISTORICAL REVIEW

INTRODUCTION.

The subject of this volume is <u>galaxies</u>, and following a natural and logical pattern in our series of observing <u>Handbooks</u> we arrive at a kind of synthesis in which all the subjects of the preceding volumes are incorporated.

Galaxies are visible in a wide variety of instruments from binoculars upwards, and although little detail can be made out in small telescopes, such objects have always had a particular fascination for visual observers. Most of the 'popular' galaxies, such as those in Messier's catalogue, are observed by all amateurs at one time or another, but this rather limited approach tends to omit a considerable number of galaxies which are not particularly difficult to reach with moderate telescopes. It is the purpose of this volume to enlarge the amateur's scope in this field, and the reader will find many lesser-known galaxies featured in the catalogue section, while for those who desire to progress further still, additional lists of some more unusual - and interesting - objects have been prepared. This volume, it should be noted, covers single and double galaxies, as well as objects comprising small, loose groups. Galaxies in groups of small angular size and large clusters will be treated separately in a succeeding <u>Handbook</u>, Volume 5 (Clusters of Galaxies).

Regardless of the instrument he uses, the visual observer will always wish to make out as much detail as possible. When we recall that spiral structure in galaxies was first detected only with the use of a 72-inch reflector. it may be thought futile to attempt to observe such features in very much smaller telescopes. That this is not the case has been proved over and over again, for structure in spiral and irregular galaxies can be seen with apertures as small as 8 or even 6-inches.

In this volume we have maintained a twofold purpose; to show the wide range of galaxies observed by Webb Society members, and to indicate the variety of lesser-known galaxies awaiting visual observation - objects not listed in <u>Atlas Coeli</u>, the standard amateur source. Our sizeable list includes both very easy and quite difficult objects to observe. In the Webb Society, our records contain some few hundred galaxies which have been observed with telescopes up to 60-inches in aperture. but of course, our object is to cater for observers who operate in the more common 6 to 10-inch range. However, these comparatively large-aperture obser-vations are extremely useful, for one of the greatest challenges in observing is finding out how much detail one can make out with one's own telescope and comparing it with the results of others with superior instrumentation. Such exercises are valuable for training

Introduction and Historical Review

the eye, and for this purpose there are no better objects to utilize
than the wide range of galaxies in all their different forms.

Finally a note is necessary regarding those sections of the text
concerned with the properties of galaxies. The literature on the
subject is vast and is accreting at a rapid rate, so we can give
only a cursory survey of this field. Readers will find that generous
space has been given to galaxy classification, while aspects of
evolutionary theory have been only briefly treated. As classification
systems are primarily morphological, we feel that the amateur
observer will find this approach more rewarding. In each field of
galaxy research, however, an adequate bibliography has been provided
for those whose interests may lie in the realms of evolution,
formation and dynamics of these great extragalactic systems.

HISTORICAL REVIEW.

The history of the observation of extragalactic systems is long
and venerable, but it was not until 1924 that the nearest and
brightest spiral nebula, M31 in Andromeda, was proved beyond dispute
to be external to the Galaxy. The subject is thus decidedly confusing
in many ways, and it will be useful to consider the matter in two
distinct aspects; a) Pure Observation, and b) Theory.

Observation.

The Great Nebula in Andromeda is clearly visible to the naked
eye in dark skies and must have been noticed, and even commented
upon, in prehistoric times. However, the first recorded observation
of this notable object was the one given by the Persian astronomer
Abd-al-rahman al-Sufi in his Book of the Fixed Stars in AD 954 where
he described it as 'a little cloud' near the star nu Andromedae.
Strangely there is no mention of the Andromeda Nebula in the star-
catalogues published subsequent to that of Al-Sufi, and the next
account we have of it was not until 1614, when Simon Marius published
his controversial Mundus Jovialis. Marius seems to have rediscovered
the nebula using an early version of the telescope on December 15,
1612: he described it as shining 'with a whitish light which is
emitted more brightly at the centre, where there is a pale and
blurred glow, about a quarter of a degree in diameter. It somewhat
resembles the light of a burning candle, shining through translucent
horn, when seen at night from afar.'

The only other extragalactic systems which had been observed up to
this time were the two Magellanic Clouds, which had been noticed and
briefly described by Dutch navigators in about 1520, but being even
brighter and more conspicuous than M31, they too must have been known
to southern hemisphere inhabitants of the earliest times.

The first true telescopic discovery of a new extragalactic system

Introduction and Historical Review.

was made on October 29, 1749 by the French astronomer G - J le Gentil, when he came upon the nearer companion of the Andromeda Nebula, which later became catalogued as M32, and which he described as 'about one minute in diameter, which appeared to throw out two small rays, one to the right and one to the left.' Le Gentil can thus be credited with the first known discovery of an extragalactic object, although, of course, he was not aware of the significance of his feat. (The other companion to the Andromeda Nebula, NGC 205 (M110) was first observed by Messier in 1773, and Caroline Herschel made an independent discovery in 1783).

The Abbé N - L de la Caille was the next discoverer of an extra-galactic nebula, when during his remarkably productive one-man expedition to the Cape of Good Hope in 1751-2, he came upon 'a small formless nebulosity' in Hydra. This object, (No. 6 in La Caille's list of 'First class nebulae') was later catalogued as M83 by Messier: it has recently gained the distinction of having produced, along with NGC 6946, more supernovae (four up to 1968) than any other galaxy.

Within the next 30 years the number of galaxies discovered increased much more rapidly, many of them being ferreted out by that assiduous comet-hunter, Charles Messier. Of the 36 galaxies listed in Messier's catalogue (described, of course, merely as 'Nebulae') Messier himself was the first discoverer of 11 of them: his colleague, Pierre Méchain, 17; J.E. Bode, 3: J.G. Koehler, 2 and B. Oriani, 1.

Thereafter, with the deep-sky penetration of William Herschel, new discoveries of extragalactic objects were made in their hundreds. However, not even that prodigious observer was able to perceive any clear distinction between purely gaseous (galactic) nebulae and the irresolvable extragalactic nebulae (galaxies). The first significant classification on these lines had to await the application of the spectroscope to astronomy by that remark-able pioneer, William Huggins, who in 1864, separated the 'green' emission-line gaseous from the 'white', continuous-spectrum nebulae. A little before this, in 1845, the third Earl Rosse had observed distinct spiral structure in M51 and this unique feature was soon perceived in a few other nebulae.

Further developments in this direction came with the application of celestial photography, especially by Isaac Roberts, who in 1880 was the first to demonstrate that M31 was a 'spiral nebula seen in perspective'. The episode of the 'new star', S And., (actually a supernova) in this same nebula in 1885, although a bewildering phenomenon at the time, gave a post-dated clue to its extragalactic origin. However, it was to be another 40 years before Hubble,

Introduction and Historical Review

Ritchey and Duncan, working at the limits of the 60-inch, and later
the 100-inch telescopes at Mt. Wilson, were able, through the study
of ordinary novae and Cepheid variables in M31 and M33, to
demonstrate that these nebulae lay at distances far outside the
environs of the Galaxy. Thus, in 1924, the scale of the Universe
suddenly expanded in the minds of men, and in another five years
or so Humason and Hubble were to reveal that the Universe was
physically expanding too. With these climactic events, the study of
galaxies as such became truly significant at last, and modern
cosmology began.

Theory.

    Cosmology, the study of the Universe as a whole, can be said to
have remained largely in the realms of myth and folk-lore until the
18th century, when it attained what can be looked upon as a state
of reasoned speculation. Naturally, conceptions of extragalactic
systems had to wait upon the idea of the organization and entity of
the Galaxy itself, and it is Thomas Wright of Durham who is
generally credited with the exposition of the form of the Milky
Way as a 'grind-stone' shaped disc of stars having the Sun at its
centre. However, Wright's Original Theory of 1750 has more
recently been shown to be more of a mystical or religious concept
than a scientific one, and it was William Herschel, some 30 years
later, who put forward a more reasoned 'structure of the heavens'.
Nevertheless, it was upon Wright's idea that the German philosopher,
Immanuel Kant, built his amazingly fruitful conception. In 1755
Kant postulated that many of the nebulae to be observed in the
heavens were distant 'Milky-ways' like our own stellar system, and
furthermore, that these 'milky-ways' were themselves organised
into super-associations. This concept of island universes - as they
were later described by Humboldt - and their multiple grouping into
what we now observe as clusters of galaxies was a remarkable example
of prophetic vision - and that is all. Kant claimed that his
hypothesis was based upon actual observation of various 'spindle-
shaped' nebulae, observations made by the French scientist Maupertuis
who had suggested in 1742 that these objects were ellipsoidal bodies
formed by rotation. None of the objects observed or quoted by
Maupertuis - with the exception of the Andromeda Nebula - were extragalactic objects at all, but objects such as M13 and M22 (globular
clusters) and sundry asterisms.

    The erroneous basis of Kant's theory is underlined by the fact
that he pointed out that 'these species of nebulous stars ... have
a very near relation to the plane of the Milky Way' - a region which
constituted a 'zone of avoidance' for later observers of galaxies.
Despite this, the island universe concept was sustained, with various
vicissitudes, during the next 150 years. The beginning of the 20th

Introduction and Historical Review

Century, however, saw the astronomical world deeply divided as to the status of the 'white' and spiral nebulae, an argument which culminated in the so-called 'Great Debate' on the <u>Scale of the Universe</u> between H.D. Curtis and Harlow Shapley in 1921. Curtis held that the Galaxy was comparatively small (about 17,000 light years in diameter) and that the spiral nebulae were truly extra-galactic at distances of 500,000 light years and upwards. Shapley held contrary views on both points: he estimated from the observed distribution of globular clusters that the Galaxy was much larger (300,000 light years in diameter) than most other astronomers accepted, and that the spiral nebulae were probably part of it. We can see that the 'Great Debate', although largely inconclusive, served to sharpen the issues involved: meanwhile, several mis-leading issues, such as the phenomenal brilliance of S Andromedae in M31 in 1885 (the existence of supernovae) and the rapid rotational values found by Van Maanen in some face-on spirals (erroneous) had to be disposed of. All these difficulties, as we have seen, were swept away in the next few years by Hubble and his colleagues: Shapley's estimates for the dimensions of the Galaxy were reduced but substantially correct, while Curtis' scale for the extragalactic distances of the spirals was upheld. At the same time the theoretical conceptions for an unstable (expanding) Universe, implied in Einstein's Relativity theory, and codified by Jeans and Eddington, were also observed and quantified by the Mt. Wilson astronomers.

Since these comparatively recent, epoch-making days our astronomical horizons have widened enormously, and there can be little doubt that the study of galaxies, in all their varied aspects, will continue to be as rewarding and as exciting in the future as it has been in the past.

1. CLASSIFICATION OF GALAXIES.

INTRODUCTION.

Galaxy classification is a subject to which amateur astronomers often feel drawn, as, with suitable apertures, some indication of the basic classes can be determined (elliptical, spiral, irregular) although extreme detail is, of course, detectable only by photographs taken by large telescopes.

The prime requisite of any classification system is that it be neither too complex nor too simple; in short, it should present in a cogent fashion such basic differences evinced by the source material, which, in the present case, consists of photographs. Astronomy is in a state of perpetual development, and in the past the classification of galaxies has shown a similar progress, but, while other fields of astronomy are nowhere near their termini, it is probably correct to say that galaxy classification has now achieved an ideal state in the de Vaucouleurs extension of the Hubble system.

Beyond the classification scheme of de Vaucouleurs there are other classes of galaxies including Seyfert, cD and N galaxies, peculiar systems, luminosity classes and detailed descriptions of galaxy images as shown on the Palomar Sky Survey prints.

At first sight, therefore, it may seem that we are now presented with an almost overwhelming array of different galaxy types, but in fact the majority of all types still fall within the classification of de Vaucouleurs, which is applicable to at least 95% of known galaxies.

Pre-Hubble Classifications.

The optimum classification of galaxies was not possible until the development of astronomical photography, yet before this era the system devised by William Herschel encompassed many galaxies, these fitting into his classes I, II, III and IV. Herschel's scheme used brightness as a classification criterion, but, regardless of the quality of Herschel's telescopes, it was left to the 72-inch reflector of Lord Rosse to show spiral structure in some systems.

Once photography had reached a suitable level, the detailed structure of many galaxies became available for study. For example, a great deal of structure in galaxies is to be seen on photographs taken by Isaac Roberts between 1885 and 1904, although Roberts made no attempt to use his plates for the purposes of classification.

The first serious classification of galaxies was developed by Wolf, who, in 1908, produced a system based upon photographs taken at Heidelberg. In this scheme planetary nebulae were also included,

Classification of Galaxies.

but if these are removed from Wolf's categories quite a thorough
spread in galaxy types remains. Notably, distinction is made between
galaxies with no spiral features and those with arms of varying
intensity and degree of resolution. The Wolf system, minus planetary
nebulae, is shown in Figure 1, while examples of some galaxies shown
in the figure are: (l) NGC 4914; (m) NGC 3705; (n) NGC 4826; (o) NGC
4565; (p) NGC 3628; (q) NGC 4631 and (r) NGC 4559.

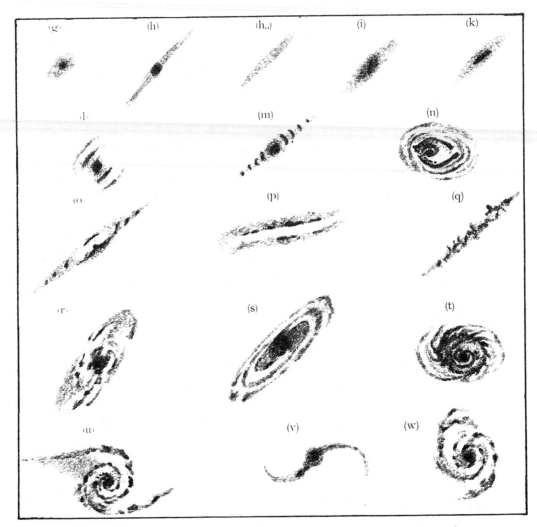

Figure 1. Wolf's Classification of Galaxies (1908).

Classification of Galaxies.

In the years between the Wolf classification and the modified
Hubble scheme of 1936, numerous researchers utilised the Wolf method
in their work, and even continued to do so into the early 1940's.
Regarding other schemes during this period, we can cite Shapley's
1928 classification which was based upon degrees of concentration,
but like other early schemes, is now no longer in use. Another early
system, however, that of Reynolds (1919) is of interest in that, in
many respects, it parallels the first classification of Hubble, upon
which many current schemes are constructed.

The Hubble Classification.

Hubble produced his first classification scheme in 1926 and a
revision appeared ten years later. This revision brought into the
fold the SO class of galaxy, one which, although not observed until
1936, had in fact been postulated by Hubble as a necessary class to
form a transition between the elliptical and spiral systems. The
reason for the late recognition of SO galaxies was due to the fact
that on small-scale plates they appeared identical to ellipticals.
While the latter have a steep intensity gradient, SO types display
an outer envelope superimposed upon an elliptical-like central
structure; this outer envelope is similar to the exponential disks
of spiral galaxies.

Other changes introduced by Hubble in 1936 were the inclusion of
a class of galaxy with a small bar in the nuclear region of an
ordinary spiral and, finally, Type II irregular galaxies, objects
showing no resolution into stars and containing much obscuring
material, of which the best-known example is M82.

It was in 1936 that Hubble also devised his famous tuning-fork
diagram, shown in Figure 2. It was felt by Hubble that this viewpoint, from elliptical to irregular, was a function of rotation,
and that the EO class galaxies would flatten as they spun, develop
spiral arms, and eventually wind up as irregular systems. This view
will be discussed further in Chapter 3.

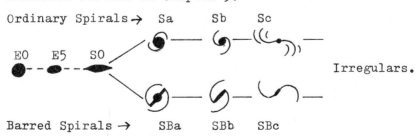

Figure 2. The Hubble Tuning-Fork Diagram.

Classification of Galaxies.

Post-Hubble Developments.

The great asset of the Hubble sequence is its simplicity, and his first (1926) classification was considered to be too simple by Reynolds, who had been struck by the great variety of structure seen within the basic galaxy types. On the other hand, Baade was convinced that no extension of Hubble's 1936 scheme was necessary, and stressed that examples of anomalistic galaxies could be counted on the fingers of one hand. From Baade's viewpoint, therefore, such later classifications as those of Sandage and de Vaucouleurs were entirely superfluous, and such were the variations in the morphology of galaxies that, beyond the Hubble system, only a study of plates could give researchers insight into the variations within a single class.

The Sandage Extension.

Here we are presented with a classification system which increases the number of compartments devised by Hubble. Being structureless objects, elliptical galaxies are left out of the picture, and the concentration is upon SO, normal and barred systems, while, as will be seen, space is given for subtle transitions within each class and sub-class, although these are not delineated.

Taking the SO class of galaxy, Sandage divided these into three sub-classes, SO_1, SO_2 and SO_3. The distinguishing features of these are as follows.

SO_1 — Similar to an elliptical system but is characterised by a flatter intensity gradient and also displays a thin plane, as with spiral galaxies.

SO_2 — Similar to SO_1 but shows outer structure in the form of 'steps', unlike the smooth gradations of ellipticals.

SO_3 — Again similar to SO_1 but with the central regions showing an absorption lane which, in the case of an almost face-on system, is discernable virtually all around the centre. More tilted galaxies show this absorption only on one side of the centre.

Many SO galaxies, however, show morphology which differs a good deal from the above examples, ranging from irregular absorption features through double nuclei to central isophotes which appear to be square. Such anomalies as these rather refer us back to the viewpoint of Baade mentioned earlier.

For ordinary and barred spirals, Sandage has added sub-divisions, depending upon whether or not ring formation is evident. Furthermore, a transition type between Sc and Irr has been introduced, which is classed as Sd or SBd. From SO and SBO to Sd and SBd, Sandage has distributed the galaxies into a box diagram, shown in Figure 3.

Classification of Galaxies.

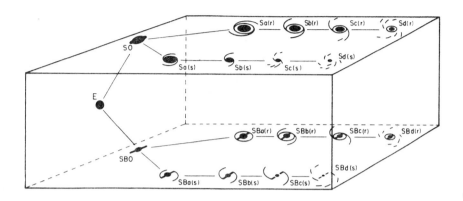

Figure 3. Sandage's box diagram showing spiral (s) and ring (r) subclasses. The full box volume is populated with types of intermediate structure.

The de Vaucouleurs Extension.

In this system the classification compartments have also been extended from the Hubble scheme, and in such an extension much more data can be accomodated in what is still a concise method. The prime distinctions made by de Vaucouleurs are:

a) The use of SA and SB for normal and barred spirals. Intermediate cases are labelled SAB.

b) The designations (r) and (s) for the presence or absence of ring structure. Transitions are designated (rs), an example of the latter being NGC 4579 - SAB(rs)b. An outer ring structure is defined by (R), and in such cases this precedes the main classification, as for NGC 4736 - (R)SA(r)ab.

c) SO galaxies are designated SO$^-$, SO^o and SO$^+$, these referring respectively to early, intermediate and late types.

d) Irregular galaxies are classed as ordinary (IA), barred (IB) and mixed (IAB). Magellanic Cloud types are (Im) and non-Magellanic types (IO). A recent addition is for compact irregulars (cI), examples being NGC 1741 C and D.

d) Compact ellipticals (cE) have been added to the E-type range, a bright example being M32, a fainter, NGC 4486B.

In Table 1 overleaf is shown de Vaucouleur's morphological types; further details of this will be covered on page 13.

Classification of Galaxies

Table 1. de Vaucouleurs' Morphological Types

Classes	Families	Varieties	Stages	Type
Ellipticals		Compact		cE
			Ellip. (0-6)	E0
			Interm.	E0-1
		"cD"		E$^+$
Lenticulars				S0
	Ordinary			SA0
	Barred			SB0
	Mixed			SAB0
		Inner ring		S(r)0
		S-shaped		S(s)0
		Mixed		S(rs)0
			Early	S0$^-$
			Interm.	S0
			Late	S0$^+$
Spirals	Ordinary			SA
	Barred			SB
	Mixed			SAB
		Inner ring		S(r)
		S-shaped		S(s)
		Mixed		S(rs)
			0/a	S0/a
			a	Sa
			ab	Sab
			b	Sb
			bc	Sbc
			c	Sc
			cd	Scd
			d	Sd
			dm	Sdm
			m	Sm
Irregulars	Ordinary			IA
	Barred			IB
	Mixed			IAB
		S-shaped		I(s)
			Non-Magell.	I0
			Magellanic	Im
		Compact		cI
Peculiars Peculiarities (all types)			Peculiarity	P P
			Uncertain	:
			Doubtful	?
			Spindle	sp
			Outer ring	(R)
			Pseudo outer	(R')

Classification of Galaxies

The (R') stage on the lower line of Table 1 results from the fact that it can at times be difficult to define real ring structure from tightly wound spiral arms. This can be seen in those Sb systems where the arms virtually make contact after each has made a full half-circle turn. Such cases as the latter are therefore classed as (R'), pseudo rings.

Many amateurs are probably aware that the structure of spiral arms can show considerable variations. In the Hubble classification, for example, spiral arms in Sc galaxies can display morphology which ranges from regular and well-developed in early Sc systems to quite chaotic in late type ones. As a result of this, de Vaucouleurs has classified arm structure; some of these classes are shown in Table 1, where in the spiral compartments c to m refer to different arm morphology. In this notation, m refers to massive arms, but not shown is an additional symbol, f, which indicates filamentary form. Further additions, such as the symbol 2^+, would indicate two main arms with branches.

At such a point as this the classification is quite complex, and further additions would overburden the system to the point of being unwieldy to use. However, a given researcher can remove such of the notation as he desires, and could eventually reach a stage where the scheme is as basic as the original Hubble classification.

In the catalogue of galaxies in this volume, many of those listed will be given both their Hubble and de Vaucouleurs classifications, but before this it is instructive to give a few examples of the de Vaucouleurs scheme. Among the well-known galaxies M31 would be classed as SA(s)b and M33 as SA(s)cd. For a more complex example we can cite NGC 1318 - (R)SAB(rs)O/a.

Van den Bergh's classification.
This scheme is a luminosity classification, being based upon the appearance of the spiral arms of Sb and Sc-Irr galaxies on the blue prints of the Palomar Sky Survey. It was found that the most luminous galaxies have the most developed spiral arms; in contrast, fainter galaxies have less bright, less well-developed arms. In this system, Sb galaxies are divided into five luminosity classes and Sc-Irr galaxies into eight half-classes.

This classification has a useful bearing upon the extragalactic distance scale, and this aspect will be detailed in Appendix 1, so we shall here give details of the notation of this classification followed by examples of each class in Table 2.

Sb or Sc I galaxies display long, well-developed arms of quite high surface brightness. Descending through I-II, II, II-III to III in the Sb group we are going down the scale towards the faintest -

Classification of Galaxies.

arm galaxies. Similarly, the Sc-Irr galaxies finish at IV-V. the latter being the faintest. Additional symbols include (n) = nebulous arms, (*) = patchy arms and (t) = tidal effects due to interaction. Double symbols indicate extremes,and symbols in parenthesis incipient structure. Table 2 shows the respective divisions with examples alongside, while in Figure 4 are shown examples of an ScI and an ScII galaxy.

Table 2. Van den Bergh's System.

Sb I	ScI	NGC 4321	IrII	NGC 3310
SbI-II	ScII	3184	IrIII	4449
SbII	ScIII	2403	Ir^+IV	5204
SbII-III	S^-IV	247	Ir V	IC 1613
SbIII	S^-IV-V	45		

A further schems by van den Bergh concerns what he has termed 'anaemic spirals, objects which appear to occur most in rich clusters of galaxies. The characteristics of these systems are found to be intermediate between gas-rich normal spirals and gas-poor SO types. The sequence for anaemic spirals parallels the Sa/SOa, Sb/SOb and Sc/SOc types, and is thus set ou as Aa, Ab and Ac.

NGC 4321 ScI   NGC 3184 ScII

Figure 4. Two examples of the van den Bergh system of classifying spiral galaxies.

Classification of Galaxies

Vorontsov-Velyaminov System.

All of the previous classifications have been concerned with varying degrees of basic structure with the Hubble type as an under-lying trend. Unlike these, the Vorontsov-Velyaminov system utilises a very large number of symbols to define the structural variations of galaxies as they appear on the Palomar Sky Survey prints. In its detailed notation, this system seems very like the answer to Reynolds wish for a more detailed classification than that of Hubble.

Vorontsov-Velyaminov is at pains to point out that his system is not a classification in the sense of all those we have detailed so far. All that his scheme does is to illustrate the wide variety of structure displayed by about 30,000 galaxies to a limiting magnitude of m_{pg} = 15.0. The full details of the notations will not be given here, but we can give a broad coverage by noting that galaxies are divided into ellipticals (E) and flat (F). Other symbols are N for large nucleus, n for small nucleus, H for halo or haze, RR for several rings, B⁻ for very short bar and BBB for very long bar. In all over 60 symbols are employed, and in Figure 5 we show examples of four galaxy types with explanations of the respective symbols alongside.

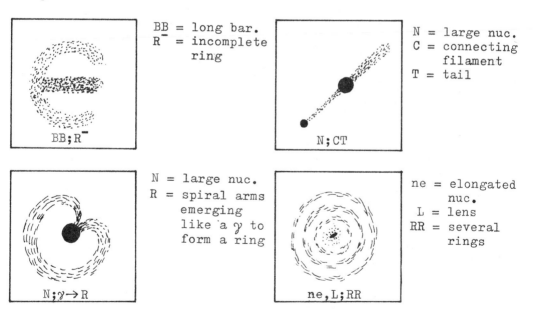

Figure 5. Four examples of Vorontsov-Velyaminov's classification.

Classification of Galaxies

Luminosity Classification.

In 1957 Morgan and Mayall reviewed earlier studies of the differences in stellar content between the central (spheroidal) and spiral arm (disk) components of galaxies. Later, Morgan developed a spectral classification of galaxies in which the spectral region is blue, and generally related to the nuclei, or, more properly, nuclear regions of galaxies.

Morgan found that the correlation between form and spectral appearance is particularly close for two galaxy types, these are, a) Irregular Magellanic Cloud-like systems and spirals with an insignificant central luminosity concentration and b) giant ellipticals, such as M87, and spirals in which a bright, amorphous central region makes up the major part of the luminosity, as in the case of M31. In a) the spectrum is dominated by early-type stars and emission nebulae while the blue and violet spectral regions show strong hydrogen absorption and bright emission lines similar to those exhibited by galactic H II regions. In b) the brightness of the central parts is due to yellow giant stars; galaxies with an intermediate degree of central brightness are shown to have an intermediate stellar population.

As a result of these observations, Morgan has classified the spectra of the central regions of these galaxies in comparison with central stars, being either a, af, f, fg, g, gk or k, depending upon which spectral types make up the greater part of the observed spectrum.

As examples of the Morgan scheme we can take M31 = kS5, M74 = fgS1 and NGC 4449 = a1. In the first two examples the 'S' refers to spiral and the arabic numerals to the degree of ellipticity of the image. This latter symbol is used for all galaxy types, in contrast to the Hubble scheme, where it is used only for ellipticals. Other symbols utilised are 'D' for dustless galaxies, 'L' for low surface brightness objects and 'N' for galaxies showing small and very bright nuclei which dominate the rest of the image, which is characterized by extreme faintness and small angular size; more on these particular objects will appear a little further on.

The final symbol used in this classification is 'p' for any galaxy with peculiar features, and these again are objects which we shall consider shortly. The combination of spectrum and form which is characteristic of this classification leads us smoothly into a further class of galaxy, the Seyfert type,

Seyfert Galaxies.

In 1942 Seyfert drew attention to a type of galaxy whose prime feature was a small, bright nucleus set in spiral structure. A further characteristic was that the nucleus of such an object

Classification of Galaxies

showed a spectrum which displayed broad, strong emission lines. The original six galaxies in Seyferts list included NGC 1068 (M77), an object in which both the nuclear region and the outer, spiral structure is bright. Another of the original six, NGC 4151, differs from M77 in that its outer material is much fainter relative to the nucleus, and, moreover, shows structural peculiarities.

Unlike other emission lines in galaxies, those observed in the spectra of Seyferts are very wide, and are interpreted in terms of gas in the nucleus moving at high velocities, indicative of some kind of violent activity in the nucleus. The velocities in the gas are in the range 500 to 10,000 km/sec, and subsequent study of these has led to the identification of two types of Seyferts. In Seyfert 1 types the spectra show very broad, strong hydrogen lines and narrow forbidden lines; Seyfert 2 galaxies show spectra in which the forbidden lines are the same width as the hydrogen lines. Furthermore, the nuclei of Seyfert 1 types are variable, although the amplitude range is small, being well below half a magnitude, while the associated time scales are also quite large, being reckoned in months.

QSOs and BL Lac Objects.

Classification concepts can often change as work on the objects concerned develops, and this is to be seen with Quasi-Stellar-Objects (QSOs). As the name implies, these objects are virtually stellar in appearance, at least on large-scale photographs, such the Palomar Sky Survey prints. This stellar appearance, along with strong ultraviolet excess (extreme blueness), an emission-line spectrum and variability at optical wavelengths, was for a considerable time the criteria by which QSOs were classified.

Currently, however, the above parameters have in part required modification. To begin with it must be remembered that many QSOs were identified initially by their radio emission, and while it is true that numbers of these are optically variable the same does not hold for those QSOs which were discovered optically, these being variable, but not to such a degree. In addition, the distance of a QSO will affect its appearance; at a large distance the redshift can shift the Lyman alpha emission line, which is responsible for the ultraviolet excess, far to the red and thus bring into the picture absorption features, resulting in either no ultraviolet emission or, at best, very little.

Further uncertainty in classification also relates to redshifts and Seyfert galaxies, as an object classed as a QSO on plates of low resolution may well turn out to be a Seyfert, or even one of Morgan's N-galaxies (page 15). We shall now briefly consider

Classification of Galaxies

the criteria by which the BL Lac objects are classified.

In 1968 a radio source known as VRO 42-22-01 was identified with an object which had for some time been considered to be a variable star in Lacerta, and which was given the nomenclature BL Lac. From a morphological viewpoint, BL Lac objects are varied, being either completely stellar, compact elliptical galaxies or nuclei of galaxies. In addition they show a non-thermal optical continuum and a complete lack of emission lines plus rapid light variations and strong polarization, which is also variable. While the optical variability is much greater than for QSOs, other BL Lac features are similar, except for their lack of emission lines. Seyfert and N-galaxies, QSOs and BL Lac objects form an interlocking group of objects with many similar characteristics, and the possible mechanisms which give rise to such vast outflows of energy, plus further excursions into classification problems, will be taken up in Chapter 6.

Markarian and Haro Galaxies.

The use of spectroscopy as a method of classification is illustrated in the case of Markarian galaxies. These are objects which display extremely strong ultraviolet continua; most are compact and posess stellar nuclei, while many have been found to be Seyfert galaxies.

Haro galaxies are, in the main, distorted or very irregular in structure, this being evident even on their small images on the Palomar Sky Survey. Selection of these objects by Haro was made on the basis of ultraviolet excess on Schmidt telescope plates.

Zwicky Compact Galaxies.

Classification of galaxies depends a great deal upon the resolution of the original classification photographs. For example, if the Seyfert galaxy NGC 4151 were situated at a greater distance, its faintish outer regions would not be observed in their entirety, and it could well thus be classed as an N-galaxy.

The aspect of plate scale and resolution is well brought out in the definition of compact galaxies given by Zwicky in 1964, viz., that they are objects just distinguishable from stars on 48-inch Schmidt plates. Also applicable is a surface brightness criterion of 21 mag sec^2, which is the lower limit. Furthermore, Zwicky also included compact parts of galaxies in his scheme, these ranging from bright nuclei to bright, small emission regions.

These compact systems do not present a homogeneous group of objects; of their morphology as revealed by high resolution photographs, there are jets, rings, spirals of various types (some distorted) as well as blue, irregular objects, which are virtually extragalactic H II regions.

Classification of Galaxies.

In common with galaxies of other types, numbers of Zwicky objects
are also Seyferts, including the first catalogued compact, I Zw I.
In recent observations Sargent has discovered that a small number of
compacts are in fact galactic stars, while others are stars superimposed upon the images of faint, distant galaxies, thus giving the
impression of a compact object.

Interacting and Peculiar Galaxies.

In 1959 Vorontsov-Velyaminov published his first Atlas of Interacting galaxies and a second Atlas appeared eighteen years later.
Arp's Atlas of Peculiar galaxies (1966) contained 338 objects, all
photographed with the Hale 200-inch telescope, and a good many of
these also feature in the Vorontsov-Velyaminov works. The objects
contained in the Arp atlas are only a sample of known peculiar
systems, and a revised and extended atlas is now in preparation,
plus a similar atlas for the southern sky.

It would be easy to accept interacting and peculiar galaxies as
new classes of objects, but such an idea is soon dispelled by an
inspection of, for example, the Arp peculiars. For all but 45 of
these a basic Hubble type is distinct, and the same can be said for
many of the Vorontsov-Velyaminov objects. Furthermore, even some
of those interacting and peculiar systems to which no Hubble type
can be currently assigned may have once been normal as regards
type, and may revert back to the same in future epochs.

Further excursions into the processes occuring in these galaxies
will be made in Chapter 7, and to conclude this chapter we show
overleaf the method by which Arp has arranged the various objects
in his atlas. The numbers occuring under each type refer to the
numbers of the respective objects in the atlas.

Classification of Galaxies

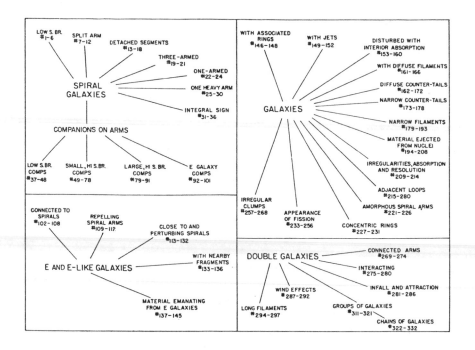

Figure 6. Arrangement of objects in the Atlas of Peculiar Galaxies. The diagram shows the major peculiarities which determine the classification. (Reprinted courtesy of H.C. Arp and <u>The Astrophysical Journal</u>, published by the University of Chicago Press: © 1966 The Americal Astronomical Society).

2. DISTRIBUTION OF GALAXIES

INTRODUCTION.

In this chapter we shall fairly briefly consider the apparent
distribution of galaxies on the celestial sphere as well as their
space distribution out to a distance of about 10 Mpc. Beyond this
lies the nearest large cluster of galaxies, the Virgo cluster.

The amateur astronomer, upon glancing at the Atlas Coeli charts,
can obtain a good indication of the distribution of galaxies
brighter than 13 mag. From the point of view of a whole-sky view of
a good percentage of galaxies down to 15 mag, the Coeli charts are
not useful, yet it is at these lower magnitudes that the numbers of
galaxies increase substantially. More galaxies are to be found on
the SAO charts, all of them NGC and IC objects, and the magnitude
limit is thus considerably lowered. A further aspect noticeable on
the SAO charts is the clumping of galaxies in regions of various
angular sizes. Many of the objects in these amalgams are members
of large clusters of galaxies, and so fall outside the scope of
this volume; other, smaller groups are valid for inclusion here,
according to the criteria explained in the introduction.

Field Galaxies.

By field galaxies we mean those systems which, as far as can be
ascertained, are not members of either large clusters or smaller
groups. In the 1930's galaxies were generally regarded as mainly
isolated objects, only a small percentage being known to occur in
clusters. Nowadays, however, it is realised that isolated systems
are not the norm; in the galactic neighbourhood, for example,
true field galaxies are not common, and among their number are
NGC 1313, NGC 2903, NGC 6744 and NGC 6946. If we take a sample
radius of 50 Mpc from the Sun, we find that many groups of galaxies,
as well as the Virgo Cluster, lie within this volume. The number of
field galaxies distributed in the area may well only amount to 10%
of the total known number, and even some of these may be members of
as yet unrecognised groups.

Groups and Clouds of Galaxies.

To begin with it is necessary to fit the words 'group' and 'cloud'
into their order of placement in the hierarchy of galaxy distribution.
Leaving aside single galaxies, the sequence is: binary, group, cloud,
cluster and supercluster.

There are two analogies which may help to define a group of
galaxies, and both of these compare with the cluster membership of
stars as described in the preceding volume of this series. A group
of galaxies comprises over 2 distinct objects that are gravitationally bound for a period of about 10^9 yr, or are related as products
of a common formative event during such a time scale, but are now

Distribution of Galaxies

no longer gravitationally bound. The former of these two is analogous to star clusters and the second to stellar associations.

The factor by which a group is first suspected or identified is by contrast with the field. In cases such as Stephan's Quintet or Seyfert's Sextet (NGC 6207 group) this contrast is obvious enough, but for more extended groups, such as the NGC 1023 one, close and obvious clumping is not the case. To be absolutely sure that a given number of galaxies comprise a group of extended angular size, certain data is required; radial velocities are neede to determine the difference in velocity (ΔV_o) between the galaxies, plus any general similarity of morphological type, apparent magnitude and angular diameter. Finally, corrections may be necessary to the magnitudes of the galaxies to allow for the effects of galactic obscuration or any absorption within the galaxies themselves.

Clouds of galaxies are larger conglomerates, and will include groups. For example, the Local Cloud comprises all groups within about 7 Mpc. Hence we are here concerned with intermediate-sized groupings, with absolute diameters of about 1 to 3 Mpc. Within such a volume is contained the galactic neighbourhood which in turn incorporates the Local Group of galaxies which we shall discuss a little further on.

The Galactic Neighbourhood.

To define such a region of space is, to a certain extent, a difficult task. If we use the 9.1 Mpc set by Tamman and Kraan (1978) this partially takes in the Local Cloud radius of 7 Mpc used by de Vaucouleurs. Within this region are considered to be 131 galaxies of which 33% are possible field systems while the remainder are concentrated into 8 groups. Noteworthy in the distribution of these systems is their strong concentration towards the supergalactic plane, which describes a band nearly perpendicular to the plane of the Galaxy, and, at greater distances, incorporates the Virgo cluster of galaxies.

There still remain problems regarding the definite assignment of nearby galaxies to groups, and further observations are needed to smooth out any existing ambiguities. While Tamman and Kraan list 8 groups within 9.1 Mpc, de Vaucouleurs considers there to be 54 within 10 Mpc, inclusive of the Local Group and the next group to it which lies in Sculptor, and comprises 6 or 7 late-type spirals. We shall consider the Local Group next, but first show in Table 3 overleaf the 14 nearest groups according to de Vaucouleurs. It is instructive to look at the angular sizes of these groups, which are quite considerable; 5 have largest diameters between 20 and 28° and the remainder, barring the NGC 5128 group (30° long) between 7 and 20°.

Distribution of Galaxies

Table 3. Groups of Galaxies within 10 Mpc.

Group/Cloud	Members def.	pos.	prob.	Group/Cloud	Members def.	pos.	prob.
Scl gp	6	1		NGC 2997 gp	5	5	
M81 gp	5	23	4	M66 gp	5	6	2
CVn I cld	5	8	6	CVn II cld	5	2	12
NGC 5128 gp	6	1		M96 gp	10	8	6
M101 gp	8	20		NGC 3184 gp	4		
NGC 2841 gp	6	10		Coma I cld	15	12	
NGC 1023 gp	6	8	2	NGC 6300 gp	5	3	

The Local Group.

Loose groups of galaxies are distinguished by a lack of concentration at the centre, and the Local Group is a good example of
such a group. The dominating members are the Galaxy and M31, and
the other members are made up of a preponderance of dwarf irregulars and dwarf ellipticals. By 1965 the known number of members
was 26, but this has risen in recent years by the discovery of
very low surface brightness systems such as the dwarf irregulars
in Sgr, Scl and Phe and the new companions to M31.

Other possible Local Group galaxies may skulk behind regions of
obscuration in the plane of the galaxy; IC 10 has been known for
many years to be a heavily obscured object, and more recently the
much more obscured Maffei galaxies have been unearthed. Many
galaxies in and beyond the Local Group are affected by interstellar
material, and even M31 and its companions are in such regions.

The Zone of Avoidance.

The most obvious region of the sky in which the effects of the
interstellar medium are to be seen on galaxies is the Zone of
Avoidance. This is formed by the great clouds of dust in the plane
of the Galaxy, and its obscuring properties are immediately
apparent when only the brightest galaxies up to 13 mag are plotted.
As galaxies of fainter magnitudes are plotted, so the Zone of
Avoidance becomes even more prominent. The effects of all this
material will either effectively dim the outer regions of galaxies,
(IC 10, IC 342) or render them completely invisible, as is the
case with the Maffei galaxies, which are only detectable at radio
wavelengths. Overleaf, in Figure 7, are plotted galaxies in the
magnitude range $m_{pg} = 15.0$ to $m_{pg} = 15.7$, and the Zone of Avoidance is clearly in evidence, along with the extremely heavy
distribution of galaxies within the given magnitude range.

Distribution of Galaxies

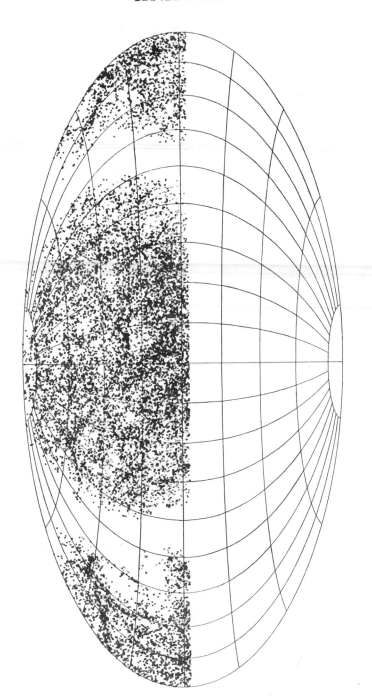

Figure 7. Distribution of galaxies in the magnitude range 15.0 to 15.7 in equatorial coordinates showing the Zone of Avoidance. (From Peterson, 1973. Reproduced by courtesy of D. Reidel Pub. Co.).

3. FORMATION AND EVOLUTION OF GALAXIES.

INTRODUCTION

The appearance of galaxies at the current epoch leads us to suppose that they are at a certain stage in their evolutionary sequence. Why do the different galaxy types look as they do; what is their past history; and what will happen to them over the large time scales of the future? These are questions which have been asked and investigated over many years, and which are still being pursued with the aid of both theory and observation.

It will be recalled from Chapter 1 that Hubble considered his morphological sequence of 1936 to be evolutionary; that from E-type galaxies succesive stages of rotation finally resulted in the Irr - type systems. The reverse of this idea has also been considered, but some indication of the actual stages of galactic evolution are now beginning to emerge.

At the present time, the evolutionary aspect of galaxies has reached a quite complex level; not only are there the obvious features of galaxies which seem to be partially explained (spiral arms) but also radio emission and the effects of the environment from which galaxies form. The topic itself is a complex one, and in this chapter we shall consider the fundamental processes by which the observed structure of galaxies is achieved, as well as the related subject of primeval galaxies.

The ages of Galaxies.

Nowadays, when we look at the Hubble sequence, we view it from a standpoint which differs from those enumerated above; it is now seen as demonstrating that it is the initial conditions which give rise to the Hubble type of a galaxy, and that the overall ages of all galaxies are about the same. The parameters of the initial gas cloud from which a galaxy forms, therefore, determine its currently observed structure.

Useful objects to utilise in the study of some galaxy ages are globular clusters. We have seen from the previous volume in this series that these are old objects, and the fact that they are to be found in irregular galaxies such as the Magellanic Clouds shows that, for all their young blue stars and associated H II regions, these galaxies are old. From such objects as globular clusters and the colours of galaxies, it appears that the ages of all normal galaxies in the Hubble sequence are about 10^{10} yr old.

Further evidence on ages can be derived from the brightest stars in nearby galaxies. Here what can be done is to use the shape of such giant branch stars which are bright enough to register on a Colour-Magnitude diagram. In the Draco dwarf elliptical galaxy, for example, the giant branch shape is very similar to those of halo globular clusters in the Galaxy and also similar to the central

Formation and Evolution of Galaxies

regions of M31 and M32, which again indicates ages of the same order. The idea that the ages of normal galaxies are on a par is to say that in all of them a large population of old, red stars must exist, and part of the red star distribution is now thought to be at the root of the formation of spiral arms.

Spiral Arm Formation.

A galaxy becomes recognisable through star formation: prior to this it exists as a gaseous cloud, mainly composed of hydrogen, and of a given size and mass. These latter parameters will determine the Hubble type of the resulting system, once contraction of the cloud has reached the point where stars begin to form. At some point, therefore, a young or primeval galaxy will appear. We shall pass on to the subject of primeval galaxies further on in this chapter, and see what evidence there is for such objects.

Young stars are blue objects, and, as colour photographs of spiral galaxies show, are arranged in spiral structure. In other systems, such as irregulars and interacting systems the blue star distribution is more random. The fact that the stars forming the arms are young shows that, on cosmological time scales, they have not been in existence for long. In looking at such photographs, it appears that the spiral regions of galaxies are free of other stellar types, but this is not the case, as an underlying layer of red stars exists. In distant galaxies particularly, these red stars can be completely masked by the bright, young stars.

In Figure 8 opposite is an illustration made up from a photograph of M33. The original plate was made up by superimposing a blue-light negative on an infrared positive, which makes the blue stars show up as black and the red stars as white. In the figure the red stars, extending out from the nuclear region of M33, can be seen to form an elliptical disk; superimposed on the disk can be seen the blue stars, forming the spiral arms. It is obvious from such stellar distribution that the young, blue stars must have formed within the red star population (in the same plane) and the currently accepted explanation of this is the density-wave theory of spiral arm formation.

This theory was first proposed by Lindblad and later resurrected and developed by Lin and Shu in 1964. Since then they, along with the Stroms at Kitt Peak, have worked on the idea in both the observational and theoretical fields. It is stressed that they do not pretend to have a theory about every spiral galaxy; however, the idea goes a long way to explain how spiral arms can be formed and maintained over quite large periods of time.

Disk galaxies (spirals and S0's) possess two components; the

Formation and Evolution of Galaxies.

central bulge and the flat disk component, the latter being the
regions in which spiral arms appear.in the case of spirals. Such
galaxies are best seen edge-on if the two components are to be
seen, and obvious examples are M104 and NGC 4565. Depending upon
type, some disk galaxies are forming stars at the current epoch,
these being late-type spirals plus some irregulars. Earlier systems
(SO's and smooth-arm spirals, which we shall discuss later) do not
show stars forming at the present time.

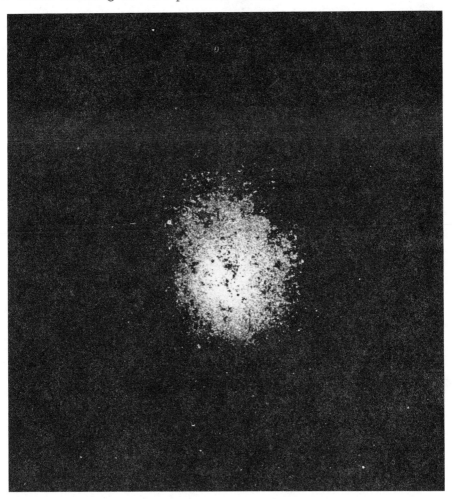

Figure 8. Disk and spiral arm star distribution in M33.
Photograph kindly supplied by M.F. Walker, Lick Observatory.

Formation and Evolution of Galaxies

Spiral arms in galaxies are believed to form in the following way. It is considered that spiral patterns are quasi-permanent density-waves in the red stars of the disk, but the initial formation of the waves is at present uncertain. With the density-wave in existence, gas in the disk of the galaxy encounters the crests of the waves at supersonic velocities. As this occurs, a shock wave results, compressing some of the gas and resulting in star formation in the observed spiral form.

Spiral arms formed in such a fashion should exhibit certain characteristics: a) dust lanes should be seen near the inner regions of the arms; b) in intermediate arm regions OB star associations should be apparent, together with H II regions formed from earlier compressed gas; and c) older clusters and associations formed from much earlier compression should populate the outer arm regions.

To date observations by Lynds have shown the dust lanes on the inner regions of the arms, while photometry by Visser and others has demonstrated that the predicted density-waves are apparent in the red, disk star distribution in M81 and other spirals.

Smooth-Arm Spirals.

Not all spirals exhibit the star and cluster populated arms seen in Sa to Sc systems; some, e.g. NGC 3860, NGC 1268 and IC 2951 are classed as smooth-arm galaxies, that is objects in which no Population I features are to be seen. Clearly in such cases there is no gas extant to encounter density-waves and thus form spiral arms of recognisable type, and star formation will be curtailed unless the gas can be replenished. The means by which gas can be removed from a galaxy are: a) galaxy-galaxy collisions; b) stripping by intergalactic material and c) the expulsion of gas by galactic winds.

Out of these three mechanisms a) and b) can be excluded in the context of this volume, but will be covered in Volume 5, as the event is most likely to occur in large clusters of galaxies. The galactic wind mechanism operates as follows. Winds are generated in the central bulge of the galaxy by either supernova heating or heating from colliding shells of gas ejected by dying stars. If either of these methods heats the gas to sufficient temperatures, the gas is no longer contained within the central bulge of the galaxy, and can be driven from both the bulge and the inner regions of the disk. A combination of b) and c) is also possible, and in such a case, once gas has been completely stripped from a spiral it would be kept in a gas-free state, and no further star formation would be possible.

Formation and Evolution of Galaxies

Elliptical and Irregular Galaxies.

Before moving on to the interesting topic of primeval galaxies, we must very briefly take up the case for the formation of the elliptical and irregular galaxies. The formation of each of these types lies at opposite poles from the spiral galaxies. For the E-type systems the early formation of stars would have been very efficient, and any gas involved soon utilised, hence the current appearance of these objects, which are composed of nothing but old, red stars. In some cases, however, gas is detectable in these galaxies, and what at first may be considered anomalistic, the presence of young, blue stars. This latter aspect, however, belongs in the field of interacting galaxies, which will be covered in Chapter 7.

With irregular galaxies, objects still forming stars, the early star formation rate was much less efficient, and hence large amounts of gas are still available for making stars. This can be seen by not only the fairly chaotic distribution of blue stars and H II regions in these objects, but also by the large amounts of neutral hydrogen (H I) in which these galaxies are embedded.

Primeval Galaxies.

The possibility that by looking back in time it may be possible to identify galaxies undergoing a first burst of star formation is intriguing. What has to be decided is what the appearance of such objects would be like and whether they would be bright enough at large redshifts to be observable.

Elliptical galaxies of giant size, forming stars rapidly, are considered to be the best candidates for primeval galaxies, as it is such systems, as we have seen, which are very efficient formers of stars. Such objects should be detectable if their brightest state of formation occurs at redshifts of about z = 5, (3,700 Mpc). For these galaxies a small angular size is expected to be the case, particularly if the rate of star formation at its greatest takes place in a region comparable to the nuclei of elliptical galaxies we see at present. For this reason it has been proposed that some quasars could be primeval elliptical galaxies. A disadvantage is that these galaxies might be very dusty objects, emitting mostly in the infrared. Given a non-dust ridden primeval galaxy and a given star formation rate, this would have an absolute magnitude of about M_V = -25, and at a redshift of about z = 3 (3,500 Mpc) would have an apparent magnitude of about 22 mag, which is a magnitude shared by many quasars.

It is now possible that numbers of primeval galaxies have been identified which are observable as blue objects, some occuring

Formation and Evolution of Galaxies

in clusters of galaxies. However, while it is very likely that these
objects are undergoing bursts of star formation, they may not, on
the other hand, actually be primeval galaxies. Possibly some of the
non-variable quasars with suitable spectra may be such objects,
lying far away in deep space, and whether or not they are identified
in the near future, the search for them is another example of the
new horizons forever opening up in extragalactic astronomy.

 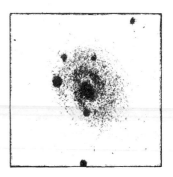

Figure 9. Two examples of smooth-arm galaxies.
On the left NGC 3860, on the right NGC I268.
(From Strom and Strom, 1978. Reproduced by
courtesy of D. Reidel Pub. Co.).

4. GASEOUS AND STELLAR CONTENT OF GALAXIES

INTRODUCTION

Direct evidence that gas has been, and still is, present in some galaxies, can be seen by the presence of stars of all types as well as by H II regions. In the latter case we have optical evidence of gas, but not all of it radiates at optical wavelengths. Neutral hydrogen (H I), as well as other gases and molecules can be observed only at radio wavelengths.

The H I in galaxies radiates at a wavelength of 21 cm, and is due to the following sequence of events. The ground state, or energy level number 1 consists of two parts, the upper and the lower. In the low-density regions of H I in space, collisions are infrequent between the hydrogen atoms, but when these take place at low-speed, the hydrogen atom can be excited in the upper part of energy level 1. The electron of the atom can remain in this excited state for an extremely long period of time, but when it eventually drops down to the lower part of energy level one it emits a 21-cm photon. Observations of the 21-cm radio emission can furnish details on the total mass of H I in a given galaxy as well as other data such as rotational measures.

Distribution of H I according to Galaxy Type.

In the previous chapter it was shown that star formation from the primordial gas clouds proceeds most effectively in those clouds which eventually form elliptical galaxies. As a consequence it is natural for such systems to be totally free of gas. In some cases, however, gas is present in E-type systems, e.g. NGC 4472, and spectra show emission-lines of once-ionized oxygen at a wavelength of 3727 Å, thus indicating the presence of gas at very low densities.

When we come to irregular and spiral galaxies we also find much more obvious signs of ionized gas in the form of H II regions. With regard to the H I in spirals and irregulars two types of H I distribution occur. In the Irr systems, the H I is centrally concentrated and can extend well beyond the optical boundaries of these galaxies, the latter aspect also being a feature of spiral galaxies.

Unlike irregular systems, however, the H I in spiral galaxies shows a peak distribution, not at the centre, but well away from it. At the centre of spirals, in fact, the H I displays a minimum of concentration, which gives the impression of a large hole. In our own Galaxy, which is probably an Sb-type spiral, the annular distribution of H I lies well away from the centre, as is the case with external spirals, and within the central hole are found giant H II regions. The presence of optical spiral arms within the

Gaseous and Stellar Content of Galaxies

central hole is not shared by M31, where the H I is seen to be co-
incident with the arms. Before continuing with the treatment of
hydrogen and other gases, we show in Figure 10 the H I distribution
in the irregular Local Group galaxy NGC 6822, in which the very
extensive contours of the gas are clearly shown

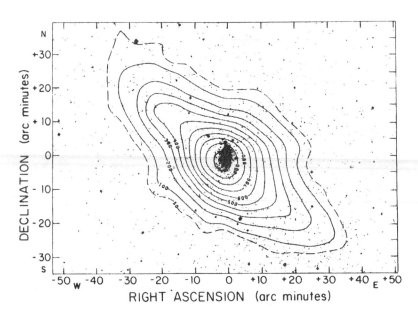

Figure 10. Contours of 21 cm emission superimposed
on a photograph of NGC 6822. (From M.S. Roberts,
1970. Reproduced by courtesy of D. Reidel Pub. Co.).

Observations of the H I content of a galaxy can aid in deriving
such parameters as rotation velocities and mass. In the case of
M101 the H I outside of the optical boundaries has a mass of about
2.4×10^9 M$_\odot$, of which about 1.5×10^9 M$_\odot$ is associated with the
south companion (or H II region) NGC 5474. The velocities observed
in the 21-cm line agree with the assumption that most of the H I
is in co-rotation with the optical features of M101.

Neutral hydrogen is not the only gaseous matter connected with
late-type galaxies; other gas, the result of processing in stellar
interiors, also being evident. Among the elements found are
Sodium (S), Calcium (Ca), Titanium (Ti), and Iron (Fe). Observations
at radio wavelengths can detect molecules of water (H_2O), Ammonia
(NH_3), Formaldehyde (H_2CO), carbon monoxide (CO) and —so far
detectable in the Galaxy only — the hydrogen molecule (H_2).

Gaseous and Stellar Content of Galaxies

Gas Distribution near Galaxies.

In cases where neutral hydrogen is detectable near galaxies, the question to be answered is whether this is remnant material, left over from the original gaseous cloud, or whether it is tidal in origin, i.e., material drawn out from one system by interaction with another.

The nearest example of the latter process is the Magellanic Stream, a loop of H I between the two Magellanic Clouds and possibly linked to the Galaxy. There is evidence that this filament of gas describes virtually a large circle, and this has been considered to be the product of gravitational interaction between the Small Magellanic Cloud and the Galaxy during a close passage (about 20 kpc) something like 5×10^8 yr ago. Part of the stream, incidentally, is a detached section once thought to be an H I companion of the southern sky galaxy NGC 300. A likely by-product of such a close encounter is that stars may have been pulled out from the SMC or the Galaxy or even both; to date, however, none have been observed.

Moving further out past the Local Group, we find other clouds of H I associated with the M81/M82/NGC 3077 triplet. All three lie within a common H I envelope, and in particular there is a strong bridge of hydrogen between M81 and NGC 3077, which could be the result of a close passage of the two galaxies. Examples of H I bridges are also known in more distant galaxies (NGC 4631 and NGC 4656; NGC 4151 and NGC 4145).

A number of galaxies, e.g. M31, IC 342, show warps in the outer structure of their H I distribution. The causes of such features can be varied, one of the most probable being the presence of an H I companion. Such an object is situated about 60 kpc away from the bright S0 galaxy NGC 1023, the velocity difference between the two objects being about 200 km/sec. No optical feature can be seen at the position of the H I object, and as other members of the NGC 1023 group are too distant to have pulled the companion from this galaxy, it is possible that the gas is remnant material left over from the time the galaxies formed.

As we have seen, elliptical galaxies are noted for their old, red star population, but anomalies can exist. The E0 system NGC 1510 lies about 20 kpc away from the SB0 galaxy NGC 1512, and this latter object is enveloped in a vast cloud of neutral hydrogen. Interestingly, NGC 1510 is quite a blue object, completely at variance with the colours of most ellipticals. If some of this gas had been accreted by NGC 1510 in the past, it is possible that this has been enough to form a population of young, blue stars.

Such possible interactions in the radio wavelengths also display

Gaseous and Stellar Content of Galaxies

optical features in some cases, and these, as well as further
excursions into relevant radio observations will form part of the
substance of Chapter 7.

Stellar Distribution in Galaxies.

The colours of galaxies show characteristic features: E-types –
red; spirals – red centres and blue disks, and irregulars – blue.
Leaving aside emission-lines in normal galaxies, which arise in
H II regions, the spectra of galaxies will display absorption lines,
and in the very nearest systems the spectra of individual stars
(and clusters) can be obtained. In more distant objects, however,
information about their stellar content can only be derived from
integrated spectra.

The composite spectral features in far-off galaxies give data
on the their stellar populations. To take two examples, low-density
dwarfs have stellar populations similar to metal-poor globular
clusters while high-density giants show spectra with super-metal-
rich characteristics, that is, they contain large numbers of giant
stars with a heavy metal content. To take every absorption feature
separately is not our purpose, but we can give brief details of
individual features and their cause, as a given absorption line or
band will relate to a certain type of star. Thus cyanogen (CN)
bands near 4220 and 3880 Å are indicative of the presence of G5
to K4 giant stars; the magnesium (Mg) band near 4800 Å means that
K to M0 dwarfs are present and the strong titanium oxide (TiO)
bands in the red and infrared refer to a population of Mira-type
stars.

A large percentage of stars of a given type does not mean that
the total luminosity which they radiate will also be large. This
can be demonstrated by taking just the nucleus of M31, the light
of which is made up by about 17 different types of stars. In this
galaxy's nucleus the greatest percentage of light (18.2%) is due to
super-metal-rich stars of K2III-IV. The percentage of the total mass
of the nucleus contributed by these stars is, however, only about
0.03%. In contrast, M8V stars contribute only 0.5% of the nuclear
luminosity but 66.92% of the total mass.

5. NUCLEI OF GALAXIES

INTRODUCTION.

In speaking of nuclei it is necessary to define exactly what is meant by this term. Often the words 'nuclei' or 'nucleus' are used to denote the central regions of galaxies, and such regions should not be confused with nuclei proper, which display angular sizes considerably less than central regions or bulges.

Almost all galaxies of intermediate and high luminosity seem to possess nuclei; exceptions are objects like the Small Magellanic Clouds and the Sculptor dwarf galaxy. Other systems at greater distances than the above two examples may show no discernable nuclei at low resolution, but higher resolution photography may show very small nuclei.

The question of resolution is an apt one in this context. It is probably not always realised that the nucleus of even a large, nearby galaxy is of very small angular size. The obvious system to quote in this regard is M31, whose nucleus has an apparent size of about 2.8 x 1.6 arcseconds, which corresponds to an actual size of 9.4 x 5.4 pc at a distance of 690 kpc. The further away we look, therefore, the smaller appear galactic nuclei; for M81 the apparent size of the nucleus is already reduced to less than one arcsecond, while for spirals at the distance of the Virgo cluster of galaxies the nuclei are less than 0.1 arcseconds in angular size. To get the best idea of the intrinsic diameters of the nuclei of spiral galaxies is to realise that these are matched by some galactic globular clusters, about 10 pc.

Types of Nuclei.

The two main types of nuclei are the passive and the active. The former is self-explanatory in that no unusual parameters are evident, while in the latter various characteristics are in evidence, ranging from violent motions of gas clouds (detected spectroscopically) to bright condensations and variations in luminosity (detected optically). Basically an active nucleus is one in which a percentage of the observed radiation appears to be the result of non-thermal radiation, a topic which will be considered further in the next chapter with regard to extreme forms of nuclear activity.

Among the nearest galaxies with active nuclei are NGC 253, NGC 4258 and NGC 4736. The former contains a powerful infrared source, while the latter has an intense radio feature in its nucleus. NGC 4258 is noted for its anomalous spiral arms, which are thought by some to be due to the high-speed ejection of material from its nucleus.

Nuclei of Galaxies.

The large infrared luminosities of galaxies like NGC 253 are due to non-thermal sources operating; if stars accounted for the infrared flux which is observed, they would need to be high luminosity O and B stars, objects with lifetimes of only about 10^6 yr, an extremely small percent ge of a galaxy's lifetime. Also in many cases the infrared luminosities of galaxies are greater than the optical luminosities, and examples of such objects are NGC 4151 and NGC 5236 (M83). The former of these is a Seyfert galaxy, and these objects will be taken up in the next chapter.

As well as dust, which is necessary for infrared emission, the nuclei of galaxies also contain gas; emission lines denote the presence of low-density gas, and often small radio sources are to be found in emission-line nuclei. Nuclear emission-lines occur more often in radio-nucleus systems, and at present this aspect is not understood; either the nuclear gas was present before the onset of radio emission or, alternatively, the emergence of the radio source coincides with the appearance of the gas.

A type of nucleus of interest is the Hot-spot nucleus, which display bright, small regions. Although no correlation exists between these nuclei and radio sources, activity is possible in galaxies harbouring them. One Hot-spot galaxy, NGC 1808, shows spectroscopic characteristics which have been interpreted as being due to material ejected from the nucleus along the minor axis of the galaxy.

In conclusion, mention must be made of the classification of galactic nuclei carried out at Byurakan Observatory. In this survey the central parts of almost 500 galaxies were studied, and these were finally divided into the following groups. Class 5: prominent star-like nuclei; Class 4: star-like nuclei not very distinct or pronounced; Class 3: general increase in brightness to the centre where no stellar nucleus is visible; Class 2: a notable increase of brightness to the centre which has somewhat peculiar irregularities in brightness distribution; Class 1: no brightness increase to the centre and, finally Class +2: Galaxies with nuclei split into two parts.

6. SEYFERT GALAXIES, QSO's AND RELATED OBJECTS

INTRODUCTION

In this chapter we shall consider the parameters that link the
Seyfert galaxies, QSO's and BL Lac objects. Also included in the
contents of the chapter will be radio galaxies, and we shall define
the properties which distinguish radio galaxies from those other
systems that emit radiation at radio wavelengths. As will be seen,
the explanations for the energy sources of radio galaxies, QSO's
some Seyfert galaxies are common to all. Both optical and radio
characteristics of these active systems will be covered, but we
can do no more than skim the surface of what is a complex subject.

Radio Galaxies.

Since the first discovery of radio emission from galaxies in
1949, it has been found that many galaxies, including our own, are
radio emitters. In the case of most spirals a small radio flux is
present. Such galaxies as these are classed as weak radio sources,
but when we come to the strong radio galaxies, not only is the
emitted flux much greater, but the source objects are all E-type
systems. These can be divided into the following: a) Classical
E-types (M87); b) D-galaxies (similar to a) but for the presence
of a large, faint envelope); c) N-galaxies and d) Dumb-bell
galaxies, showing double nuclei.

The absolute magnitudes of radio galaxies are very high, of
the order of -20.5, thus making them among the optically brightest extragalactic objects. Also of large intrinsic size are the
angular sizes, particularly if we include the detectable limits
of the radio emission.

It will be recalled from Chapter 4 that the H I distribution in
spiral and irregular galaxies extends beyond the optically determined boundaries, and a similar situation prevails in radio galaxies, where the radio-emitting material is present well outside
the optical image. However, in radio galaxies the phrase 'well
outside' gives no idea of the vast extent of the radio sources.
Furthermore, these are not distributed symmetrically around the
source galaxies, but aligned on each side of the visible galaxy.
Typically these radio lobes are separated by a few times their
diameters, the emitting regions being of a size about two thirds
to one-fifth of their separation, although some, e.g. 3C 33, appear
much wider. The double nature of the radio lobes appears to exist
for all sources where the intrinsic diameter is greater than about
20 kpc. If we realise that the linear diameters of giant ellipticals can be 50 kpc, and that the largest radio sources have
intrinsic diameters over ten times that of the associated galaxy,
then some idea of their extent can be gauged. Nothing really

Seyfert Galaxies, QSO's and Related Objects

succeeds like an illustration, however, and in Figure 11 is shown
the distribution of the radio emission around NGC 5128 (Cen A). As
a further point of interest this galaxy also displays a secondary
double radio source contained within the optical image, and this is
also shown in the figure.

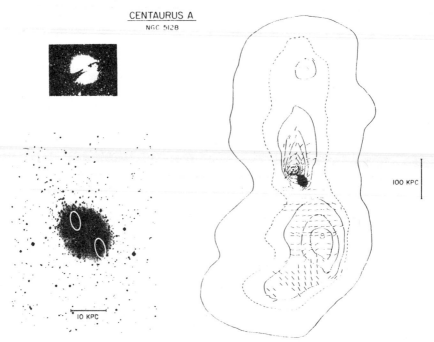

Figure 11. NGC 5128 (Cen A). The extent of the radio
emission is shown on the right extending from a photograph of the galaxy. A larger scale photograph of the
galaxy is at bottom left with the position of the
secondary double radio source marked. The top left
positive photograph shows the well-known absorption
feature. (Reprinted courtesy of Alan T. Moffet and
The Astrophysical Journal, published by the University
of Chicago Press; © 1975 The Americal Astronomical Society.)

NGC 5128 is a prime object of study as it is the nearest radio
galaxy, and hence very important in investigations of these objects,
and at the heart of these observations lies the problem of deter-
mining the mechanisms which give rise to the radio emission.

Physical Processes giving rise to Radio Emission.

Here we are back once more in the realms of galactic nuclei, as

Seyfert Galaxies, QSO's and Related Objects

it is in these regions that the energy sources must lie. An ideal
starting point is the giant elliptical galaxy M87, which displays
two jets of material extending out from the centre. These jets are
apparent at optical wavelengths, and spectroscopy of the brighter
one shows a featureless continuum; photographs, however, reveal
a number of structureless knots, with linear sizes of about 20 kpc.
The light from this jet is partially polarised, and this, plus the
continuous spectrum, indicates that the radiation producing the
feature is synchrotron radiation.

Synchrotron radiation occurs when an electron, moving at a
relativistic velocity, comes into contact with a magnetic field
which is aligned in the direction of the electron's trajectory.
Upon contact, the electron spirals around the magnetic field line,
and as it does so emits radiation in a small cone. Thus, as the
radiation vector sweeps round, it is detected by the observer as
a pulse. The diagram in Figure 12 shows this action.

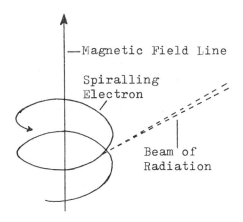

—Magnetic Field Line

Spiralling
Electron

Beam of
Radiation

Figure 12. Diagram
of Synchrotron
Radiation Process.

We have seen that the light from synchrotron radiation is
polarised, and in typical radio galaxies the polarisation decreases
with increasing wavelength. Apart from M87, another well-known
galaxy emitting polarised radiation is M82. Originally this was
thought to be an exploding system, but later the idea was put
forward that the cause of the polarisation and optically-observed
filaments was due to interaction with an intergalactic dust cloud.
In the following chapter we shall again return to the subject of
galaxies in interaction with clouds of intergalactic material, in
which mention will again be made of NGC 5128.

What triggers the activity in radio galaxies? It now appears tha·
large amounts of energy are released in one or more violent events
occuring in the nuclei of these galaxies, and that this is sub-

Seyfert Galaxies, QSO's and Related Objects

sequently flung out from the nucleus in opposing directions. Theories
as to the triggering mechanism are: a) a QSO is the perpetrator; b) a
multiple supernova event, causing a chain reaction with other stars;
c) gravitational collapse of an object or objects; d) following on
from the supernova theory, that a number of pulsars are the cause, and
e) accretion of material on to a black hole. Out of these, the supernova mechanism is somewhat out of fashion, for, while the energy
emitted by a typical supernova is about 10^{51} ergs, many such events
are needed to occur within about 10^4 yr to provide the necessary
energy.

It is therefore obvious from the above that an active nucleus is
at the root of the radio emission, so we shall now pass on to very
obvious manifestations of active nuclei – Seyfert galaxies, QSO's and
the BL Lac objects.

Seyfert Galaxies.

Radio emission is detectable in Seyfert galaxies, but in most cases
it is of weak intensity, and only a few are strong sources such as
3C 120 (BW Tau) which was discovered to be a galaxy by its radio
emission. As can be seen, it was once classified as a variable star.
Of the strong radio Seyferts, it is mainly Seyfert 2 objects that
come into this category, and the radio emission appears to be linked
with the emission-lines seen in the spectra of Seyfert nuclei.

Forbidden lines in spectra are the result of transitions occuring
in very low density gas, as was explained in Volume 3 of this series,
and in Seyfert galaxies forbidden lines of Iron, Oxygen, Argon and
other elements are to be found. With regard to the permitted lines
of Hydrogen seen in Seyfert spectra, these furnish information on the
internal motions of the gas in the nuclei. The widths of these lines
in both classes of Seyferts indicate the following velocities: in the
Seyfert 1 class gas velocities extend up to 18,000 km/sec while in
class 2 Seyferts the lines indicate velocities of around 500 km/sec.
Once gas exceeds a given velocity it can escape from the parent
galaxy, and the limiting velocity can be quite low compared with the
above-mentioned figures, only about 1000 km/sec. The mass loss in
NGC 4151, due to gas ejection, has been calculated at up to 10,000
$M_\odot$ yr. At lower velocities than 1000 km/sec, ejected gas would fall
back into its galaxy, and such an occurence seems to taking place in
our own Galaxy.

Our Galaxy, therefore, has an active source in its nucleus, but
this is, of course, nothing like the energy sources in Seyferts.
Gravitational activity can be very energetic, as is shown for case
e) at the top of this page, which has been used to explain the
energy source in the nucleus of NGC 5128. Accretion is also a possible
explanation of Seyfert nuclear activity, and on a grand scale. The

Seyfert Galaxies, QSO's and Related Objects.

accretion of material on to a very large mass black hole or a very
sizeable number of neutron stars could account for the energy out-
flow from Seyfert nuclei. As a comparison object we can take the
Crab nebula, which has an intrinsic size and radiation characteristics which could be very similar to Seyfert nuclei. The difference
between the two, however, is in the amount of energy given off, which
in a Seyfert nucleus could be as much as 10^7 times that of the Crab.

Quasi-Stellar Objects.

The first QSO was identified in 1960 (3C 48) and was optically
seen to be a blue, 16 mag stellar object with faint associated
nebulosity. In the case of 3C 273 there are two distinct optical
features, a stellar body with a jet of material nearby. While
some QSO's are radio emitters, others are radio quiet; in all cases,
however, they appear to have extremely high luminosities, of the
order of 10^5 that of normal galaxies, and this, plus other characteristics, made them initially regarded as highly unusual objects.
Since then it has been found that the spectra of the nearer (low
redshift) QSO's are very similar to the spectra of strong radio
galaxies and Seyferts, and that the spectra of the more distant QSO's
are in fact continuations of such spectra into the ultraviolet. The
current explanation of QSO's is that they are the excessively active
nuclei of galaxies.

In Chapter 3 it was suggested that some QSO's may in fact be
primeval galaxies in early bursts of star formation. What evidence
is there that QSO's are galaxies, bearing in mind their unusual
properties? Very distant galaxies, in clusters for example, display
images that are virtually stellar, and a large percentage of QSO's
follow this example. Examples do exist, however, of QSO's in which
other material can be seen. PKS 0837-12 exhibits outer nebulosity of
average galaxy size and shape, while Ton 256 is surrounded by an
elliptical galaxy; both this and the bright QSO centre have the same
redshift.

A feature of the spectra of QSO's is that both absorption and
emission lines are present, the former being less redshifted than
the latter. Two explanations can account for this; either the
material responsible for the absorption is connected with a given
QSO or it arises in material connected with intervening galaxies or
gaseous clouds. At the present time it seems that the latter case
is the most likely, and this would, of course, nicely account for
the redshift difference between the two spectral features.

The emission lines, on the other hand, occur within QSO's, and
are in all probability due to nearby gas surrounding the power
source, which is thought to be gaseous matter entering a massive

Seyfert Galaxies, QSO's and Related Objects.

black hole, the origin of the gas being possibly due to a range of occurences including material from stellar collisions and stars which have been totally disrupted by tidal forces produced by a black hole. The origin of a black hole can be due to a wide variety of prior events including supermassive stars and dense star clusters. In the latter case clusters of stars of 100 $M_\odot$ could eventually form giving rise to multiple supernova explosions which will produce a cluster of neutron stars or black holes. Whatever form their evolutionary sequences take, black holes represent extremely high power sources, producing the vast amounts of energy which enable QSO's to be detected at such great distances.

BL Lac Objects.

With these objects we are still concerned with sources of small angular diameter and high luminosity. The prototype of these galaxies was once considered to be a variable star, BL Lac, and it is only comparatively recently that its extragalactic origin has been recognised. A similar object, AP Lib, was also originally catalogued as a variable star. Other BL Lac objects have been discovered quite recently, while similar objects with lower luminosities include B2 1652+39, B2 1101+38 and NGC 6454.

In the cases of OJ 287 and 0735+178 no galactic envelopes are observable, but these are to be found in BL Lac and AP Lib. These outer envelopes are faint with regard to the central regions of these galaxies, and show absorption lines in their spectra which are quite typical of those in normal giant galaxies, and in essence BL Lac is an elliptical galaxy with a nucleus displaying certain characteristics. The properties of BL Lac objects, or rather the strong central regions, consist of nonthermal radiation, rapid variability, strong and variable polarisation and infrared emission. Unlike the QSO's, the nuclei of BL Lac objects display no emission lines, although in a few cases some very faint ones are likely. The cause of the lack of emission lines is thought to be due to radio frequency heating, which can give rise to hot coronae around emission-line clouds, and in extreme conditions this can blot out emission lines. BL Lac objects, therefore, are best considered as a variant of the QSO's, as in both types of object the dominant feature is nonthermal radiation.

7. INTERACTING AND PECULIAR GALAXIES

INTRODUCTION

We have lumped these two classes of galaxies together due to the fact that many interacting galaxies display peculiarities, and as a consequence cross classification occurs in many instances.

The definition of interacting galaxies is self-evident, but it is necessary to define just what constitutes a peculiar galaxy, as it is possible, but wrong, to regard them as new galaxy types. In the large majority of cases, peculiar galaxies are objects showing unusual structure but which still fall within the Hubble or the de Vaucouleurs classification scheme. Objects outside the basic galaxy types are those like ring galaxies, although it appears that even these once posessed a Hubble type; ring systems are also good examples of objects which are both interacting and peculiar.

In Chapter 1 we showed the classes into which Arp has divided peculiar galaxies, and at this point it is necessary to define the various classes into which Vorontsov-Velyaminov has divided inter-acting galaxies. The definition of these galaxies, as given by Vorontsov-Velyaminov is: a) Systems where regular shapes are perturbed as a result of interaction with another another galaxy, and b) Systems where galaxies are embedded in a common luminous haze. Such objects have been grouped into 10 categories, ranging from peculiar distribution of H II regions to disrupting nests of galaxies, M51-type systems and chains of galaxies.

From here on we shall detail examples of a few selected objects which fit the title given to this chapter. The obvious method is to use bright, well-known objects for some of these examples, and since such objects are not too common among nearby galaxies, they are naturally seized upon when they are relatively close. In the course of this chapter, therefore, we shall mention M51, NGC 5128, NGC 4038/9 plus other, less well-known objects. As a prelude, a few lines will be taken up by a brief survey of the processes which produce the observed structures.

Both Toomre and Vorontsov-Velyaminov, who have studied peculiar and interacting systems for many years, have estimated that 15% or more of galaxies have suffered mergers or collisions during their existence. Collision or interaction can result in bursts of star formation, and as examples we can take NGC 2623 and NGC 7252, both of which seem to show evidence of large bursts of star formation which occured a few hundred million yr ago. M82 and NGC 5128 also provide evidence for ongoing star formation, but in the former case it is not a case of galaxy-galaxy interaction, as mentioned on page 39.

After a period of star formation has occured due to interaction

Interacting and Peculiar Galaxies

the respective galaxies should eventually appear as ordinary-looking systems with regard to color and structure. This implies that many objects currently appearing normal could have undergone large-scale disturbances during past epochs. We shall now consider individual objects, beginning with NGC 5128, which has already been alloted a degree of space, but which displays characteristics not yet covered.

NGC 5128.

The radio properties of this object have already been broadly sketched in, and here we shall concentrate upon the optical aspects. Figure 13 shows in more detail than Figure 10 the photographic appearance of NGC 5128. Noted as being a striking object in the NGC, the galaxy was once thought to be the result of a collision between two systems, but for a time this idea fell out of favour, only to be resurrected again later.

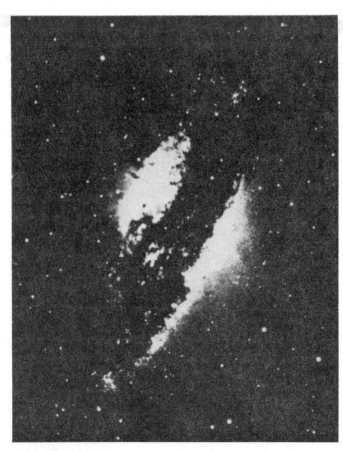

Figure 13. NGC 5128 taken in ultraviolet light by Dufour with the CTIO 4-m tele- scope. (From van den Bergh, 1978. Repro- duced by courtesy of D. Reidel Pub. Co.).

Interacting and Peculiar Galaxies

In the photograph oppositr we see a main, luminous body, like that of a normal giant elliptical galaxy. This is bifurcated by a band of dark material, which is interpreted in terms of a ring or disk of dusty material. The elliptical component contributes 90% of the light, and is composed of old, red stars. However, old as this component is, active star formation is visible along the edges of the obscuring band as well as behind it. In Figure 12, note in particular the distribution of the young stars below the dark material and towards the lower part of the photograph. While young, blue stars and clusters populate both edges of the dust band, other stars are reddened due to the heavy absorption produced by the dust.

Such features may be the result of the merging of an inter-galactic gaseous cloud, or a small galaxy, with a giant elliptical system about 10^9 yr ago. As we have seen, however, uncertainties exist regarding the presence of intergalactic material, so it is quite possible that a galaxy-galaxy interaction is responsible for the observed features. A further fact relative to this is that a moderate abundance of metals are found in the dust band, and as the most likely explanation of this is prior processing in a galaxy, this reinforces the two-galaxy merger idea.

A percentage of the dust must fall on to the elliptical galaxy, and almost twenty years ago, Schlovskii theorised that violent nuclear activity may result from the penetration by infalling material of a galactic nucleus, an accretion process which has already been mentioned with regard to active nuclei, with the added requirement of a black hole. Finally, another peculiar object may be an example of a similar occurence, NGC 2685 (Arp 336).

NGC 5194-5, M51.

Objects of this type appear to be fairly common, many examples being found in the photographic atlases of Arp and Vorontsov-Velyaminov. There is no doubt that with the example of M51 we have two galaxies to consider. In the photographs of this object which are normally seen, no real structural peculiarities are in evidence. Different use of photographic material, however, can bring to light very different morphology, as is shown on the following page in Figure 14. This photograph has been made up from a print of M51 in which the normal appearance of the galaxies (white images) has been superimposed upon the result of five deeply-exposed IIIa-J photographic plates (dark images). In particular, note the two plumes or streamers (A and B in the figure) extending from the region of the smaller galaxy.

Recent models by Alar Toomre, using computer test disk particles, have been constructed to try to duplicate structure in interacting galaxies, and Figure 15 shows these results for the M51 doublet.

Interacting and Peculiar Galaxies

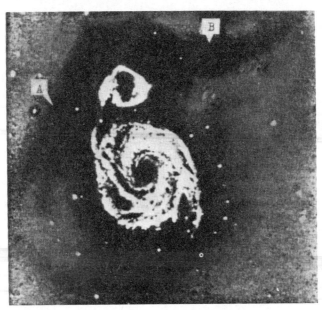

Figure 14. Composite photograph of M51
by Burkhead. (From Toomre, 1978. Reproduced by courtesy of D. Reidel Pub. Co.).

In Figure 15, the left-hand views are as seen from the Sun and
the right-hand views as seen from the west, both of them clearly
showing how the plumes or streamers are associated with the small
galaxy as a result of the interaction.

NGC 4038-9.

In 1977 Toomre presented eleven examples of NGC galaxies which
were considered to be merging systems; heading the list was the
NGC 4038-9 pair.

In the late 1960's, these two objects were regarded as repres-
enting a single, exploding galaxy, but the identification of them
as two systems in interaction is now certain. Recent observations
by Schweizer show extensive tails, which are 20 arcminutes from
end to end. UBV photometry shows that the tails are composed of
stars similar to those found in late-type spirals, and with ages
much younger than the determined time of interaction. As a result
of these observations it is concluded that the tails were formed
from material pulled from the two galaxies. In addition, at the
tip of the southern tail is a stellar system of very low surface
brightness which is composed of young, blue stars, bluer than in
the average irregular galaxy. It thus appears that dwarf irregular
galaxies can be created out of tidal interactions between two

Interacting and Peculiar Galaxies

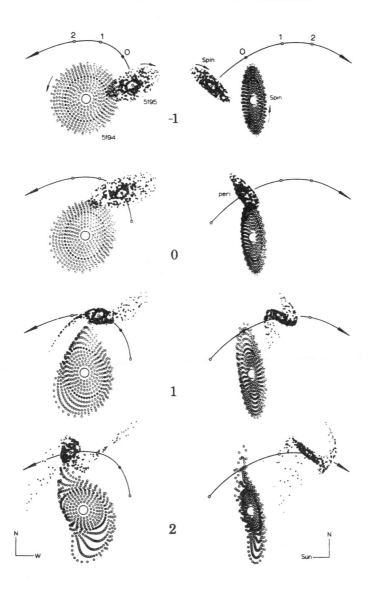

Figure 15. Model of the tidal encounter in M51.
(From Toomre, 1979. Reproduced by courtesy of
D. Reidel Pub. Co.).

Interacting and Peculiar Galaxies.

large systems. Further particle tests by Toomre show the process of
the interaction well, while the optical structure is well-seen in
Schweizer's photographs, two of which are shown in Figure 16.

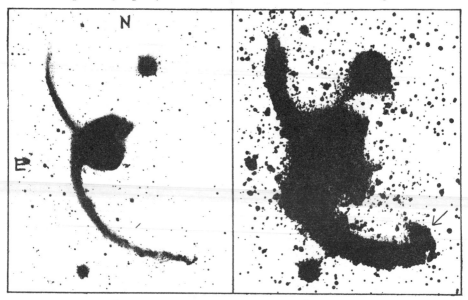

Figure 16. NGC 4038-9 photographed by Schweizer with the
CTIO 4-m telescope. The left-hand photograph is of 50
minutes exposure, the right-hand one a superimposition
of two plates totalling 3.5 hours exposure time. In the
latter the dwarf system mentioned above is arrowed.
(From Schweizer, 1977. Reproduced by courtesy of
D. Reidel Pub. Co.).

Ring Galaxies.

With these objects we are still in the realms of galaxy interactions, although the results produce different structures from
the examples enumerated above.

First, however, it is necessary to define ring galaxies. There
are many examples of systems displaying various degrees of ring
structure; these range from objects with small, inner ring form-
ations (NGC 1343, NGC 3310) through systems with rings of apparently gaseous material away from their centres (M101, IC 10) to ring-
like structures seeming to result, as Vorontsov-Velyaminov has
stressed, from a spiral arm which, seen from earth, appears to
curve back and give the impression of a ring.

Such objects are not true ring galaxies, as the latter are dom-

Interacting and Peculiar Galaxies.

inated by a ring of stars and emission regions within which is set
a nucleus which appears offset from the centre of the ring. Fainter
material is also visible inhabiting the space between ring and
nucleus.

Ring galaxies such as these are not common in the sky, and only a
few have been studied thoroughly; of these, A0035 ('The Cartwheel')
and II Hz 4 are the best known, and it was the latter object which
was first utilised by Toomre and Lynds to explain the unusual
structure displayed by these galaxies. The method of formation is
as follows. A large, spiral galaxy is penetrated by a smaller galaxy
which passes through the plane of the larger. As the intruding system
passes through, the extra gravitational attraction causes gas in the
disk of the larger system to move towards its centre. At a given time
this gravitational attraction will cease, due to the emergence of the
smaller galaxy. At this point the inwardly-moving gas in the large
system will spring back violently, giving rise to an outward-moving
density wave, which triggers star formation. Eventually a ring is
formed which is made up of O and B stars and associated H II regions
while remnants of the original disk material, falling back towards
the centre of the larger galaxy, may be aligned in an arrangement
like wheeel spokes, due to differential rotation. This latter type
of structure is most prominent in A0035. Finally it is expected that
the smaller, intruder galaxy will be swept free of its gas by the
encounter, and such a small, gas-free system is evident near A0035,
as depicted in Figure 17.

Figure 17. A0035 taken by
Blanco with the CTIO 4-m
telescope. The gas-free
intruder galaxy is indic-
ated by an arrow. (From
Toomre, 1979. Reproduced
by courtesy of D. Reidel
Pub. Co.).

Interacting and Peculiar Galaxies.

Models of ring galaxies have also been constructed by Toomre. He
has shown examples of six penetrations of a disk of 2000 test part
icles by an intruder particle, and one of these displays a marked
similarity to A0035, as Figure 18 shows.

Figure 18. Vertical penetration of a disk of 2000 test particles. (From Toomre, 1979. Reproduced by courtesy of D. Reidel
Pub. Co.).

It is very likely that tidal effects do not account for all of
the observed connections between galaxies, and that in some cases
we are observing galaxies in varying degrees of fragmentation.
This idea originated over twenty years ago, and its conceiver,
Ambartsumian, believes that the splitting of a nucleus lies at the
heart of the fragmentation process. A large number of objects in
which Vorontsov-Velyaminov considers dispersion to be likely are
presented in Part II of his Atlas of Interacting Galaxies (1977).
Currently, preliminary observations are being carried out in order
to study the relative motions of the components of chains and
nests of galaxies.

Finally it must be realised that in many cases we may still be a
long way from understanding the activities occurring in peculiar
and interacting galaxies. In the introduction to his Atlas, Arp
stresses this point, and remarks that galaxies are more than
amalgams of stars, radiation and gravitation. He stresses that the
importance of dust is obvious in certain of his peculiar systems,
as well as the apparent action of magnetic forces, an aspect which
is not easy to study but may be of great importance. By further
studies it is to be hoped that at least some indication of the
processes holding sway in these often strange-looking objects will
be forthcoming.

8. CATALOGUES OF GALAXIES.

It is not too great an exaggeration to say that the catalogues and lists of galaxies now extant seems almost as endless as the objects with which they are concerned. Overlaps, however, do occur, as we have seen for compact and Seyfert galaxies and peculiar and interacting systems. In this chapter we shall not be concerned with the galaxy list in the Atlas Coeli catalogue, but will briefly cover a selection of the publications in the professional field. The Coeli list is very useful to amateurs, and covers all the bright, plus a number of fainter objects. Where professional sources often score over Coeli is from the point of view of additional data on individual objects plus references for further research.

The basis of present day catalogues is the Shapley-Ames list of over I000 galaxies to I2.8 mag (1932, Harv. Ann. Vol. 88, No. 2). A revised edition is now being prepared, while an extension of it is the Revised Catalogue of Bright Galaxies by de Vaucouleurs (1976, University of Texas, Austin). This is a very detailed work, giving many references, lists of radio sources and sources of photographs. In passing it is necessary to state that no catalogue is I00% complete to its quoted limiting magnitude, and for the RCBG the completeness is 98% to 11.5 mag and 50% complete to I2.5 mag.

Smaller in conception, but very useful, is the Uppsala Catalogue of Galaxies (Nilsen, 1973), but if we wish to study a much more comprehensive publication we must turn to the Morphological Catalogue of Galaxies (Vorontsov-Velyaminov et al,, 5 vols, I962-8) and the Catalogue of Galaxies and Clusters of Galaxies (Zwicky et al, 6 vols, 1961-68, Calif. Inst. of Technology, Pasadena). In both these the limiting magnitude is I5.5 mag, while the former includes charts of the regions plotted from 48-inch Scmidt plates. While magnitudes are given, angular diameters are not, unlike the MCG, which gives inner and outer diameters.

Regarding photographic atlases and associated catalogues there is that of Holmberg (1937, Ann. Lund Obs. No. 6) comprising 827 double and multiple galaxies down to 16 mag and covering 52% of the sky. In recent years it has been found that a number of the smaller objects included are stars, but the work is still a useful reference point. The original edition of Arp's Atlas of Peculiar Galaxies is out of print, although a new one is being prepared. However, smaller copies can be obtained very cheaply from the University of Chicago Press, (1966, Ap.J. Supp. No. 123, Vol. XIV). Also very useful is the Atlas of Interacting Galaxies (Vorontsov-Velyaminov, 1977, Astron. & Astrophys. Supp. Vol. 28, No.I), which contains very detailed notes as well as a wide variety of photographs. Finally mention needs to be made of the Palomar Sky Survey prints, which are extremely useful as identification checks. Details of prices plus a catalogue of the prints can be obtained from California Institute of Technology Book-

Catalogues of Galaxies.

store, Pasadena, California, 91109). The 5-volume Catalogue of Galaxies
and Clusters of Galaxies (CGCG), Zwicky et al, can also be obtained
from the Caltech bookstore, while the Catalogue of Selected Compact
Galaxies and Post-Eruptive Galaxies (Zwicky) is obtainable from
Miss Margrit Zwicky, Bahnhofmatte 1, CH - 3113 Rubigen (BE) Switzerland.

The currently-known examples of Seyfert galaxies are to be found in:
Weedman, D.W.   1976, Q.J. Roy. Astr. Soc., 17, 227.
                                1977, Ann. Rev. Astr. & Astrophys., 15, 69.
                                1978, Mon. Not. Roy. Astr. Soc., 184, 11p.

Finally, for an up-to-date list of QSO's there is:
Hewitt, A.   1980, Ap. J. Supp. 43, No. 1.
Burbidge, G.

9. OBSERVATION OF GALAXIES

INTRODUCTION.

External galaxies present the visual observer with various features which, in many cases, he hopes to be able to observe. The success with which such observations are carried out depends upon numerous factors; these are a) Galaxy type; b) Distance; c) Galaxy inclination on the plane of the sky; d) Effects of galactic absorption (if any); e) Altitude and f) Telescope in use, observing site and the observer's experience. In this chapter we shall be considering each of these aspects plus related factors.

Selection effects are natural in astronomy, and in the field of galaxies these can colour the composition of catalogues and hence the number of galaxies available to the observer. Brightness is a natural criterion in the recognition and hence classification and cataloguing of galaxies, but it is not the only one; allied to it must be an angular size that is enough to differentiate galaxies from stars on large-scale plates. This combination of brightness and large angular size will allow many galaxies to be easily recogniseable, and hence a good proportion of the 4000 odd NGC galaxies are objects of this type. Objects of quite high brightness but small angular diameter were not extensively catalogued until after the completion of the Palomar Sky Survey, which enabled large regions of the sky to be studied with relative ease. In this category fall many galaxies in the Morphological Catalogue of Galaxies (MCG), the Zwicky compact systems, Markarian galaxies, N-galaxies and many other objects.

For visual observers an analogous situation prevails; in the main it is only the brighter, larger galaxies which are selected for observation. Partly this is probably due to the moderate-aperture telescopes used by large numbers of amateurs, as if more observers owned or had access to well-sited telescopes of 16-inches aperture and over, many galaxies of smaller angular size and low surface brightness would be available. A further reason is that the standard source of galaxies for many amateurs is the Atlas Coeli and its associated catalogue. With a limiting magnitude of 13, Coeli omits large numbers of galaxies which can be of interest to visual observers.

Magnitudes.

In leafing through a catalogue of galaxies, the first thing that an observer will generally look for are the quoted magnitudes. These seem to often have a hypnotic effect, the attitude toward them being virtually that of Holy Writ. Consequently it is easy to become ensconced in the strait-jacket of magnitude figures, and find that all other factors are, consciously or unconsciously, relegated to oblivion.

Observation of Galaxies

For the majority of catalogued galaxies the quoted magnitudes are photographic. If the observer seeks out photovisual magnitudes as being of more use, he will find that only a small percentage have been assigned these. Numbers of these magnitudes appear in the Atlas Coeli while others are due to observations made with Holmberg with the 60 and 100-inch reflectors on Mt. Wilson in 1958.

Magnitudes of galaxies are difficult to derive, and can involve various corrections due to the effects of absorption within a given galaxy, absorption in the Galaxy itself and other factors. In particular the faintness of the outer regions of galaxies presents problems, and these are best solved by taking a particular isophote and using only the light within this to derive a magnitude. The most accurate pv magnitudes are those of Holmberg for 300 galaxies, the majority of these being spirals. With irregulars and ellipticals thus pretty well excluded from Holmberg's sample, there is no universal spread of pv values which would be useful to amateurs. In the circumstances the best that can be done is use the Holmberg figures where available and pg values for the remainder.

Magnitude figures alone do not always give a good indication of the visibility of a galaxy; in particular late-type spirals and irregulars suffer in this way, as the distribution of material in them is far from being similar to elliptical galaxies with their smooth intensity gradients. In stressing the fact that magnitudes of galaxies do not always tell all, we in no way intend to convey the impression that they are of no use. On the contrary, they are of great value, but the other factors that contribute to a galaxy's visual appearance must also be taken into account. As a postscript, it is best to say that the only way to see whether a galaxy is visible or not, or displays any detail, is to observe it, preferably in the best transparency and seeing that can be found. We shall now discuss the other aspects of galaxies which bear directly upon their appearance at the eyepiece.

Surface Brightness.

The surface brightness distribution across the faces of galaxies will vary considerably as a function of galaxy type. We have already mentioned the strong increase in central brightness which is a feature of elliptical galaxies, barring dwarf types. This steep increase in luminosity results in high contrast with the sky, and contrast is a major factor in the observation of galaxies or other objects with nebulous regions. It is contrast which makes edge-on galaxies present more easily detectable images than face-on ones, although there are exceptions to this, such as the edge-on Sc galaxy IC 2233, with its overall low surface brightness.

Observation of Galaxies.

Visibility, therefore, can be defined as an increasing function of intensity gradient at sky level. A diagrammatic rendering of these factors shows the situation best, using a late-type spiral as an example. Face-on, such a galaxy displays a low intensity gradient, resulting in low contrast with the sky brightness, while in the edge-on position the steep intensity gradient produces a high contrast with the sky, as shown in Figure 19.

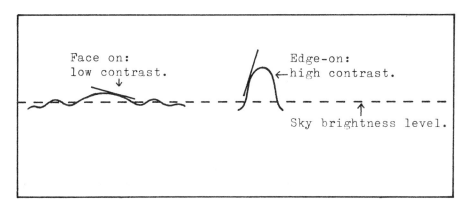

Figure 19. Respective intensity gradients of an edge-on and a face-on late-type spiral.

The surface brightness distribution within an object is defined as the apparent magnitude per square arcsecond (mag sec^{-2}), and very detailed surface brightness figures can be obtained for galaxies. These can show just how a given galaxy type will colour the results of visual observation, in particular with regard to late-type systems, Some irregulars, for example, may only show a small region of relatively high surface brightness, while in the case of dwarf elliptical galaxies like the Draco, Fornax or Sculptor systems, there is no real concentration of stars to give rise to regions of high surface brightness. The star distribution in such objects is rather analogous to a fairly rich star cluster, and as a result of this morphology such objects are detectable mainly in the galactic neighbourhood, and even at these nearby distances are very low in surface brightness. While suitably located observers should be able to register the Fornax and the Sculptor systems, others are totally beyond visual observation, as can be seen by taking the Local Group of galaxies.

The nearness of a galaxy does not mean that it is of suitably high surface brightness to be seen visually. Numerous dwarf irr-

Observation of Galaxies

egulars and ellipticals are nearer than M31 but none are bright enough
to be seen in telescopes. Such objects also furnish confirmation of
the fact that magnitudes are not the only criteria regarding galaxy
visibility; many of them have apparent magnitudes of between 9 and
11 mag, the lowest being for the dwarf elliptical Leo II (12.9 mag).
Other, larger Local Group systems are not observable visually, in
particular IC 1613 and A1009. Inspection of photographs of the former
shows a very faint object in which the region of highest surface
brightness in the blue is 23.76 mag sec^{-2}; similar figures are to be
found for A1009.

In contrast to the above nearby galaxies, high luminosity objects
of lower integrated magnitudes are visible out to considerable
distances, well beyond the Local Group. For such objects it is only
their type which allows them to register in moderate apertures.

To conclude this section on surface brightness we shall take two
galaxies of identical type and see how these relate to observation.
NGC 1569 and A1009 are both Magellanic-type irregulars (IBm), the
former being at a distance of 3.3 Mpc and the latter 1.1 Mpc. The
respective V magnitudes are: NGC V = 11.16; A1009 V = 11.63. Despite
the distance differences, NGC 1569 is much brighter and of smaller
angular size; it is also the more inclined of the two.

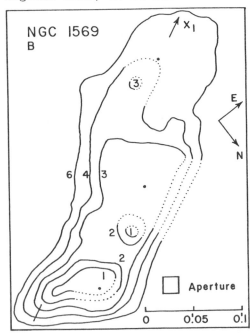

Figure 20. SB measures
of NGC 1569.

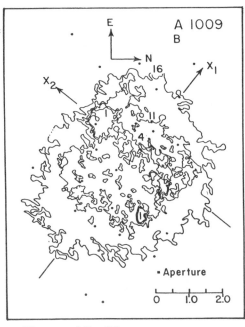

Figure 21. SB measures
of A 1009.

(From Ables, 1971. Reproduced by courtesy of U.S. Naval Obs.).

Observation of Galaxies

In Figures 20 and 21 on the opposite page are shown isophotes of
these two galaxies, depicting respectively the central region of
NGC 1569 and the total area of A1009. For Figure 20 the number 1
indicates a surface brightness of V = 18.18 and the number 4 of
V = 18.48. The regions outside of this have surface brightnesses
ranging from V = 18.69 to V = 24.82. In Figure 21 1 indicates a
surface brightness of V = 23.4 and 2 of V = 24.42. Areas exterior
to the latter have surface brightnesses going down to B = 28.49.

From this it can be seen that the brightest region in A1009 is
not too different in surface brightness to the faintest region in
the NGC 1569 isophotes. Add to this the more compact distribution
of material in NGC 1569, and the combination accounts for the fact
that whereas NGC 1569 is an easy object in quite small telescopes,
A1009 is very much the opposite, as the brightest region of
surface brightness in this is due to a number of blue supergiant
stars. As a further comparison we can take the nucleus of the
face-on Scd galaxy IC 342, which is all that is visible of this
galaxy to the eye, but which, for all its small angular size, is
easily recogniseable optically; this has a surface brightness of
18.56, a sizeable increase in brightness over both the brightest
regions of NGC 1569 and A1009.

Degrees of Inclination.

The extent to which a galaxy may be inclined with respect to the
observer contributes to their visual observability. Edge-on systems,
epitomised by NGC 4565 and M104, can display bright images due to
their steep intensity gradients and high contrast with the sky.
The more that a galaxy approaches the face-on position, the less
contrast will there be, although a considerable part is played by
galaxy type.

With spirals the sequence Sa- Sb- Sc will show different degrees
of central bulge and disk morphology. From Sa through to Sc the
arms in the disk become less pronounced and the central bulge less
prominent. Late-type spirals (Sc) will thus suffer most when their
inclination is face-on, a good example being M74, where the outer
regions of the disk is of very low surface brightness. A similar
object is M100, where in moderate apertures only the nuclear region
and its immediate surroundings are visible, the spiral arms being
of very low luminosity, even in photographs.

With Sa and Sb galaxies the structure of the spiral arms is a
good deal more pronounced, and they are more tightly wound, thus
presenting regions of higher surface brightness, even in the face-
on position. As distances increase the problems of visual sightings
●f spirals become more acute, until eventually only high luminosity
SO and E-types are within the light grasp of amateur telescopes.

Observation of Galaxies.

Some edge-on galaxies display no indications of nuclear bulges, and perhaps the most well-known example is IC 2233. This object is not too faint to register in the larger amateur telescopes, but other examples such as MCG 4-29-60 are very faint. Such objects would probably pose extreme problems for the average amateur telescope, but determined observers may feel inclined to attempt the feat, and therefore details of some of these objects will appear in the list of additional objects.

In conclusion it is instructive to note that the degree of internal absorption shown by an edge-on galaxy will radically alter its apparent radius. The absorption lane in M104 is a good example, this running right through the major axis, and if this galaxy were to be seen in a face-on position its radius would probably be effectively increased.

Spiral Structure.

While the detection of very faint galaxies can be a satisfying excercise in itself, the resolution of spiral arms and other features in galaxies is often even more so. Spiral structure is relatively easy to discern in the larger amateur telescopes, but there are various indicators of spiral form which can be seen in smaller apertures. As dust lanes are as effective spiral arm tracers as young stars, open clusters and associations, spiral form may be detected as regions of dark nebulosity, which, although not always seen in their entirety, are often reasonably prominent at the eyepiece.

The nearest galaxies in which spiral form is detectable are M31 and M33. In the former the spiral arms are partially delineated by two lanes of dark nebulosity running along the W edge of the galaxy. These features are visible in apertures as small as 8-inches, and although some observers seem unable to detect them, it is possible that they are looking for something less sizeable than these lanes appear. Even if, for some reason, the lanes are not seen, their presence can be inferred from the distribution of light in the galaxy. On the E border of M31 the glow of integrated starlight falls away gradually to sky brightness level. In contrast, the W border of the galaxy can appear to be rather abruptly cut-off, due to the presence of the lane nearest to the central regions.

In M33 telescopes of 8-inches aperture are able to resolve traces of spiral structure, and the same can be said, although in lesser degree, for more distant systems. Individual examples will be found in the catalogue and selection of drawings further on in this volume.

Nuclei and Central Regions.

The nuclear and central bulges of galaxies can form the basis of interesting visual observations, although these are, by the very nature of the instrumentation utilised, very crude. In bright Local Group galaxies nuclei and central parts are easily seen, but nothing

Observation of Galaxies

of interest morphologically is apparent. If we wish to see more of interest, therefore, we must extend observations to more distant objects. Here angular sizes will be much reduced, and consequently we must adopt the term 'nuclear regions' or, better perhaps, central regions', in accordance with the data presented earlier.

Many features grouped closely around nuclear regions are too small and often too faint to be resolved with amateur telescopes. There are numerous galaxies with such inner morphology, such as M95 and NGC 5383. In NGC 1087 and NGC 6607 the true nuclei lie at the end of a bar of bright regions. Observations by a well-sited $16\frac{1}{2}$-inch reflector in southern California have failed to show any of these features, so there is no likelihood of their being seen with lesser apertures.

Visually, many galaxies will contain central regions which are blanketed by high surface brightness nebulosity, as is the case with NGC 4473, where amid the luminous material a tiny central region is visible at high powers. Other objects present fairly diffuse images, and the use of high magnification will decrease the overall image brightness of such a galaxy to an unacceptable level, if not complete invisibility. Such a step up in magnification, however, will not too detrimentally affect bright central regions. For such observations the very best seeing is necessary in order that the small region under scrutiny does not suffer distortion. There will, of course, be artifacts produced by the lack of really adequate resolution, but at least in many instances some apparent structural aspects can be perceived.

The relation of the central regions to the parent galaxy can also display interesting aspects. In some cases the central regions are offset from the apparent centre of the object, either along the major axis or along the minor, while duplicity may appear to be the case for some systems. Here, however, care must be taken with the observation, as often superimposed stars are involved, and in the case of NGC 6207 the apparent nucleus is actually a superimposed galactic star.

In conclusion we can take Seyfert galaxies, where the relative brightness of nuclear regions to envelope varies considerably. The intensity of a few of these regions is extremely high, attaining in a few examples a surface brightness of 11 mag sec^{-2}. It hardly needs to be said that such central regions are of very small angular size, and display no structure at all. It is of interest to note that the nucleus of the Seyfert NGC 4151, small as it is on large reflector plates, is considerably reduced when observations are made by balloon-borne instruments, where atmosphere-dictated seeing is considerably depleted.

Observation of Galaxies

Emission Regions.

All emission regions in external galaxies are of small angular diameter when compared with the overall apparent size of the parent galaxy. Small as these are visually, it needs to be realised that these are only the largest, and are, in intrinsic size, much greater than any in the Galaxy which lie relatively near to the Sun. In addition, a further snag is that extragalactic emission regions are generally well immersed in quite bright areas made up by the light of innumerable stars. This may be compared with bright emission regions in the Galaxy itself, where, visually at least, contamination by field stars is not at all great.

The number of known emission regions varies from galaxy to galaxy; most are beyond visual scrutiny, but a number are bright enough and large enough to be seen in suitable amateur telescopes, and for many high quality seeing is required in order to differentiate them from stars. The nearest large, bright emission region in an external galaxy is the 30 Doradus nebula in the Large Magellanic Cloud, which has a mass of about 10^6 $M_\odot$, and is a bright telescopic object. Apart from this object, the most obvious emission region is NGC 604 in M33, with a mass of about 2×10^6 $M_\odot$. While a good deal farther off than 30 Doradus, NGC 604 is nevertheless not a difficult object to observe.

As in the galactic emission regions, the extragalactic ones emit a degree of their radiation in the forbidden lines of twice-ionized oxygen ([OIII]) at wavelengths of 4959 and 5007 Å. This is near to the eye's peak response at 5500 Å, and this, plus the strength of the [OIII] emission, accounts for the greeny tinge to galactic nebulae of sufficient brightness. The extragalactic emission regions, however, are too faint for the colour to register in amateur telescopes, even when their abundances are similar to those in galactic nebulae. M42, for example, has an oxygen abundance similar to that of NGC 604.

In the final analysis, the observer will have to make up his own mind as to the actual nature of suspected emission regions, unless photographs are on hand which can be referred to. In some galaxies nebulae are well within the light grasp of the larger amateur telescopes, and may be seen as being located within spiral arm regions or, in the case of irregular galaxies, at any point within the overall image. In the Local Group irregular galaxy NGC 6822 are four emission regions of quite large size. For observers at mid-northern latitudes these will be very difficult, if not impossible, to see, but for those who may feel inclined to try, details of these objects will be found in Appendix 2.

As an example of the emission regions within a galaxy, and how a large amateur telescope is incapable of registering them, we can take the Sc galaxy NGC 2403. A drawing of this object, made with a 16-inch reflector, will be found on page 168, and notable in the drawing is an emission region situated towards the end of a gradually fading spiral

Observation of Galaxies

arm, which is the brightest emission region in the galaxy, NGC 2404. No other such regions are visible with the 16-inch, but there are a good many, and numbers are visible with a much larger aperture, as will be shown in the catalogue. However, concentrating upon the single emission region seen with the 16-inch, and comparing this with the larger, brighter regions as shown on photographs, we find a great difference. Figure 22 shows over 80 of these regions, and very apparent in their distribution is the delineation of spiral structure.

Figure 22. Bright emission regions in NGC 2403. The cross marks the position of the nucleus.

Observation of Galaxies

Peculiar, Interacting and Compact Galaxies.

Many Peculiar and interacting systems are easily visible with small
telescopes, but with regard to the observation of any of the material
giving rise to these classifications it can be categorically stated that
in the overwhelming number of cases nothing will be seen. The reason for
this is that the relevant structures are mainly of very low surface
brightness, this being the case whether they are in inner or outer
regions.

These types of galaxies, however, still afford much of interest to
the visual observer, who can select objects within a given group for
observation. A good group of objects for such a programme are those
double systems of the M51 type, of which many examples exist, although
many are faint, particularly the smaller associated systems. A further
group of objects are those whose makeup differs from ellipticals or
spirals but are akin to irregulars in that they contain ionized gas.
These galaxies are notable for the fact that most of their radiation
comes from young stars and associated emission regions, and with so
much of the latter being present, which radiates effectively at
visible wavelengths, particularly the $[OIII]$ lines of forbidden oxygen,
they can be of quite high apparent brightness. Many are compact objects,
which will be covered shortly, but others are of quite large angular
size in comparison with the compacts. A good introduction to such
systems is the double galaxy NGC 3690/IC 694, which, although having
a fairly low magnitude, can be seen with ease in moderate apertures.

Ring galaxies, as a class of interacting objects, are all rather
faint and of small angular size. The first visual detection of ring
structure in a galaxy was made in 1886 with the 26-inch refractor of
the Leander McCormick observatory in the U.S.A. The galaxy was NGC 985,
which, however, is not a true ring galaxy, as the annular structure is
formed by a curling spiral arm.

True ring systems will not show their structure in the usual run of
amateur telescopes, but, as with other objects, a real interest can be
achieved in just finding them. The writer has made numerous attempts to
observe the ring galaxies Arp 148, II Hz 4 and VII Zw 466; in all cases
the observations were foiled by poor seeing. As well as transparency of
a high order, good seeing is essential in the observation of objects of
small apparent size, as they could in many instances be mistaken for
stars.

So much overlaps in the context of classification that it will come
as no surprise to learn that ring galaxies can also be classed as
compact systems, and the above-mentioned VII Zw 466 is such a case.
Furthermore, there are still compact parts of galaxies which come into
the present category, such as the ring around the nucleus of NGC 1343,
which is catalogued as VII Zw 8. At 14 mag, this is nonetheless not
exceptionally difficult for telescopes of about 8-inches upwards.
VII Zw 8 is, however, still quite sizeable in extent when compared with

Observation of Galaxies.

some of the compact galaxies proper. A glance through the lists of
these objects demonstrates this well, and we find that although some
of the outer regions may extend to 30 arcseconds in angular diameter,
such areas are very faint, and the brightest parts of the galaxies are
much smaller, between 2 and 18 arcseconds. Observations of such
objects, therefore, will require high-quality seeing in order that
they are able to be differentiated from stars. Although such observations can do no more than identify these small galaxies, eventual
success is really a reward in itself, considering the difficulties
which abound. In concluding this section we show in Figure 23 a small
selection of the structures exhibited by compact galaxies; angular
sizes are also shown, giving an indication of the structure which,
although beyond the light grasp of moderate telescopes, is compressed
in such small angular sizes.

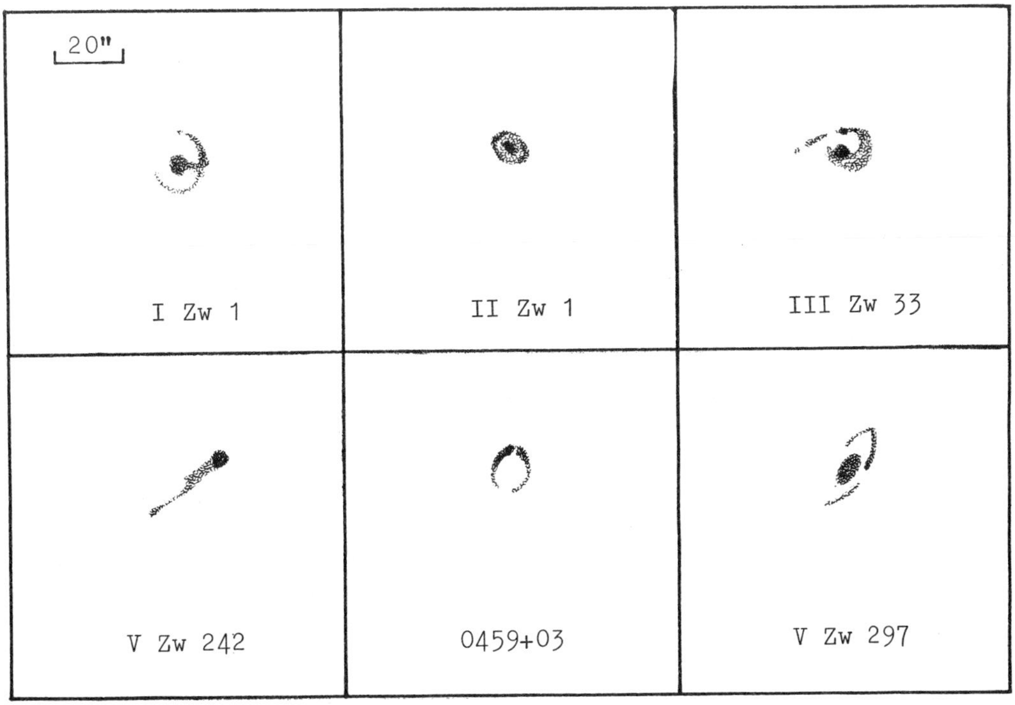

Figure 23. Six compact galaxies from Zwicky's
catalogues. The scale applies to all the six.

Observation of Galaxies.

Supernova monitoring.

In the field of extragalactic astronomy there is little that the amateur can do, and any useful work should therefore be welcomed unreservedly. Monitoring selected galaxies for supernovae is a case in point, and the only requirement is a suitable telescope, (upwards of 6-inches aperture), a field drawing of each galaxy and finally perseverance and good luck.

The first visually detected supernova in an external galaxy was S Andromedae, which occured near the centre of M31 in 1885. Since this first sighting the number of known supernovae has increased considerably, and since the 1885 sighting 478 have been recorded up 1979 Dec. The majority of these occur in the 14 to 20 magnitude range, with a peaking in the 16 to 17 magnitude bracket (85). If we take a mean limiting magnitude of 14 for the majority of amateur telescopes, we find that 61 supernovae have been discovered up to this limit, and that 30 of them are in the 13 to 14 magnitude range.

The visual observer, therefore, has only a chance of catching a small percentage of future supernovae, and should prepare a thorough set of drawings of each selected galaxy showing all nearby field stars to the galaxy, being careful to remember that the outer regions of galaxies, where many supernovae occur, are far too faint to register in telescopes, and that therefore a supernova may well appear well beyond the apparent optical boundaries.

It is late-type galaxies which mainly produce supernovae, and some of these have produced more than one outburst, NGC 6946, for example, having spawned five. Judging from past discoveries, it is not the assiduous supernova hunter who discovers one of these events, but a random sweeper of the sky or a comet-hunter. Also many seem to regard the activity as irksome, but once the initial groundwork has been covered, then the actual checking of each object is a relatively rapid affair, and the observations can be quite easily fitted in with other programmes.

Variable Extragalactic Sources.

Many galaxies are variable, the nuclei of some Seyfert galaxies, for example, plus QSO's and BL Lac objects. In the case of the former, the flux variations are of small amplitude, and accurate photometry is requires in order to realise the light curves. The BL Lac objects, as well as the QSO's, unfortunately reach low magnitudes, even when at maximum, so will only be within the light grasp of the larger amateur telescopes, and even then only at odd periods. An alternative method of obtaining light curves is to photograph the object and then compare any brightness changes with well-calibrated field stars. Photography, however, is not within the bounds of the present volume, but a list of a few variable sources is given in Part Three. Finding charts

Observation of Galaxies.

and comparison star sequences are also given, as for the visual
observer even the random checking of such objects is of interest for
those with suitably large instruments.

In conclusion, galaxies can be observed for a variety of reasons.
The search for a faint object, large or small, can be reason enough,
particularly when earlier attempts have been unsuccessful.
Alternatively various objects can be checked for any structural
detail, spiral or otherwise, or random observations can be made with
no particular scheme in mind. Whatever the approach, the seeking out
of these often faint, often historic and often unusual extragalactic
systems will continue to attract future generations of observers.

PART TWO : A CATALOGUE OF GALAXIES.

INTRODUCTION.

The catalogue contains observations of 275 galaxies made by 19 observers using telescopes of 152 to $2\frac{1}{4}$-inches aperture. Following this will be found 156 field drawings of galaxies, most of which are in the catalogue, although a few have been included which are not. In certain cases more than one drawing has been assigned to an object to show the effect of different apertures upon it.

The extreme left sides of the left-hand pages show the Webb Society catalogue number (WS); these continue in sequence from the last catalogue entry in Volume 3 of this series. Each WS number is followed by the actual designation of the galaxy. In many cases there is more than one designation, and these appear below the NGC or IC number, and comprise the Messier number, (M), the number in the catalogue of Interacting Galaxies of Vorontsov-Velyaminov, (VV), the number in Arp's Atlas of Peculiar Galaxies (Arp) and the number from the lists of galaxies showing ultraviolet excess of Markarian (Mkn). In some instances a galaxy will be found to have two NGC numbers or an NGC and an IC number, this being due to errors in these catalogues.

The remaining data, covering the greater parts of the pages, is as follows.

Upper Line.

(a) Positions for 1950.0.

(b) Magnitudes of the galaxies. Those magnitudes with two places after the decimal point are the very accurate pv magnitudes of Holmberg (1958).

(c) Angular diameters in arcminutes. Holmberg diameters are shown to two decimal places.

(d) The abbreviated form of the relevant constellations.

Second and Subsequent Lines.

First the galaxy Hubble type is given followed in some cases by the revised type of de Vaucouleurs. Following this will be found radio source identifications, where these occur. PKS sources are from the Parkes survey, and 3C and 4C sources from the Cambridge surveys. After this any X-ray and IR source will be shown. Completing these sections will be any structural aspects of the galaxies of interest, all supernovae (SN) known up to 1979 Dec, and finally any membership of a group or cloud. (DDO = David Dunlap Observatory).

Visual Observations.

The data below the dotted lines display the visual observations. Observations are set out in order of decreasing aperture, the figures in parenthesis, (16) ($8\frac{1}{2}$) etc., being the respective apertures in

A Catalogue of Galaxies.

inches. All quoted magnitudes and angular sizes are eye estimates
only.

Field Drawings.

These number four to a page, and are shown in circles of 56 mm
diameter, regardless of the actual field diameters in arcminutes.
For most the whole field is shown, but in a few cases only the
object and its immediate surroundings, this being done mainly for
observations with large apertures, in order that the detail
recorded is presented at a suitable scale. In a few instances no
scale was available, but for most objects the total field is shown
in arcminutes.

List of Observers.

The following list gives the names of the observers whose work
appears in the catalogue, plus details of the telescopes used and
their locations.

D.A. Allen	152-inch	Anglo-Australian Observatory. Siding Spring, Australia.
	60	Mount Wilson, U.S.A.
	12	Cambridge, U.K.
R.J. Buta	107	McDonald Observatory. University of Texas, U.S.A.
	82	" " "
	36	" " "
	30	" " "
	12½	" " "
J.K. Irving	18	Salford, U.K.
J. Toone	18	" "
	2¼	" "
M.J. Thomson	16½	Santa Barbara, U.S.A.
G.S. Whiston	16	Witley, U.K.
J. Perkins	14	Kirkby-in-Ashfield, U.K.
G. Hurst	10	Earls Barton, U.K.
R.J. Morales	10	Tucson, U.S.A.
	8	
S. Selleck	10	Santa Barbara, U.S.A.
	6	
E.S. Barker	8½	Herne Bay, U.K.
D. Childs	8½	Luton, U.K.
T. Davies	8½	LLandudno, U.K.
S.J. Hynes	8½	Crewe, U.K.
A.P. Wilson	8½	Scunthorpe, U.K.
P. Brennan	8	Regina, Canada
	6	
K.G. Jones	8	Winkfield, U.K.
K. Sturdy	6	Helmsley, U.K.

A Catalogue of Galaxies.

Observers and Accredited Galaxies.

    The following list shows all the galaxies that appear in the first
section of the catalogue plus the initials of the respective observers.

NGC	16	MJT, DC.
	23	RJB, JKI.
	55	RJM.
	147	MJT, PB.
	160	GW.
	169	MJT.
	181	GW.
	185	MJT, SS.
	·205	SS.
	221	PB.
	224	SS. KS.
	247	SS.
	253	MJT, RJM.
	278	GH, SJH, PB.
	300	RJM.
	404	GSW.
	407	GSW.
	410	GSW.
	414	GSW.
	467	GSW.
	488	GSW, SS.
	520	MJT.
	524	MJT, SS.
	523	DAA, ESB.
	584	SS, PB, JT.
	596	SS.
	598	RJB, GW, DC, KS.
	615	SS.
	628	RJB, MJT, KGJ, SS.
	636	SS.
IC	1727	RJM.
	672	MJT, RJM, SS.
	691	GSW.
	697	GSW, DAA, SS.
	720	JT.
	736	MJT, RJM.
	750	GSW, RJM, DC.
	751	GSW.
	761	GSW.
	772	MJT, DC.
	779	PB.
	784	RJM.
	890	GSW.
	891	RJB, GSW.
	925	RJB, MJT, RJM,

NGC	936	GW, DAA, JT.
	949	GW, RJM.
	972	RJB, MJT, ESB.
	1023	MJT, KR.
	1052	GH, SS.
	1055	DAA, SS, RJM.
	1068	RJB, GW, KGJ.
	1073	SS.
	1087	GH.
	1090	GH.
	1084	MJT, SS.
	1156	RJB.
	1169	MJT.
	1300	RJB, MJT.
	1309	MJT.
	1332	SS.
	1337	MJT.
	1343	ESB.
	1421	MJT.
IC	342	ESB.
	1465	SS.
IC	356	ESB.
	1560	MJT.
	1569	RJB, ESB.
	1637	RJB, MJT.
	1784	MJT, SS.
	1888	MJT
	1889	MJT
	2146	MJT.
	2207	SS.
	2276	MJT.
	2403	RJB, RJB, MJT, KGJ, KR.
	2537	RJB, MJT.
IC	2233	MJT.
	2523	MJT.
	2549	ESB.
	2608	GSW.
	2613	MJT.
	2639	JP, ESB.
	2655	PJM, KS.
	2672	MJT.
	2681	MJT, SS.
	2683	KJI, MJT, DC.
	2685	MJT, ESB.
	2692	ESB.

A Catalogue of Galaxies.

NGC	2713	DAA.
	2719	DAA, MJT.
	2775	SS.
	2782	PB.
	2787	JT, KS.
	2841	MJT, ESB.
	2859	GSW, RJM.
	2872	GSW.
	2874	GSW.
	2903	RJB, MJT, TD, KS.
	2911	GSW
	2964	MJT.
	2968	MJT.
	2976	MJT, SS, KS.
	3031	RJB, MJT, SS.
	3034	RJB, MJT, KR.
	3067	SS.
	3079	JP, SS.
	3077	MJT, ESB.
	3115	RJB, MJT.
U	0549	DC.
	3166	GSW, SS, KS.
	3169	ESB, KS.
	3185	GH, SJH,
	3184	MJT, SS.
	3187	MJT, SJH.
	3190	MJT, GH.
	3193	MJT, KR.
	3226	MJT, TD.
	3227	MJT, TD.
	3245	ESB.
	3310	RJB, MJT, RJM, KS.
	3351	RJB, SS.
	3353	GH.
	3368	DC.
	3377	JP.
	3379	DAA, SS.
	3384	SS.
	3389	SS.
	3412	GSW.
	3414	DAA, TD.
	3430	TD.
	3432	GSW, ESB, KS, DB.
	3445	GH.
	3458	GH.
	3504	SS.
	3521	JKI, ESB.
	3556	RJB, MJT, ESB.
	3593	GSW. SS.

NGC	3627	GSW, TD.
	3628	GSW, KGJ.
	3631	JP, KS.
	3646	RJB, MJT.
	3665	KGJ.
	3765	GSW, ESB.
	3690	DAA, ESB.
IC	694	DAA, ESB.
	3718	DAA, MJT, KS.
	3726	MJT.
	3729	RJB, MJT, KS.
	3938	JP.
	3810	SS.
	3877	APW, KGJ, KS.
	3893	RJB, MJT, SS.
	3898	MJT, KGJ.
	3921	JP.
	3949	MJT, APW.
	3953	RJB, MJT, KGJ.
	3963	MJT, ESB.
	3982	KGJ.
	3992	MJT, GH.
	4026	MJT, KGJ.
	4027	RJB, MJT.
	4038	RJB, MJT, RJM.
	4039	RJB, MJT, RJM.
	4041	MJT.
	4051	MJT, ESB.
	4088	RJB, MJT, SS.
	4100	RJM.
	4111	JKI.
	4138	JP.
	4144	GH.
	4151	RJB, JKI, ESB.
	4157	SS.
	4179	MJT, KS.
	4203	KGJ.
	4206	MJT, RJM.
	4214	RJB, ESB.
	4216	MJT, KS.
	4217	MJT, ESB.
	4236	RJM, ESB.
	4244	MJT, KGJ.
	4251	DAA, KS.
	4258	RJB, MJT, ESB, SS.
	4274	RJM, KS.
	4278	GSW.
	4290	RJM.
	4314	GSW, KS.

A Catalogue of Galaxies.

NGC	4319	GSW.	
	4346	RJM.	
	4395	MJT.	
	4414	JT.	
	4419	PB.	
	4448	ESB.	
3C	273	CC.	JT.
	4449	RJB, JKI, RJB, ESB, KGJ	
	4485	RJB, GSW, KGJ.	
	4490	RJB, GSW, KGJ.	
	4494	DAA, JT.	
	4527	DAA.	
	4565	RJB, MJT, ESB, KS.	
	4605	MJT, ESB, KS.	
	4618	RJB, ESB.	
	4625	RJM, DC.	
	4627	RJB, MJT.	
	4631	RJB, MJT, ESB.	
	4651	SS.	
	4656	RJB, GSW, KGJ.	
	4657	RJB, GSW, KGJ.	
	4665	DAA.	
	4666	GSW.	
	4670	MJT, ESB.	
	4676	RJB, MJT.	
	4710	RJB, GSW.	
	4725	RJB, PJM, KS.	
	4762	MJT, ESB.	
	4775	MJT.	
	4793	MJT, ESB.	
	4826	DAA. RJB, GSW, KGJ.	
	4861	RJB.	
	4868	GSW.	
	4900	RJB, KS.	
	5005	MJT, GSW, KGJ.	
	5033	RJB, RJM, KGJ.	
	5055	MJT, KGJ.	
	5128	MJT, DD.	
	5194	RJB, GSW, GH, KGJ.	
	5195	RJB, GSW, GH, KGJ.	
	5198	MJT, GSW.	
	5221	GSW.	
	5222	GSW.	
	5236	RJM.	
	5248	RJB, MJT, KS.	
	5273	JP.	
	5297	MJT, JP.	
	5371	RJB, MJT, GSW.	
	5457	RJB, GSW, KGJ, KS.	
	5583	GSW, RJM.	

NGC	5600	DC.
	5665	DC.
	5676	GSW.
	5678	RJB, MJT.
	5746	RJB, JKI, KS.
	5820	MJT.
	5846	GSW, DAA, KGJ.
	5850	RJB, DAA.
	5866	RJB, MJT, ESB.
	5879	GSW, KS.
	5907	GSW.
	5929	GSW.
	5930	GSW.
	6052	DAA, RJM.
	6181	RJB, MJT.
	6217	MJT.
	6207	JKI, DAA, KGJ.
	6384	MJT.
	6503	GSW, ESB.
	6643	MJT, ESB.
	6764	RJB.
	6822	ESB.
	6946	RJB, MJT, KGJ.
BL	Lac	KJI.
	7217	MJT, GSW.
	7331	RJB, MJT, DC, KR.
	7335	RJB, MJT, DC.
	7448	ESB.
	7463	GSW.
	7464	GSW.
	7465	GSW.
	7469	GSW, SJH.
IC	5285	ESB.
	7479	RJB, MJT, EJC, ESB.
	7603	DAA.
	7640	RJB, GSW, ESB.
	7678	RJB, ESB.
	7973	ESB.

A Catalogue of Galaxies.

A few words are necessary regarding the composition of the following catalogue. By no means every galaxy observed by Webb Society members is included in it, and the reason for this is as follows. If every object were listed it would run the risk of being a rather monotonous amalgam of faint, featureless objects interspersed with those which display some kind of structure to amateur telescopes. While the search for very faint objects can be most interesting and challenging, to read of the results, comprised of a few words, is not inspiring. Consequently in the present catalogue we have mainly selected those objects which display varying degrees of morphology to different apertures and cut down heavily on those which do not. The latter include ellipticals and SO types, by their natures featureless, plus many spirals and irregulars. For those who wish to extend their telescopes to near the limit, many faint objects will be found in the list of additional objects, together with brighter examples, and we trust that a sufficient variety is set out to cater for all types of telescopes and observers.

The following observers' names were omitted from the list on page 68.

Denis Dutton, $12\frac{1}{2}$-inch, California.

Chris Clayton, Bath, U.K., 10-inch.

Dave Branchett, Bishopstoke, U.K., 5-inch.

The following catalogue entries should appear on page 144.

NGC 5474 MJT, PB.

NGC 5533 GSW, SS.

WS	Cat		RA	Dec	m	AD	Con
430	NGC	16	00 06.5	+27 27	13.2	1.0 x 0.7	Peg

E3. NGC 22, $14^m.9$, 1.8×1.4, lies 11.5 N.f.

- -

(16) Round, with a slightly brighter centre; the outer nebulosity is of uniform surface brightness. ($8\frac{1}{2}$) Almost stellar at LP; a little outer material visible at MP.

WS	Cat		RA	Dec	m	AD	Con
431	NGC	23	00 07.3	+25 39	12.5	2.2 x 1.6	Peg

Sb.

- -

(36) Bright, extended ellipse; a bright nuclear structure is noticeably elongated; two weak spiral enhancements emerge from opposite sides of the nucleus, one curving towards a bright star attached on the S end. A close double star
(18) Slightly pointed at the SE end; stellar nucleus with a star quite close to SE and a star suspected on the NW side.

WS	Cat		RA	Dec	m	AD	Con
432	NGC	55	00 12.7	-39 28	7.8	25.0 x 3.0	Scl

SB. PKS 0012-394. The spiral structure is weaker in the W part. Member of Sculptor Group. Other members not in this volume are NGC's 45, 7793 and possibly IC 5332.

- -

(36) Nearly edge-on and appears asymmetrical with some signs of dust near the bulge, which is diffuse, broad and somewhat elongated with the S edge sharp; SE of the bulge it is strongly curved and lined with 4 or 5 faint knots; N edge of the curve is sharp.
(8) Large and very long; bright nucleus shows two almost stellar condensations and is off-centre; mottling evident in the central area.

WS	Cat		RA	Dec	m	AD	Con
433	NGC	147	00 30.4	+48 14	12.0	15.0 x 9.0	And
	DDO	3					

dE5. Member of Local Group.

- -

(16½) Large, quite faint, irregularly round; it brightens in the middle to a stellar nucleus.
(6) Faint stellar nucleus in faint nebulosity; brightest part about 30" diameter.

| 434 | NGC | 160 | 00 33.4 | +23 41 | 13.3 | 3.5 x 1.1 | And |

Sa. Contains a very small, isolated nucleus in a faint, double outer ring.

- -

(16) Small, faint, diffuse ellipsoid.

435	NGC	169	00 34.2	+23 43	13.3	3.5 x 1.1	And
	Arp	282					
	Mkn	341					

Sb + comp in contact to S. NGC 162, 2.8 S.S.f. is probably a star. IC 1559, $13^m.2$, lies 1.0 S.

- -

(16½) Easily visible x84; x176 appears bi-nuclear, the second nucleus being on the S end; x351 both nuclei surrounded by a nebulous envelope.

| 436 | NGC | 181 | 00 35.4 | +08 22 | 14.3 | 2.8 x 2.3 | Psc |

SBc:SB(rs)bc.

- -

(16) Faint, small, slightly elongated in PA 135°.

| 437 | NGC | 185 | 00 36.2 | +48 03 | 11.0 | 14 x 12 | Cas |

E2. A globular cluster lies 1.1 S.f. the nucleus. Member of the Local Group.

- -

(16½) Fairly bright, large, irregular; brightens towards the centre.
(8) Possibly slightly extended E-W with a hint of mottling; slightly irregular at MP.

WS	Cat	RA	Dec	m	AD	Con
438	NGC 205	00 37.6	+41 25	8.17	26.0 x 16.0	And

E5. The brightest stars have M_{ab} = -5.2. Member
of the Local Group.

- -

(8) Elongated N-S; brightens gradually to the
centre, which appears offset; at HP a star
suspected S.p. the centre.

439	NGC 221	00 39.9	+40 36	8.16	12.0 x 8.0	And
	M 32					
	Arp 168					

E3. A faint, diffuse plume of material associated.
Member of the Local Group.

- -

(8) Slightly extended in PA 150° - 330°; stellar
nucleus within gradually fading nebulosity.

| 440 | NGC 224 | 00 40.0 | +41 00 | 3.47 | 200 x 80 | And |
| | M 31 | | | | | |

Sb. Radio source. Nucleus about the size of a large
globular cluster but nearly 100 times greater in
mass and 20 times greater in luminosity. 688 H II
regions. Over 120 known novae. SN: 1885 - $5^m.8$.
Member of the Local Group.

- -

(8) Very bright, large spherical core with a stellar
nucleus; surrounding this a large halo with extensions running NNW-SSE; two dark lanes run along the
W part of major axis, the one closer to the nucleus
the more obvious and about 15' long; the star cloud
NGC 206 shows as a nebulous knot in the SSW end; a
second, fainter knot in the same extension, about
midway between the nucleus and NGC 206.
(6) Nebulosity cuts off sharply to the W and fades
more gradually to the E; nuclear region stellar at
x24, and of distinct size at x120.

WS	Cat	RA	Dec	m	AD	Con
441	NGC 247	00 44.6	−21 20	10.7	18.0 x 5.0	Cet

SAB. Member of Sculptor Group. DDO 6, 14^{m}9, lies 40$'$ ESE. A chain of faint, mostly spiral, galaxies, lie close to the NE.

- -

(10) Large, fairly bright with a slightly brighter centre; difficult at powers over x59.

442	NGC 253	00 45.2	−25 33	7.0	22.0 x 6.0	Scl

Sc. PKS 0045−25. SN: 1940 − 14^{m}0. Member of the Sculptor Group.

- -

(16½) Very bright, large and long, the major axis extending N.f., S.p.; central area non-stellar and extends along major axis; a number of dark lanes evident, especially on the N edge of p extension.
(8) Bright; very small core inside mid region with mottling evident in the latter; impressive.

443	NGC 278	00 49.2	+47 17	10.5	2.8 x 2.8	Cas

Sc:SAB. Contains several knotty, massive arms.

- -

(10) Very bright and small, appearing as a round glow without any defined nucleus; 8^{m}0 star N.f.
(8½) x111 a pretty faint stellar nucleus in faint diffuse nebulosity.
(6) x50 small, faint and round; suspected stellar nucleus at x155; lies in a fine LP field.

444	NGC 300	00 52.5	−37 54	9.68	20.0 x I0.0	Scl

SA.

- -

(8) Bright, starlike nucleus with a very large faint nebulous shell, the latter not too prominent and somewhat difficult.

WS	Cat	RA	Dec	m	AD	Con
445	NGC 404	01 06.7	+35 27	11.3	6.0 x 6.0	And

E/S0. Possible member of the Local Group.

- -

(16) Very bright and round; diffuse outer halo and much brighter to the middle; β And, close to the N swamps the field.

| 446 | NGC 407 | 01 07.8 | +35 21 | 14.3 | 2.0 x 0.35 | Psc |

S0/a. In group of ellipticals. NGC 408, lying at $01^h 09^m.5$, $+32° 58'$ is probably a star.

- -

(16) Quite bright and small; elongated approximately N-S; brighter towards the middle.

| 447 | NGC 410 | 01 08.2 | +32 53 | 12.6 | 2.3 x 1.8 | Psc |

E . In group of ellipticals.

- -

(16) Round and bright; much brighter to the middle.

| 448 | NGC 414 | 01 08.5 | +32 50 | 14.5 | 0.8 x 0.4 | Psc |

?. In group of ellipticals. Double system.

- -

(16) Small, round, brighter to the middle.

| 449 | NGC 467 | 01 16.6 | +03 02 | 13.3 | 2.4 x 2.4 | Cet |

S0. Contains a weak, narrow dark lane. Member of NGC 467, 470, 474 group.

- -

(16) Quite bright; slowly brightens to the middle and a faint, stellar nucleus; slightly elongated approximately N-S; in same LP field as NGC 470 and NGC 474 (Arp 227).

WS	Cat	RA	Dec	m	AD	Con
450	NGC 488	01 19.2	+05 00	11.6	6.0 x 4.3	Psc

Sa. Contains a weak, smooth outer ring. NGC 490, $15^m.5$, lies 8' N.f.

- -

(16) Considerably bright, large and circular; a bright, central core is surrounded by diffuse nebulosity easily visible at x160 and x222.

(10) Faint, diffuse patch; no detail seen.

WS	Cat	RA	Dec	m	AD	Con
451	NGC 520	01 22.1	+03 33	11.54	6.8 x 2.9	Psc
	VV 231					
	Arp 157					

Irr II. Strongly peculiar. Two apparent objects plus two streamers.

- -

(30) Irregular shape split into two sections by a weak dust lane, the section to the E being the more conspicuous, long and nearly straight; the brightest part of the galaxy is on the N tip of this section, and appears round and diffuse; the section W of the dust lane is bent with a very faint knot at the kink; a second faint knot lies directly opposite this on the E side; not a very bright object.

(16½) Quite large but not bright; elongated N.p., S.f.; x222 wider on f end while the p end ends in a point.

WS	Cat	RA	Dec	m	AD	Con
452	NGC 524	01 22.1	+09 17	11.5	3.5 x 3.5	Psc

S0 or E pec. In group of S0's, Sa's and others.

- -

(16½) Circular with very bright centre and faint surrounding nebulosity; dark mottling suspected in outer material, especially to N and E.

(8) Mottling possible x48; quite large and bright.

WS	Cat	RA	Dec	m	AD	Con
453	NGC 523	01 22.5	+33 46	13.5	3.2 x 0.8	Psc
	Arp 158					
	IV Zw 45					

Pec. Possibly comprises three objects, including a dwarf system.

- -

(60) Very elongated nebulosity; two bright regions involved, the W one brighter and compact.

(8½) Faint, extended nebulous blur at LP and HP.

454	NGC 584	01 28.8	−07 07	11.6	2.0 x 1.2	Psc
	IC 1712					

E4. PKS 0128-07. Member of Cetus II Cloud.

- -

(10) Round with ill-defined edges; brighter centre with stellar nucleus; x178 possible star on N edge.

(6) Round and faint; prominent stellar nucleus.

(2¼) Difficult; gradual central brightening.

455	NGC 596	01 30.6	−07 17	12.2	0.6 x 0.5	Psc

E2. Contains a distorted envelope with a faint tail leading to a small spiral. Similar to NGC 7135. Member of Cetus II Cloud.

- -

(10) Small, faint and gradually brighter towards the centre; x148 a very small, bright nucleus is apparent and the edges seem mottled; on the N.p. edge a star suspected.

456	NGC 598	01 31.0	+30 24	5.79	83.0 x 53.0	Tri
	M 33					

Sc:SA(s)cd. PKS 0131+30. Contains over 360 known emission nebulae. Its globular clusters are bluer than those in M31. Member of the Local Group.

- -

(82) NGC 604 - knot at end of NE spiral arm. At x820 a fascinating object; 17 stars down to $18^m.0$ or $18^m.5$ plus definite signs of the associated nebulosity, in particular on the W side.

(36) Spiral structure clear but contrast poor; both

WS	Cat	RA	Dec	m	AD	Con

(NGC 598 - M33 - continued).

arms are lined by knots and enhancements, some including a few very faint stars; near and to the W of centre is a conspicuous straight, narrow filament with two knots in its S half; the central bulge appears very diffuse, broad and somewhat extended N-S; NGC 604 appears like a nebulous version of the Pleaides as seen with the naked eye; IC 139, at the tip of the S arm, shows as about a dozen very faint stars about 1' across. A chart of the knots in M33, plus 36-inch observations, will be found in Appendix

(16) Clearly spiral; contains three bright patches, NGC 604 being the brightest; the other two are near the nucleus and are more diffuse.

(8½) Definite spiral form in the shape of a reversed 'S' projected upon a uniform haze; N arm of uniform brightness, the S arm appearing to have two brighter regions; NGC 604 prominent and about 1' in diameter; other nebulosity suspected only.

(6) Large, diffuse with nucleus displaced to the W; just visible to the naked eye on a clear night.

| 457 | NGC 615 | 01 32.6 | -07 35 | 12.6 | 2.7 x 0.8 | Cet |

Sc. Contains a very bright nucleus in a bright, outer ring. Member of Cetus II Cloud.

- -

(10) Small, faint and fairly even in brightness; a small, bright nucleus appears to be situated more towards the W edge; x148 seems elongated N-S.

| 458 | NGC 628 | 01 34.0 | +15 32 | 9.33 | 12.0 x 12.0 | Psc |
| | M   74 | | | | | |

Sc:SA(s)c. Contains 193 H II regions.

- -

(30) Two arms clearly visible, each with a faint

WS	Cat	RA	Dec	m	AD	Con

(NGC 628 – M74 – continued)

knot at the end and with patchy areas; the S arm
is the brighter; nuclear region is quite small
and contains no nucleus, being immersed in a
diffuse halo to which the arms appear only weakly
connected.

(16½) Fairly bright, large and circular; brighter
towards the middle and x222 and x333 a small,
curving arc of brighter nebulosity suspected on
the N.f. outer edge.

(8) Round, with a fairly sharp nucleus which is
almost stellar and surrounded by a diffuse area
about 6' diameter; too faint and diffuse to
stand anything more than LP.

(6) Faint mass of light of even intensity.

| 459 | NGC 636 | 01 36.6 | −07 45 | 12.6 | 0.7 x 0.7 | Psc |

E3

(10) Small and faint; slightly brighter towards
the centre; appears mainly circular with a star
suspected on the S.f. edge.

| 460 | IC 1727 | 01 44.6 | +27 05 | 12.0 | 1.0 x 0.5 | Psc |

Irr I.

(10) Quite faint and small, requiring averted
vision at first; very close to NGC 672.

| 461 | NGC 672 | 01 45.0 | +27 11 | 10.88 | 11.3 x 4.1 | Psc |
| | VV 338 | | | | | |

SBc. Possibly linked to IC 1727 by an H I bridge.

(16½) Bright, large, much extended almost E-W; it
appears mottled and shows little increase in brightness along its length; a dark lane appears to run

WS	Cat	RA	Dec	m	AD	Con

(NGC 672 continued)

along the major axis; stars lie off the N end.

(10) Even brightness throughout; easily seen.

(8) Suspicion of mottling x121.

| 462 | NGC 691 | 01 47.9 | +21 30 | 13.5 | 3.8 x 2.7 | Ari |
| | Mkn 363 | | | | | |

Sb:SA(rs)bc. Member of NGC 678 - 697 group.

- -

(16½) Bright, well-developed centre in diffuse
envelope of uneven brightness; a bright star lies
close to the N.f. edge.

| 463 | NGC 697 | 01 48.4 | +22 06 | 12.7 | 5.1 x 1.7 | Ari |

Pec. Member of NGC 678 - 697 group.

- -

(16) Elongated in PA 135°; bright object which
slowly brightens to the middle.

(12) Difficult; 12^m.0 star close to the N.

(6) Faint, small; appears circular at LP but more
extended at x305.

| 464 | NGC 720 | 01 50.5 | -13 59 | 11.7 | 1.3 x 0.7 | Cet |

E. Member of Cetus II group.

- -

(2¼) Very difficult; about 2' diameter with a much
brighter nucleus; lies in a well-sprinkled field.

| 465 | NGC 736 | 01 55.3 | +32 55 | 13.5 | 1.8 x 1.6 | Tri |
| | VI Zw 111 | | | | | |

E1. Member of NGC 733 - 740 group.

- -

(16½) Elongated almost E-W; x160 and x222 two main
areas of brightness appear at each end, the N one
being brighter; area between relatively dark.

(10) Elongated; faint star on N edge.

WS	Cat	RA	Dec	m	AD	Con
466	NGC 750/1	01 54.6	+32 58	13.0	2.5 x 1.7	Tri
	VV 189					
	Arp 166					
	VI Zw 123					

E + E. Compact cores plus bridge. A long plume to the NW ends in a small spiral.

- -

(16) Both round and brighter to the middle; small and not bright; NGC 750 larger and brighter.

(10) Elongated with one side slightly brighter.

(8½) x111 a small condensation at N end while the S end is more diffuse; prolonged observation shows two nuclei in a common envelope.

| 467 | NGC 761 | 01 54.9 | +33 08 | 14.5 | 1.7 x 0.5 | Tri |

SB0. NGC 760, close to the N, is a double star.

- -

(16) Round, quite bright; much brighter to the middle and a stellar nucleus; NGC 760 shows as a stellar nucleus and halo joined to NGC 761.

| 468 | NGC 772 | 01 56.6 | +18 46 | 10.43 | 10.5 x 6.8 | Ari |
| | Arp 78 | | | | | |

SBc. NGC 770, $14^m.2$, a very small spiral, lies at $01^h 56^m.8$ $+18^o 42'$.

- -

(16½) Extensive envelope surrounding a much brighter centre and a stellar nucleus; patchy nebulosity lies S.p. the nucleus; faint star close p.

(8½) x51 seen as a diffuse glow; x102 shows a stellar nucleus set in a round, bright centre; does not bear magnification well.

| 469 | NGC 779 | 01 57.2 | -06 12 | 11.3 | 3.0 x 0.5 | Cet |

SBc. Spiral arms very weak and poorly resolved.

- -

(8) Very much elongated in PA 170° - 350°; about $2' x 0'.5$ in size and quite faint overall with a slightly brighter centre; 12 mag star lies S.p.

WS	Cat	RA	Dec	m	AD	Con
470	NGC 784	01 58.4	+28 35	11.78	9.7 x 2.6	Tri

Sc.

- -

(10) Elongated N-S; very faint core with a very patchy appearance; a hard object.

471	NGC 890	02 19.0	+33 02	12.7	0.9 x 0.4	Tri

E. Indication of a dark crescent of material near the nucleus.

- -

(16) Small, quite bright and slightly elongated N.f., S.p.; brighter centre.

472	NGC 891	02 21.0	+42 14	10.03	15.0 x 3.8	And

Sb. Member of NGC 1023 group.

- -

(30) An enormous edge-on spiral; the dust lane is prominent and cuts the bulge in half but is clearly detectable only for 2$'$ across the bulge, being difficult to trace further out; the disk is longer on the N side.
(16) Low, almost uniform surface brightness, being slightly brighter near central region; the dark lane is very obvious across the centre; the rich star field gives an interesting 3-D effect.

473	NGC 925	02 24.2	+33 21	10.13	14.0 x 8.6	Tri

Sc/SBc. Contains 99 known H II regions. HS nucleus. Member of NGC 1023 group. DDO 25, $13^m.0$, is at $02^h 30^m.3 +33° 16'$.

- -

(30) Low surface brightness; the bar is conspicuous and shows some structure including an elongated bulge with a weak enhancement to the SE; two very short, faint arms curve gradually from the ends of the bar; some very faint detached nebulosity

WS	Cat	RA	Dec	m	AD	Con

(NGC 925 continued)

is visible about 3$'$ N of the bulge.

(16½) Brightest part elongated N.p., S.f. with faint surrounding nebulosity; the f end curves to the S and then to the W.

(10) Easily seen irregular patch of light; no sign of a nucleus but brightens gradually in the centre.

| 474 | NGC 936 | 02 25.0 | −01 22 | 10.33 | 6.3 x 5.5 | Cet |

SB0/SBa. Nucleus a radio source.

- -

(16) Quite bright, elongated; suddenly becomes much brighter to the middle.

(12) Bright, easy object; about 4$'$ in diameter and very nearly circular.

(2¼) Very faint and elliptical in shape; very much brighter in the centre with a stellar nucleus.

| 475 | NGC 949 | 02 27.7 | +36 55 | 12.0 | 3.6 x 2.3 | Tri |

Sb. The outer envelope is very faint.

- -

(16) Slightly elongated; much brighter centre.

(10) Fairly bright and elongated; easy object.

| 476 | NGC 972 | 02 32.8 | +29 13 | 12.7 | 2.0 x 1.9 | Ari |

Sa/b. Contains a very complex central bulge and smooth spiral arms.

- -

(36) Bright elliptical shape with a mottled bulge; a weak enhancement is on the NW side, close to the bulge, and on the SE side an extremely faint wisp is suspected; no nucleus visible.

(16½) Elongated N.p., S.f.; the S.p. edge is brighter; quite large and very bright.

(8½) x102 fuzzy ellipse with indications of a slightly brighter, extended central region.

WS	Cat	RA	Dec	m	AD	Con
477	NGC 1023	02 38.9	+38 57	9.51	11.6 x 4.3	Per
	Arp 135					

SO. Radio source. An H I complex lies in the region. Member of NGC 1023 group. IC 239, $12^m.1$, another group member, is at $02^h 33^m.3 +38° 45'$.

- -

($16\frac{1}{2}$) Very bright and large, being greatly elongated E-W; an extremely bright, stellar nucleus is surrounded by an elliptical lens which becomes long extensions; three stars are projected on the W extension and one on the E.

(6) x50 small and rather faint; x155 symmetrical oval with a bright centre and surface brightness falling off rapidly towards the edges.

478	NGC 1052	02 38.6	-08 28	10.89	4.5 x 2.9	Cet

E. Nucleus a radio source. Active elliptical galaxy with spectrum showing [O II] at 3727 Å.

- -

(10) Small, faint stellar centre in faint nebulosity; suspected condensations.

(8) x48 fairly large and bright and much brighter towards the centre to a stellar nucleus; x241 a faint star on the S.p. edge.

479	NGC 1055	02 40.5	+00 20	10.60	11.9 x 4.8	Cet

Sb. PKS 0239+002. Member of NGC 1068 group.

- -

(12) Extended nebulosity orientated N.p., S.f.; rather difficult due to nearby 7 mag star.

(10) x59 large, faint and of fairly even brightness x148 N.p. extension appears wider than the S.f. one appears a bit mottled.

(8) Elongated patch of light with a star on the NW edge; no other detail seen.

WS	Cat	RA	Dec	m	AD	Con
480	NGC 1068	02 40.1	-00 14	8.91	10.0 x 8.0	Cet
	M 77					
	Arp 37					

Sb. 3CR 71. PKS 0240-00. IR and X-ray source.
Class 2 Seyfert. The nucleus is not as optically
compact as in some Seyferts.
- -
(36) A remarkable object; small spiral with a
conspicuous nucleus and inner ring structure, the
latter being the most interesting feature, being
quite well-defined with a conspicuous knot at one
end of the major axis; the ring is broken on one
side; outside the ring is an extensive diffuse
glow containing weak spiral features, the most
conspicuous being on the S side.
(16) Very bright indeed; the diffuse halo brightens
abruptly to a brilliant core containing a bright,
stellar nucleus; the core contains a notch on the
S side, apparently a short, inner spiral arm.
(8) At LP appears as a faint, circular nebulous
patch; it stands higher magnification well, and on
MP the surrounding nebulosity is more distinct; the
nucleus is very small and virtually stellar.

| 481 | NGC 1073 | 02 41.1 | +01 10 | 12.5 | 5.5 x 5.5 | Cet |

SBc. Member of NGC 1068 group. SN: 1962 - $13^m.9$.
- -
(10) x59 faint with slightly brighter centre; the
edges are ill-defined; becomes increasingly difficult with higher magnification.

| 482 | NGC 1087 | 02 43.8 | -00 42 | 10.02 | 5.9 x 3.9 | Cet |

Sc:SA(rs)c. HS nucleus. 8 superassociations.
- -
(10) A fairly easy object; the nucleus is quite
large and oval in shape; the remainder is rather
faint but an oval outline is easily discerned.

WS	Cat	RA	Dec	m	AD	Con
483	NGC 1090	02 44.0	−00 27	11.98	7.9 x 3.0	Cet
	I Zw 100	SBb. Member of NGC 1068 group. SN: 1962 − $12^m\!.8$.				

- -

(10) Excessively faint, small and oval; no nucleus
is detectable; an 11 mag star about 1' N.p.

484	NGC 1084	02 44.7	−07 41	11.0	2.2 x 0.8	Eri
		Sc. PKS 0243−07. SN: 1963 − $11^m\!.2$.				

- -

(16½) Very large and bright and elongated N.f., S.p.;
the ends of the extensions do not narrow but remain
quite wide; the central area is very bright and the
area immediately surrounding the centre is mottled,
especially on the f side.
(8) At LP fairly bright and large; brighter centre;
x121 the minor axis quite broad and mottling seems
possible; x241 mottling easily seen.

485	NGC 1156	02 56.7	+25 03	11.47	5.9 x 5.9	Ari
		Irr I. A highly resolved dwarf system with traces				
		of spiral structure; 2 emission patches W of centre.				

- -

(36) Bright, large box-shaped galaxy with some
extremely faint, extremely small knots equally
spaced along the major axis; the underlying light
distribution is weakly enhanced along the latter;
a pretty bright star is close to the W edge.
(8½) x69 a faint, amorphous patch with a 12 mag
star in contact to the N; no discernable nucleus
and at higher power seems elongated; higher powers
show no other detail.

486	NGC 1169	03 02.9	+25 03	13.0	5.0 x 2.8	Per
		Sb. Peculiar twisted plane. Star close to nucleus.				

- -

(16½) x176 appears as round and diffuse with a

WS	Cat	RA	Dec	m	AD	Con

(NGC 1169 continued).

bright stellar nucleus; x422 the area S of the nucleus is darker while the N.f. edge is brighter, looking like a bright patch.

487	NGC 1300	03 18.6	−19 29	10.58	8.0 x 4.8	Eri

SB. AN nucleus.

- -

(30) Bright barred spiral; the bar and spiral form are clearly visible, both appearing as a soft glow; the bar shows enhancements, including individual knots near the ends; the W spiral arm emerges from the bar at a sharp right angle and remains intact while the E arm fades near the middle and then brightens at the end near a field star; a stellar nucleus is at the centre.

($16\frac{1}{2}$) Greatly elongated N.p., S.f. with faint extensions; x176 a nucleus is visible in nebulosity which is oval in shape.

488	NGC 1309	03 20.9	−15 30	11.4	1.4 x 1.4	Eri

Sb. One arm is stronger and both well resolved.

- -

($16\frac{1}{2}$) Bright centre surrounded by fading nebulosity; a 7 mag star lies close S.p.

489	NGC 1332	03 24.0	−21 30			Eri

E . Member of NGC 1315 − 1332 group, an amalgam in the Eridanus cloud of galaxies.

- -

(8) x48 fairly large, bright and much brighter at the centre to a stellar nucleus; x241 suspicion of a star or nebulous knot S.p. the nucleus.

WS	Cat	RA	Dec	m	AD	Con
490	NGC 1337	03 26.8	−08 29	12.0	6.0 x 1.0	Eri

S.

- -

(16½) A little brighter at the centre with the remainder being of uniform surface brightness; the S extension is narrower than the N.

491	NGC 1343	03 32.4	+72 24	14.1	2.7 x 1.8	Cas
	VII Zw 8					

Pec. A ring encloses the nucleus of this object, the remainder being considerably fainter.

- -

(8½) Too diffuse to stand powers in excess of x102, but the central part is faint but quite clear at the latter power; a fairly bright star lies close to the N.

492	NGC 1421	03 41.4	−13 35	12.0	3.0 x 0.5	Eri

SAB(rs)bc. The central parts are very complex. A wide, dark lane runs along the major axis.

- -

(16½) Extended almost E-W; it widens to a bright, extended nuclear region; x351 a knot is suspected in the W extension; Y-shaped group of stars S.f.

493	IC 342	03 41.9	+67 54	9.1	27.4 x 24.2	Cam

Sc:SAB(rs)cd. The outer, spiral regions of this object are quite faint due to galactic obscuration.

- -

(8½) A small, nebulous spot about 15 - 20$''$ in size is all that is visible, but this is easily found; a line of 5 stars of 10 - 11 mag, PA 150° - 330°, lie about 3$'$ S.p.

WS	Cat	RA	Dec	m	AD	Con
494	NGC 1465	03 52.0	+32 24	14.9	2.2 x 0.4	Per

S0/a.

- -

(6) Faint and fairly small at LP; at HP at least 3 stars seem to be superimposed and the centre appears a bit brighter.

WS	Cat	RA	Dec	m	AD	Con
495	IC 356	04 02.5	+69 40	10.5	7.8 x 6.6	Cam
	Arp 213					

Sa. Radial bands of dark nebulosity cut across the NW regions. Outer spiral arms very faint due to galactic obscuration.

- -

(8½) Just discernable x51 and quite clear although not too bright x102; image quality becomes too poor at higher powers; no real central brightening.

WS	Cat	RA	Dec	m	AD	Con
496	NGC 1560	04 29.9	+71 49	11.59	11.9 x 2.2	Cam

Sc. No definite nucleus. Possibly in M81 group.

- -

(16½) Elongated N.f., S.p.; the ends of the extensions do not narrow and the S one is brighter; an involved star or small nucleus is visible towards the p end; a star is visible in each extension.

WS	Cat	RA	Dec	m	AD	Con
497	NGC 1569	04 28.5	+64 47	11.17	6.9 x 3.2	Cam
	Arp 210					
	VII Zw 16					

Irr I. Radio source. 2 field stars lie S.p. the centre. Possibly in M81 group.

- -

(36) Bright, large, very much extended; it appears nearly edge-on and shows 4 very faint, nearly stellar knots along its W half, appearing brightest in these regions; the E half is faint. (8½)x204 shows mottled areas; appears wider at the S.f. end and x308 quite irregular light distribution seen; BD+64°450, 9 mag, lies close to the N.

WS	Cat	RA	Dec	m	AD	Con
498	NGC 1637	04 38.9	-02 57	10.75	7.7 x 6.3	Eri
	Sc.					

- -

(30) A bright asymmetric spiral; the central region
is bright and round but has no nucleus; surrounding
this is a faint, slightly oval glow about 1 - 1.5
in diameter from which a spiral arm emerges on the
W side and winds about 90° until it points E.
(16½) Quite bright, slightly extended and brighter
to the middle

499	NGC 1784	05 04.4	-11 54	11.82	5.8 x 3.7	Lep
	Sc.					

- -

(16½) Irregular shape; x176 the centre is extended;
a faint star is close S an close S.f.
(10) Appears almost circular at LP and at HP slightly
brighter towards the centre; edges ill-defined.

500	NGC 1888	05 21.4	-11 30	14.1	1.4 x 0.8	Lep
	1889	Sb + E0		13.8	3.5 x 1.1	
	Arp 123					

- -

(16½) NGC 1888 is slightly extended N.p., S.f.; it
shows a well-developed centre with short, narrow
extensions; x351 the centre is extended and the f
edge is straight and sharply defined. NGC 1888 is
almost stellar with a brighter centre; the area
between it and NGC 1889 is dark and sharp.

501	NGC 2146	06 14.7	+78 22	10.68	8.4 x 4.8	Cam

Sb pec. 4C 78.06. Optically disturbed. NGC 2146A
lies 19' N.f.

- -

(16½) Elongated N.p., S.f.; the centre is wide and
extended; x176 mottling and a dark patch p the
centre; x351 the ends fade at the extremities.

WS	Cat	RA	Dec	m	AD	Con
502	NGC 2207	06 14.4	−21 21	11.8	3.0 x 2.0	CMa

S. SN: 1975 − $14\overset{m}{.}6$.

- -

(10) x59 faint and fairly uniform in brightness
with slightly brighter centre; a little extended
N.p., S.f.; very difficult at higher powers due
in part to low altitude.

503	NGC 2276	07 19.0	+85 50	11.54	4.0 x 4.0	Cam
	Arp 114					
	VII Zw 134					

Sc. A bright, very knotty arm lies on the W side.
4 superassociations. SN: 1966 − $16\overset{m}{.}9$, 1968 − $15\overset{m}{.}7$,
$16\overset{m}{.}6$. NGC 2300, $12\overset{m}{.}2$, is at 07^h $15\overset{m}{.}7$ $+85°$ $48'$.

- -

($16\frac{1}{2}$) Large, round, very diffuse and brighter in
the centre; resembles a puffy cloud; no nucleus is
visible at x176.

504	NGC 2403	07 34.4	+65 40	8.48	29.0 x 15.0	Cam

Sc:SAB(s)cd. Radio source. Contains 109 H II
regions. SN: 1971 − $16\overset{m}{.}0$. NGC 2404, at 07^h $32\overset{m}{.}1$
$+65°$ $48'$, is a bright knot in the galaxy.

- -

(82) Very large so that the large scale-structure
is difficult to see; x820 definite signs of partial
resolution into individual stars in some of the
brighter knots.
(30) A magnificent spiral with knots strewn all
over the field; more than a dozen are visible,
mostly in the outer extremities; two spiral arms
are visible, the brighter winding NW from the S
side and then curving E; two bright knots are near
the end of this arm, one being NGC 2404; the other
arm is very low in surface brightness, and has an
extremely faint enhancement; the central bulge is
mottled and quite extensive.

WS	Cat	RA	Dec	m	AD	Con

(NGC 2403 contined).

(16½) At first sight resembles M33; the central core is well-developed and is a little brighter than the rest of the galaxy; two spiral arms are visible plus a nebulous knot (NGC 2404).

(8) Fairly bright, very extensive but diffuse; PA is about 100° and 2 stars are superimposed on the E and W sides; no nucleus is apparent but there appears a denser portion in the middle and an arc to the W, almost like a spiral arm.

(6) x50 a large, fairly bright, shapeless patch; x82 elongated and slightly pointed at the p end plus a small vacuity just visible on the S side.

505	NGC 2537	08 11.5	+46 04	12.3	1.0 x 0.7	Lyn
	VV 138					
	Arp 6					
	Mkn 86					

S pec. "Bear-paw" galaxy. The largest associated H II region is about 200 kpc in size. Member of the NGC 2841 group.

- -

(36) Small and of relatively high surface brightness; shaped like a bear-paw, the structure consisting of a single spiral arm winding from W to E around the N side; this ring-tail includes 3 knots, one of about 15 mag; a bar-like feature shows in the interior region of the arm and extends to the S edge of the galaxy; there is a faint glow between the arm and bar feature.

(16½) A strange object, bright, quite large and of circular shape; near the centre is a large, dark area and a small, bright spot is excentric towards the N.p. edge; a bright star lies S.f. and a fainter star very close to the f edge; it rather resembles a planetary nebula such as M97.

WS	Cat	RA	Dec	m	AD	Con
506	IC 2233	08 10.4	+45 53	12.64	6.7 x 1.3	Lyn

S. One of the flattest known galaxies.

- -

(16½) Extremely narrow and very long, being aligned almost E-W; a star lies close to the N extension.

507	NGC 2523	08 12.2	+73 39	12.4	x	Uma
	Arp 9

SB(r)bc. A bifurcated arm emerges from the NW end of the bar structure.

- -

(16½) Shows a small core in diffuse nebulosity; the outer nebulosity is variable in brightness and a dark area is seen around the centre, being more pronounced to the S.

508	NGC 2549	08 14.9	+57 57	12.5	1.5 x 0.7	Lyn

S0/E6. Contains a bright, elongated nucleus. The outer lens shows traces of brightening at the ends.

- -

(8½) Slightly brighter centre; faint extensions.

509	NGC 2608	08 32.2	+28 38	12.9	1 7 x 0.7	Cnc
	Arp 12

SBb/SBc. Contains a double nucleus or a single nucleus and a superimposed star. The W spiral arm divides into three branches. SN: 1920 - $11^m.8$.

- -

(16) Dim, fairly elongated; slightly brighter centre.

510	NGC 2613	08 32.2	-22 53	11.3	6.0 x 1.9	Pyx

SA(s)b.

- -

(16½) Very elongsted N.p., S.f.; a bright centre is visible in extended lens and x176 the f extension appears wider; x351 a nebulous knot shows on the S edge of the f extension and there is also one f the central lens.

WS	Cat	RA	Dec	m	AD	Con
511		(NGC 2613 continued).				

(8) Faint, very elongated and mottled; x241 shows central brightening and the N.p. extension extends out to a bright star.

WS	Cat	RA	Dec	m	AD	Con
512	NGC 2639	08 40.1	+50 24	11.6	1.0 x 0.5	UMa

Sa/Sb.

- -

(14) Spindle elongated E-W; a bright centre is seen to extend for much of its length.

(8½) Faint oval with slightly brighter centre.

WS	Cat	RA	Dec	m	AD	Con
513	NGC 2655	08 52.4	+78 19	10.16	7.7 x 6.2	Cam
	Arp 225					

SO pec. The nucleus is a strong radio source.

- -

(18) Large, round and very diffuse; despite the latter it is quite bright; indications of a very slight elongation.

(6) Nebulous glow brightening to a diffuse centre.

WS	Cat	RA	Dec	m	AD	Con
514	NGC 2672	08 47.9	+19 10	12.2	0.4 x 0.3	Cnc
	Arp 167					

E + comp. The companion has a faint, curved plume extending to the E.

- -

(16½) Bright, irregularly round; the bright centre encloses a stellar nucleus; the companion shows as a faint, nebulous knot and could be mistaken for a star; it lies on the f end of NGC 2672.

WS	Cat	RA	Dec	m	AD	Con
515	NGC 2681	08 50.0	+51 31	10.65	5.4 x 5.4	UMa

Sa. Contains both inner and outer rings. Member of NGC 2841 group.

- -

(16½) Bright and circular with a much brighter centre weak surrounding nebulosity.

(8) Circular with a stellar nucleus; hazy edges.

WS	Cat	RA	Dec	m	AD	Con
516	NGC 2683	08 51.2	+33 38	9.72	12.1 x 3.9	Lyn

Sb/Sc. Contains a small, very bright peanut-shaped nucleus and possibly an outer ring.

- -

(18) Visually about 6' x 1'; displays a brighter centre and N of the nucleus there appears to be an indentation; the N edge is more diffuse; easily seen in the 4-inch finder.

(16½) Bright, very elongated and of high surface brightness in the central region; bright centre.

(8½) x56 shows as a long streak which looks mottled along its entire length; x111 the majority of the mottling is concentrated around the centre.

517	NGC 2685	08 52.2	+58 39	11.38	5.5 x 3.6	UMa
	Arp 336					

S pec.

- -

(16½) Quite bright, small and elongated N.f., S.p.; the central area is extended along the major axis; a bright star lies close N.

(8½) Quite faint, extended nebulosity; no detail.

518	NGC 2692	08 55.2	+52 10	14.1	1.3 x 0.4	UMa

SB. 90" N.p. is an Anon. spiral, $13^m.6$.

- -

(8½) Very difficult, appearing as a featureless diffuse blur; no sign of the Anon. spiral.

519	NGC 2713	08 54.7	+03 06	12.9	4.1 x 1.4	Hya

SBb. 2 filamentary arms form an outer ring.

SN: 1968 - $14^m.3$.

- -

(12) Oval nebulosity lying N.p., S.f.; bright centre; the supernova observed S.f. the nucleus.

WS	Cat	RA	Dec	m	AD	Con
520	NGC 2719	08 58.7	+35 49	13.5	1.3 x 0.3	Lyn
	Arp 202	Pec. Disrupted.				

(60) Double galaxy 40" apart; the N component is
a little brighter on the NE edge.
(16½) Very faint, small and elongated N.p., S.f.;
appears bi-nuclear x222.

521	NGC 2775	09 09.0	+07 09	10.7	2.1 x 1.2	Cnc

Sa:SA(r)ab. NGC 2777, $\overset{m}{.}$, is at $09^h08^m.4 +07°24'$.

(8) x48 fairly bright and much brighter at the
centre to a stellar nucleus; x241 appears a little
mottled; a bright star lies to the W.

522	NGC 2782	09 10.9	+40 19	11.7	1.8 x 1.8	Lyn
	Arp 215	Sb pec. HS nucleus. Removed from Seyfert class.				

(6) Shows a slightly brighter centre in round
nebulosity; a 9 mag star lies 5' to the N.

523	NGC 2787	09 14.9	+69 25	10.9	3.5 x 2.3	UMa
		SBa.				

(18) Egg-shaped galaxy with bright nucleus; two
faint stars on p and S.f. edges.
(6) Oval with small, stellar nucleus.

524	NGC 2841	09 18.6	+51 12	9.38	11.3 x 5.7	UMa

Sb. Radio source. SN: 1912 - $13^m.0$, 1957 - $14^m.0$,
1972 - $16^m.0$. Member of NGC 2841 group.

(16½) Elongated N.p., S.f.; a stellar nucleus is
seen in a bright lens from which broad extensions
point; a possible small, dark area p the nucleus.
(8½) Stellar nucleus in extended nebulosity; the

WS	Cat	RA	Dec	m	AD	Con

(NGC 2841 continued)

outer areas appear hazy and a dark section is suspected near the centre.

525	NGC 2859	09 22.8	+34 38	10.7	1.9 x 1.2	LMi

SBc. Contains a weak, diffuse outer ring.

- -

(16) Bright, round and much brighter to the middle; stellar nucleus.

(8) Small, round with bright centre; rather like a star out of focus; easy object.

526	NGC 2872	09 24.2	+11 34	13.0	2.0 x 1.8	Leo
	2874	E + Sc.		13.5	2.2 x 0.7	
	Arp 307					

Position given is between the two. 2872 is a Seyfert, 2874 is distorted. NGC 2871 and 2875 close by are stars.

- -

(16) 2872 is quite bright and much brighter in the middle to a stellar nucleus; quite small; 2874 is similar in brightness distribution but is oval in shape with PA about 110°. NGC 2873 appears almost stellar and about 2' N of 2874.

527	NGC 2903	09 30.7	+21 36	9.01	13.9 x 9.0	Leo

Sc. PKS 0929+21. HS nucleus. 74 known H II regions. NGC 2905 is part of it. A small, interacting group of galaxies lies 33' WSW.

- -

(30) Four-armed spiral with weak bar, the latter split into 3 sections; at each end of the bar 2 arms emerge; the arms on the NE side are shortest, although mottled while one of the SW arms fades appreciably partway around; the nuclear region is round and non-stellar.

WS	Cat	RA	Dec	m	AD	Con

(NGC 2903 continued).

(16½) Elongated N.f., S.p.; the nuclear region is bright and extended and considerable dark mottling is seen around it; an arc of bright nebulosity shows near the end of the N extension and a similar area occupies the S end.

(8½) x53 a diffuse, nebulous glow which gradually brightens towards the middle and a stellar nucleus; dark patches highly suspected near the nucleus; x212 the nucleus is elongated and the dark regions still suspected; PA 30° - 210°.

(6) Oval nebula with diffuse, oval nucleus.

| 528 | NGC 2911 | 09 31.0 | +10 22 | 13.3 | 4.0 x 3.0 | Leo |

S. Contains compact radio source. Seyfert-like spectra. A star lies 25" N.p. the nucleus. Member of NGC 2911 - 2919 group.

- -

(16) Small, round and brighter to the middle; the close companion, NGC 2912, at $09^h 31^m.1 +10^\circ 09'$, was not detected.

| 529 | NGC 2964 | 09 39.9 | +32 04 | 11.38 | 4.3 x 2.4 | Leo |

Sc. PKS 0939+32B. Mkn 404 is an H II region in it.

- -

(16½) Oval with a stellar nucleus; x333 a ring-like structure seen in the outer regions, this being most definite on the f side.

| 530 | NGC 2968 | 09 40.2 | +32 09 | 11.9 | 1.2 x 0.7 | Leo |

Irr. SN: 1970 - $13^m.0$.

- -

(16½) Quite bright and circular; a brighter centre is surrounded by dimmer nebulosity.

WS	Cat	RA	Dec	m	AD	Con
531	NGC 2976	09 43.2	+08 08	11.4	3.2 x 1.1	UMa

Sc. The inner structure is quite chaotic with a
good number of dark lanes. Member of M81 group.

- -

(16½) Elongated N.p., S.f., with a diamond shape;
x333 brightness variations are evident plus a star
or nebulous knot N of centre.

(8) Even brightness; x152 slightly mottled with a
suspicion of a star on the edge of the S.f. end.

(6) Faint, nebulous glow without any nucleus.

WS	Cat	RA	Dec	m	AD	Con
532	NGC 3031	09 51.5	+69 18	7.00	35.0 x 14.4	UMa
	M 81					

Sb. Contains relatively few large emission nebulae.
Nucleus is a radio source. Enveloped in an H I
envelope with NGC 3034 and NGC 3077. DDO 66, $13^m.7$,
is at $09^h53^m.5 +69°16'$.

- -

(30) An enormous central area evident but only one
spiral arm; the main problem is the size of M81, as
the faint outer parts have little contrast with the
sky because the field of view is not large enough;
the observed (S) arm has two faint knots and is
patchy near them; the central bulge has a small
concentration near the centre, with a bright peak.

(16½) A very bright, well-developed core is seen
with wide extensions; there are 2 bright stars in
the f extension beyond which the nebulosity curves
and brightens; the N extension widens further out.

(6) x183 the S.f. extension appears a little more
bright than the N.p. one; suspicion of a dark lane
running parallel to the major axis on the f side of
the nucleus,which is stellar in a bright core.

WS	Cat	RA	Dec	m	AD	Con
533	NGC 3034	09 51.9	+69 56	8.39	13.4 x 8.5	UMa
	M 82	Irr II. 3CR 231. A number of infrared sources				
	Arp 337	are distributed within. Member of M81 group.				

- -

(36) The surface brightness is quite high; the dust lane at the centre is very strong, and at least 8 knots are near it, 4 on either side; six of these are very faint, but two are pretty bright; another, much weaker dust lane is on the NE side.

(16½) A number of dark bays are visible along its length, all being highly inclined to the major axis; the two most prominent are f the centre, the one closest to the centre being wider as it reaches the p edge; a number of bright knots are visible, two of them being positioned each side of the main bay.

(6) The dark absorption lane near the centre appears as a wedge-shaped intrusion from the S; one or two more dark bands suspected towards the f end, which may may explain why the p part appears brighter; a faint, diffuse glow fans out from the centre on the S side.

533	NGC 3067	09 55.4	+32 36	12.7	2.2 x 0.8	Leo

Sa/b. The $15^m.8$ QSO 3C 232 is at $09^h55^m.4$ $+32°38'$.

- -

(10) x59 faint, slightly brighter towards the centre and somewhat extended; x148 a thin, edge-on object aligned N.p., S.f.; x296 no change.

534	NGC 3079	09 58.6	+55 57	10.59	11.0 x 2.3	UMa

Sc. 4C 55.19. Strong absorption makes it difficult to see the central region on photographs.

- -

(10) Edge-on, wispy and a little brighter centre.

(8) Extended N-S; x241 a star seen in the N end plus the possibility of slight mottling.

WS	Cat	RA	Dec	m	AD	Con
535	NGC 3077	09 59.4	+68 58	10.9	3.0 x 2.0	UMa

Irr. A normal emission-line galaxy, not a Seyfert as was once thought. Member of M81 group.

- -

(16½) Stellar nucleus seen in bright, oval material; dark areas seen in the outer parts.
(8½) Ellipse with strong central condensation.

| 536 | NGC 3115 | 10 04.0 | −07 35 | 9.3 | 4.0 x 1.0 | Sex |

E. Deep plates show a strong halo component and many globular clusters. Suspected SN - 1935.

- -

(36) A perfectly edge-on lenticular galaxy with a bright central core; the width is very narrow compared with the length.
(16½) Very bright centre with narrowing extensions.

| 537 | U 05459 | 10 04.8 | +53 20 | 13.8 | 4.3 x 0.5 | UMa |

S.

- -

(8½) x77 just visible as an extremely faint streak of nebulosity extending from a 7 mag star; x111 and x154 it displays even surface brightness with no nucleus being apparent.

| 538 | NGC 3166 | 10 12.5 | +03 33 | 11.4 | 5.0 x 2.8 | Sex |

Sa/Sc.

- -

(16) Very bright and very much brighter in the middle to a brilliant nucleus.
(8) Broad minor axis; slight mottling at x362.
(6) Oval with hazy nucleus.

| 539 | NGC 3169 | 10 12.9 | +03 36 | 10.54 | 6.1 x 5.1 | Sex |

Sa. Distorted. Member of NGC 3166 group.

- -

(8½) Elongated with bright centre and uneven light.
(6) Similar to 3166 but with no definite nucleus.

WS	Cat	RA	Dec	m	AD	Con
540	NGC 3185	10 16.3	+21 49	12.20	3.9 x 2.6	Leo

Sa. Weak outer arms form an external ring.

- -

(10) Rather indistinct; no apparent nucleus but brighter in central area; slightly extended.
(8½) Quite difficult; shows as a spindle about 2' x 1' in size.

| 541 | NGC 3184 | 10 16.8 | +41 33 | 9.84 | 9.5 x 9.5 | Leo |

Sc. Contains 56 H II regions. SN: 1921 - $13^m.5$, $11^m.0$, 1937 - $13^m.5$.

- -

(16½) Slightly brighter nucleus with a star close N.f. it; x222 a star on the N edge with a dark area to the S.
(6) x61 quite large though pretty faint; circular in shape with gradual central brightening; x152 a star is close to the nucleus and at higher powers the galaxy is very difficult.

542	NGC 3187	10 16.4	+21 59	13.27	4.3 x 1.6	Leo
	VV 307					
	Arp 316					

S. Distorted. No definite nucleus.

- -

(16½) Very faint, large and elongated; best image at x222 and when NGC 3190 is out of the field.
(8½) Spindle; slightly brighter centre.

543	NGC 3190	10 16.7	+21 57	11.10	5.9 x 2.4	Leo
	3189					
	VV 307					

Sa. Contains a very bright, condensed nucleus.

- -

(16½) Very bright and elongated N.p., S.f.; the stellar nucleus is surrounded by a bright lens which extends into thin arms; x222 a very strong impressic of a dark lane S of the centre.
(10) Strongly Oval-shaped; the nucleus is bright and oval and the N edge appears brighter.

WS	Cat	RA	Dec	m	AD	Con
544	NGC 3193	10 17.1	+22 01	11.02	4.8 x 4.6	Leo
	VV 307	E2.				

- -

($16\frac{1}{2}$) A bright central area is surrounded by a
region of mottled nebulosity; a bright star lies
just to the N.
(6) x82 very small, faint and round; being rather
diffuse it appears like a small ghost image.

545	NGC 3226	10 20.7	+20 09	13.3	3.0 x 2.5	Leo
	VV 209	E. Possibly linked to NGC 3227 by an H I flow.				
	Arp 94					

- -

($16\frac{1}{2}$) Bright and circular with brighter centre.
($8\frac{1}{2}$) Uniform brightness with a very sudden central
brightening.

546	NGC 3227	10 20.7	+20 07	12.2	5.0 x 4.5	Leo
	VV 209	Sb. Seyfert. Nucleus radio source. X-ray source.				
	Arp 94					

- -

($16\frac{1}{2}$) Elongated N.p., S.f.; it has a stellar
nucleus with bright extensions, the N one reaching
almost to NGC 3226; the extensions do not narrow
to points.
($8\frac{1}{2}$) Brighter and larger then NGC 3226; gradually
brightens towards the middle where a small, bright
nucleus is placed.

547	NGC 3245	10 25.9	+28 38	11.2	2.9 x 1.8	Leo
		Sa.				

- -

($8\frac{1}{2}$) Bright centre with stellar nucleus; seems a
little brighter along the major axis.

548	NGC 3310	10 35.7	+53 46	10.1	1.5 x 0.8	UMa
	Arp 217	Sb pec. Nucleus radio source. Spectrum shows strong				

UV continuum and emission lines. SN: 1974 - $16^{m}\!.5$.

- -

(36) A fascinating object; the nuclear region looks

WS	Cat	RA	Dec	m	AD	Con

(NGC 3310 continued).

like a small cluster of knots or nearly stellar
objects, arranged like water droplets in a small,
ring-like structure; there may be a very small
nuclear knot off-centre in the ring; outside the
ring there is weak structure, consisting of a very
short pointing NE and a small, very faint diffuse
knot on the opposite side.

(16½) Very bright and round; x84 it resembles an
unresolved globular cluster and x176 the core is
well-developed within the outer envelope.

(8) Small, quite bright, bluish; slightly elongated
approximately 80° and feathery at the ends of the
major axis; centre brighter.

(6) Small object with 30″ diameter nucleus; very
like a planetary nebula in appearance.

549	NGC 3351	10 41.3	+11 58	9.76	9.3 x 6.4	Leo
	M 95					

Sb. 3C 245. HS nucleus near 7 emission regions
14″ in diameter. Member of M96 group.

- -

(30) The bar is a weak extension from the bulge,
extending E-W; outside the bar the inner ring form
is suspected, but only with great difficulty; the
ring resembles a pair of spiral arms, since it does
not quite close and appears brightest to the S; no
nucleus is visible in the central section.

(8) x48 Large and bright with circular shape; a
stellar nucleus is seen x121 plus some mottling;
no change at higher powers.

550	NGC 3353	10 42.2	+56 13	13.0	1.4 x 1.0	UMa
	Mkn 35	Pec.				

- -

(10) Rather small, fairly bright and round with no
distinct nucleus; 11 mag star about 1′ SE.

WS	Cat	RA	Dec	m	AD	Con
551	NGC 3368	10 44.2	+12 05	9.29	10.8 x 7.8	Leo
	M 96					

Sa. Member of M95 group.

- -

$(8\frac{1}{2})$ x69 quite bright, large and elongated in PA
120° - 300°; the nebulosity brightens towards a
nucleus of about 11.5 mag; x111 the nucleus is
seen to be slightly elongated or even double.

552	NGC 3377	10 45.0	+14 15	10.5	1.5 x 0.8	Leo

E6. NGC 3377A = DDO 88 is at $10^{h}44^{m}\!.7$ $+14^{\circ}20'$.

- -

(14) Elongated N.f., S.p.; a stellar nucleus is
seen in bright surrounding nebulosity which ends
in slight extensions.

553	NGC 3379	10 45.1	+12 50	9.6	4.5 x 4.5	Leo
	M 105					

E. Member of M95 group.

- -

(12) Oval nebulosity with brighter centre; major
axis aligned almost N-S.
(8) Stellar nucleus; edges ill-defined.

554	NGC 3384	10 45.6	+12 53	10.2	3.0 x 2.0	Leo

SBa. Member of NGC 95 group.

- -

(8) x48 Fairly large, bright and shows a stellar
type nucleus; mainly circular in shape.

555	NGC 3389	10 45.8	+12 47	12.5	2.0 x 0.9	Leo

Sc. Contains very blotchy arms. SN: 1967 - $13^{m}_{.}0$.

- -

(8) Quite large but faint with even light; x121
seems rather circular and is slightly brighter at
the centre; at higher powers appears mottled and
slightly extended E-W.

108

WS	Cat	RA	Dec	m	AD	Con
556	NGC 3412	10 48.2	+13 40	10.4	2.5 x 1.3	Leo

SBa. Member of Leo I cloud.

- -

(16) Bright spindle elongated approximately N-S; much brighter in the middle to a stellar nucleus; a faint star almost in contact with the N edge.

557	NGC 3414	10 48.5	+28 14	11.0	1.8 x 1.0	LMi
	Arp 162					

SB0 pec. 2 faint fan-shapes extend from the centre region through the outer halo.

- -

(12) 2' in diameter; weak nucleus.
(8½) x56 a moderately bright oval of nebulosity with very slight central brightening; PA about 125° - 305°; higher powers show no more.

558	NGC 3430	10 50.8	+33 05	12.2	4.5 x 2.4	LMi
	IC 2613					

Sc:SAB(rs)c.

- -

(8½) Definition difficult owing to a nearby 8 mag star; LP shows faint, irregularly-shaped nebulosity of low surface brightness; HP shows elongation in PA 35° - 215° plus indications of nuclear bulge.

559	NGC 3432	10 50.8	+36 48	11.28	8.2 x 2.4	Leo
	VV 11					
	Arp 206					

SB. A dwarf companion lies close to the SW end. Member of NGC 3184 group.

- -

(16) Bright and slowly brighter to the middle; much extended in PA about 35°; 2 faint stars at SW end.
(8½) The NE end appears wider and is cut-off in PA 90° - 270°, the SW end tapering to a point; some faint but definite mottling is apparent; no nucleus
(6) Large, rather faint nebula which contains 3 stars, 2 of which form a double.
(5) Bright, large, elliptical; very opaque.

WS	Cat	RA	Dec	m	AD	Con
560	NGC 3445	10 51.5	+57 15	12.5	1.2 x 1.2	UMa
	VV 14	Irr.				
	Arp 24					

(IO) Diffuse; not much brighter at the centre.

561	NGC 3458	10 52.9	+57 23	13.2	1.4 x 0.8	UMa
		SO.				

(10) Rather faint, small and round; stellar nucleus; in a barren field; 10 mag star about 3' S.

562	NGC 3504	11 00.5	+28 15	10.9	2.0 x 1.0	LMi
		SBb. PKS 1104+28. Peculiar nucleus.				

(10) x59 fairly bright and gradually more so near the centre to a stellar nucleus; x148 extended N.p., S.f.; x296 a faint star just off both ends.

563	NGC 3521	11 03.3	+00 15	9.23	13.6 x 7.0	Leo
		Sb. The nucleus is a radio source.				

(18) Quite bright but difficult to decide on any structure; appeared fuzzy, very elongated and with diffuse edges.

($8\frac{1}{2}$) High surface brightness with very extensive envelope around very bright centre.

564	NGC 3556	11 08.7	+55 57	10.12	11.1 x 4.5	UMa
	M 108	Sb. SN: 1969 - $16^{m}.0$.				

(30) Dusty edgewise spiral; no nucleus, but an elongated patch near the centre; at least 4 other knots visible, the 2 brightest being at opposite ends of the galaxy; dust is obvious on the W side.
($16\frac{1}{2}$) The centre has either a small, bright star on it or a stellar nucleus; appears very mottled with a nebulous knot on the p extension while the

WS	Cat	RA	Dec	m		AD	Con

(NGC 3556 continued).

N end of the following arm is also brighter.
($8\frac{1}{2}$) Extended with patchy areas to E and W of
the centre, the former being the brightest;
the E end possibly somewhat wider.

| 565 | NGC 3593 | 11 12.0 | +13 05 | 12.0 | | 5.0 x 2.3 | Leo |

S0. Contains large amounts of dust. Probably a
member of M66 group.

- -

(16) Elongated and quite bright centre; no nucleus.
(8) Small, faint, possibly elongated in PA 60°;
looks like an elliptical; no nucleus seen.

566	NGC 3623	11 17.6	+13 14	9.37		11.9 x 4.5	Leo
	M 65						
	Arp 317						

Sa. Nucleus is a radio source. Distorted major axis
- -
(16) Very large and bright; elongated centre with
circular nuclear region surrounding a stellar
nucleus; a faint star lies close E of the nucleus.
($8\frac{1}{2}$) A dark lane is visible to the W of the nucleus
extending for about $2'.5$; it is seen as a darkening
of the background sky.

567	NGC 3627	11 18.9	+13 44	9.02		13.8 x 6.5	Leo
	M 66						
	Arp 16						

Sb. HS nucleus. PKS 1117+132. 25 H II regions.
- -
(16) Extended approximately N-S; diffuse, irregular
extensions to a brilliant, extended core which is
dominated by a circular nuclear region and stellar
nucleus; a spiral arm leaves the main body to the
S and curves off to the E.
($8\frac{1}{2}$) Large and very bright; the centre gradually
brightens to a stellar nucleus slightly N.p. centre
x212 a dark lane is suspected E of the nucleus.

WS	Cat	RA	Dec	m	AD	Ccn
568	NGC 3628	11 19.0	+13 44	9.53	18.0 x 4.3	Leo
	VV 308					

Sb. Nucleus is a radio source. 8 known H II
regions. Strong absorption makes the centre
difficult to see on photographs.

- -

(16) Very bright and extended almost E-W; a very
broad and obvious equatorial dark lane runs along
most of the length; the central region ia much
brighter to the N.
(8) Only very slightly brighter in the centre; the
S side appears more sharply cut-off.

569	NGC 3631	11 19.6	+53 19	10.45	7.2 x 7.2	UMa
	Arp 27					

Sc:SA(s)c. Contains a very large superassociation
on the W edge. HS nucleus.

- -

(14) Quite round, showing a brighter middle with a
very bright central spot; the outer halo quite faint
(6) Faint, circular with stellar nucleus.

570	NGC 3646	11 20.4	+20 19	11.28	5.0 x 3.7	Leo

Sc pec.

- -

(36) Bright, with an unusual appearance; a diffuse,
central bulge is surrounded by an elliptical, somewhat pointed ring structure; the ring is completely
closed and is knotty, especially on the N side;
about half a dozen knots or enhancements outline
the ring; a conspicuous nucleus is at the centre.
(16½) A large nucleus in an elongated lens of
lesser surface brightness.

571	NGC 3665	11 22.0	+39 02	11.4	1.0 x 0.8	UMa

Sa. PKS 1122+39. Strong absorption at the centre.

- -

(8) Quite bright with a glowing nucleus and diffuse
outer area; too faint for HP.

WS	Cat	RA	Dec	m	AD	Con
572	NGC 3675	11 23.5	+43 52	10.6	3.0 x 1.0	Uma

Sa. Contains a strong absorption lane. Possibly
a member of the CVn II cloud.
- -
(16) Very elongated; bright with brighter middle;
(8½) PA 170° - 350°; bright, extended centre in
fainter elliptical envelope; 56 Uma, 5^m.0, 40' p.

573	NGC 3690	11 26.0	+58 49	12.0	1.4 x 0.4	Uma
	IC 694					
	VV 118					
	Arp 296					
	Mkn 171					

Pec. Consists of 2 large systems + 3 or 4 dwarfs
and possibly one E-type. Dust in abundance.
- -
(60) Two objects in contact; a short extension is
to the S and a slightly longer one to the N; both
objects have brighter, extended centres.
(8½) Shows as a nebulous patch x51; x204 appears
as patchy and mottled with a brighter section at
the W end which is pointed, the remainder of the
material extending in a fan-like shape.

574	NGC 3718	11 29.9	+53 21	11.2	3.0 x 3.0	Uma
	Arp 214					

SBb. Narrow absorption lanes cross the centre.
- -
(60) Very faint; suspected to be bi-nuclear.
(16½) Slightly extended N.f., S.p.; a bright,
elongated centre with a brighter S end; a star
lies on the E edge.
(6) Faint with no nucleus.

575	NGC 3726	11 32.0	+47 10	11.7	4.6 x 3.5	Uma

Sc. Contains very patchy spiral arms.
- -
(16½) Elongated with stellar nucleus; star on the
N edge; x175 outer nebulosity mottled and a bright,
curving arm runs from the S to the E; the area N
of the arm is darker.

WS	Cat	RA	Dec	m	AD	Con
576	NGC 3729	11 32.5	+53 16	11.41	4.6 x 3.1	UMa

SB. Distorted.No definite arms in outer areas.

- -

(30) Pretty bright and small; a weak bar is
suspected with a couple of extremely faint knots
and a nucleus in an oval glow; a faint arc is on
the E side, with a dark interior; a faint star
is attached on the S side.

(16½) Major axis aligned almost E-W; a bright,
extended nucleus is seen plus a bright patch close
to the end of the S extension.

(6) Bright and small; a star is on the S.p. edge.

577	NGC 3738	11 33.1	+54 48	11.8	1.1 x 0.7	UMa
	Arp 234	Irr.				

- -

(14) Small, round and very faint; a brightening
of the middle is glimpsed but nothing else; does
not stand higher powers well.

578	NGC 3810	11 38.3	+11 45	10.8	4.1 x 2.8	Leo

Sc:SA(rs)c.

- -

(8) x48 fairly large and bright with a slightly
brighter centre; elongated N.f., S.p.; x145 there
is a suspicion of the f end appearing a little
brighter.

579	NGC 3877	11 43.5	+47 46	10.9	4.4 x 1.8	UMa

Sc. A star is superimposed on the nucleus.

- -

(10) Irregular shape; patchy in parts with no
definite nucleus; a 13 mag star lies close p.

(8½) A quite bright streak in PA 40°; a good,
bright nucleus in the 2' - 3' long nebulosity.

(6) Spindle with large, faint nucleus.

WS	Cat	RA	Dec	m	AD	Con
580	NGC 3893	11 47.3	+48 51	11.3	4.5 x 2.3	UMa

Sc. Distorted.

- -

(36) A fine one-armed spiral; a round, fairly
small central bulge is surrounded by an oval glow
with a sharp edge; winding from the W is a very
conspicuous arm with patchy areas; the arm curves
smoothly to the E and decreases a little in its
surface brightness until it reaches a knot where
it turns NW; a faint knot suspected on the edge
of the glow N of the nucleus, which is faint.
(16½) Oval with brightness variations in the outer
regions; a bright section is on the S.p. edge.
(8) Slight mottling; star on the S.p. edge.

581	NGC 3898	11 47.9	+56 14	11.4	2.7 x 0.7	UMa

Sa. Member of NGC 3846 - 3898 group.

- -

(16½) Bright and somewhat elongated N.p.; S.f.;
it brightens considerably in the middle to a
small nucleus surrounded by a fairly wide, diffuse
lens; an arc of faint stars lies close N.f.
(8) Quite bright but small although detectable at
LP; the centre is bright and elongated and the
outer area faint and diffuse.

582	NGC 3921	11 49.5	+55 15	13.4	2.2 x 1.3	UMa
	VV 31					
	Arp 224					
	Mkn 430					

Pec. A loop of nebulosity extends from the W edge
curves to the S and makes contact with the E edge.

- -

(14) Shows a stellar centre in a faint halo; no
other detail evident.

WS	Cat	RA	Dec	m	AD	Con
583	NGC 3949	11 51.1	+48 08	11.0	2.9 x 1.6	UMa

Sc. A faint companion lies 4.'4 to the W.

- -

(16½) Large, bright and extended N.p., S.f.; it appears to be tilted with a stellar nucleus; a bright surrounding lens has extended arms, and x333 considerable mottling is visible around the edge of the lens while a definite dark area is apparent on the S.p. side.

(8½) Contains a bright nucleus with a bright condensation closely f; the p end is much more bulky and rounded than the f end.

WS	Cat	RA	Dec	m	AD	Con
584	NGC 3953	11 51.2	+52 37	10.14	9.4 x 6.5	UMa

SBb:SB(r)bc.

- -

(36) Bright, very large and much extended; the structure is very subtle, consisting of a small, round nuclear region immersed in an extensive glow of non-uniform surface brightness; a very weak bar crosses the centre from E to W, being more conspicuous on the W half; an extremely faint arc winds S from the W end of the bar and quickly fades; signs of spiral structure are on the SW side, specifically two weak arms, the brighter ending with a diffuse knot; both arms are most apparent near the edge of the disk; on the NE side there is very little structure.

(16½) A small nucleus is contained within a lens which extends into arms; the centre is extensive and x176 a dark patch lies in the S extension about ⅓ the distance from the centre.

(8) Outer edges irregular and diffuse, the centre somewhat brighter; a small, faint star seems to be on the E edge.

WS	Cat	RA	Dec	m	AD	Con
585	NGC 3963	11 52.4	+58 46	12.7	1.9 x 1.9	UMa

SBb.

- -

($16\frac{1}{2}$) Appears irregularly round with a bright
centre; a bright knot in visible in the N.p. part
and a faint star on the S.p. edge.
($8\frac{1}{2}$) A diffuse, low surface brightness object.

| 586 | NGC 3982 | 11 53.9 | +55 24 | 11.3 | 2.4 x 2.2 | UMa |

S.

- -

(8) Small, very bright and stands HP well; seems
quite round with an exceedingly bright centre
in a hazy surround, which on LP makes it hardly
distinguishable from a star.

| 587 | NGC 3992 | 11 56.3 | +53 51 | 9.92 | 9.6 x 6.5 | UMa |
| | M   109 | | | | | |

SBc. SN: 1956 - $12^m.3$.

- -

($16\frac{1}{2}$) Very bright, large and greatly elongated
N.f., S.p.; x422 there is a dark area near the
core, especially near the S side; a bright patch
lies close to the tip of the S extension
(10) Oval with a small, bright nucleus in uniform
nebulosity; 13 mag star near the N edge.

| 588 | NGC 4026 | 11 56.9 | +51 14 | 10.7 | 3.0 x 0.6 | UMa |

SBa. DDO 102, $13^m.6$, lies 9' WSW.

- -

($16\frac{1}{2}$) Elongated almost on the meridian; a very
small nucleus is surrounded by a lens from which
project very long arms; x176 the extensions are
pointed at the ends.
(8) Quite bright with stellar nucleus; elongated
with pretty faint outer portions.

WS	Cat	RA	Dec	m	AD	Con
589	NGC 4027	11 58.3	−19 07	11.6	2.0 x 1.5	Crv
	VV 66					
	Arp 22					

SB. Dwarf companion NGC 4027 A lies 3.7 S.

- -

(30) A pretty ring-tail system; one of the arms
is quite conspicuous, and extends N from the W
end of the bar; a second arm curves round the
bar from the E and connects to the W end; the
bar is small and of fairly high surface brightness; no distinct knots were seen.
(16½) Irregular in shape with a bright centre;
a faint star lies on the f edge.

590	NGC 4038	11 59.3	−18 35	11.0	2.5 x 2.5	Crv
	4039					
	VV 245					
	Arp 244					

S pec. PKS 1159-18. 2 objects in a common envelope
with 2 tails.

- -

(30) A peculiar object of high surface brightness;
NGC 4038, the brighter component, is broad and
elongated with a hole in the p side; E of the hole
is a luminous patch and at several points around
the hole are a number of stars or stellar objects;
NGC 4039 is a broad wisp emerging S from and
curving around NGC 4038; the wisp has a knot and
two stellar objects along its length; at the point
where the two parts meet is a faint knot.
(16½) Appears as two irregularly-shaped nebulae
attached at their f ends; the northernmost appears
brighter and has a star just off the N.p. edge.
(10) Shows as an irregular looking object of even
texture and no bright core; looks like a shrimp
with a tail bent over the main portion; with a
6-inch it looks similar only smaller and fainter;
averted vision helps on the tail.

WS	Cat	RA	Dec	m	AD	Con
591	NGC 4041	12 00.9	+62 17	11.0	2.0 x 2.0	UMa

Sc. The centre shows very complex structure.

- -

(16½) Bright, round, with a bright central core
surrounded by fainter nebulosity; well seen at
x176, but no further detail noted.

WS	Cat	RA	Dec	m	AD	Con
592	NGC 4051	12 02.9	+44 41	10.20	8.0 x 5.8	UMa
	Mkn 79					

SBc. PKS 1208+39. Class 1 Seyfert. The nucleus
has varied by $0\overset{m}{.}25$ in 28d. Probably a member of
the CVn II cloud.

- -

(16½) Shows a pronounced stellar nucleus in large,
surrounding nebulosity; x176 dark areas seen to
lie around the nucleus and curved, spiral arcs
N.p. and S.f.; the former arm is brighter, and
curves towards a star which p the nucleus.
(8½) Elliptically-shaped, even nebulosity around
a well-defined but not very bright nucleus.

WS	Cat	RA	Dec	m	AD	Con
593	NGC 4088	12 04.3	+50 41	10.58	6.5 x 2.8	UMa
	Arp 18					

Sc. The optical and dynamic centres are not co-
incident. A large chunk of the high surface
brightness NW arm appears to be receding. Probably
a member of the CVn II cloud.

- -

(30) A conspicuous, very bright and considerably
large spiral with patchy arms appearing detached
in places; the brighter, more extensive arm is on
the E side, winding S from a small nuclear region
and then turning slightly E; at the turning point
it weakens considerably, brightens for about 1',
and then fades again; thereafter it brightens
again into a detached island feature that looks
cometary; the second arm is fainter and shorter,

WS	Cat	RA	Dec	m	AD	Con

(NGC 4088 continued).

and ends about due W of the nucleus with a faint
star or knot.

(16½) Extended N.f., S.p. with the N extension
being narrow and curved; dark mottling is visible
around the centre.

(8) Brighter towards the centre and showing small
extensions; x183 irregular in brightness.

594	NGC 4100	12 04.9	+49 44	11.9	4.0 x 1.0	UMa

Sc. Contains a weak, outer ring.

- -

(10) An easy object; elliptical in shape, it shows
a fuzzy outer shell and slight central brightening.

595	NGC 4111	12 04.5	+43 21	10.91	6.3 x 1.8	UMa

SO. The nucleus is cut through by a dark lane.
Probably a member of the CVn II cloud.

- -

(18) Small, very elongated with a bright, star-like
middle; SAO 044039, 8^{m}0, lies about 5' N.f.

596	NGC 4138	12 08.3	+43 50	11.9	2.9 x 1.7	CVn

Sa.

- -

(14) Extended N.p., S.f.; shows a mottled surface
with a brighter bar of nebulosity across the major
axis.

597	NGC 4144	12 08.8	+46 36	12.4	5.3 x 0.7	UMa

Sc.

- -

(10) Elongated N.p., S.f.; shows a suggestion of
mottling and dark regions.

WS	Cat	RA	Dec	m	AD	Con
598	NGC 4151	12 09.3	+39 33	11.6	2.5 x 1.6	CVn

Sb. SAB(rs)ab. Class 1 Seyfert. Radio, X-ray
and IR source. The nucleus brightened by $0^m.5$
between 1967 Jan and 1968 Nov. NGC 4156, $14^m.0$,
appears on the end of one of the arms.

- -

(30) Considerably bright with very interesting
structure; a very bright nucleus is surrounded by
a large, round diffuse glow; this is situated in
an extended, low surface brightness region which
brightens into faint arcs at each end, one being
brighter; NGC 4156, about 5' or 6' NE, appears
pretty faint and slightly extended with a conspicuous stellar nucleus.
(18) Appears as a blue star of about 11 mag with
slightly fuzzy edges; an extremely faint glow of
no definite dimensions surrounds this; a star was
seen in the position of NGC 4156, and may have
been the nucleus of this object.
($8\frac{1}{2}$) Quasi-stellar nucleus in a faint, oval halo.

599	NGC 4157	12 09.9	+50 38	11.9	5.9 x 1.0	Com

Sa. SN: 1937 - $16^m.2$, 1964 - $16^m.0$.

- -

(8) Elongated N.f., S.p.; at LP it appears to be
of uniform brightness, but x152 the brightness is
a little uneven.

600	NGC 4179	12 11.6	+01 27	11.6	2.2 x 0.9	Vir

Class uncertain, possibly an E7.

- -

($16\frac{1}{2}$) Extended N.f., S.p. with a stellar nucleus
and needle-thin extensions.
(6) Stellar nucleus in small nebulosity.

WS	Cat	RA	Dec	m	AD	Con
601	NGC 4203	12 13.9	+13 10	11.0	2.3 x 2.3	CVn

SBa. Member of Coma I cloud.

- -

(8) Fairly faint, small and round with a distinct nucleus which is practically stellar.

| 602 | NGC 4206 | 12 14.0 | +13 10 | 12.14 | 6.6 x 1.6 | Vir |

Sb. In a multiple system with NGC 4216, 4222 and IC 771.

- -

(16½) Faint, although not difficult to see; it is greatly elongated N.f., S.p. and appears fairly uniform in brightness with only a slight brightening in the centre.

(10) A small, extended patch S of NGC 4216; it is elongated in a N-S direction and of even brightness.

| 603 | NGC 4214 4228 | 12 14.4 | +36 28 | 9.85 | 10.6 x 10.6 | Vir |

Irr I:IABm. Spectrum shows Hα and [OIII] . The surrounding H I extends towards NGC 4190, and suggests possible tidal interaction. SN: 1954 $9^m.8$. DDO 113, $15^m.4$, lies 10' SW.

- -

(30) Bright, mottled and fan-shaped with a wisp on one end which ends in a double knot; six very faint, very small knots line the major axis, including what appears to be a conspicuous nucleus.

(8½) Large and bright; magnifies well but no detail is to be seen.

| 604 | NGC 4216 | 12 14.6 | +13 17 | 9.94 | 10.4 x 3.7 | Vir |

Sb.

- -

(16½) Elongated N.f., S.p.; the centre is well-developed. the p side appears darker while the N

WS	Cat	RA	Dec	m	AD	Con

(NGC 4216 continued).

arm is mottled and contains a bright patch.
(6) Shows a non-stellar nucleus displaced to
the p side of the major axis.

| 605 | NGC 4217 | 12 14.6 | +47 14 | 11.9 | 3.9 x 1.2 | CVn |

Sb.

- -

($16\frac{1}{2}$) Elongated N.f., S.p.; a slight central
brightening is visible, and the N extension is
brighter.
($8\frac{1}{2}$) Brightish centre in extended nebulosity.

| 606 | NGC 4236 | 12 15.5 | +69 37 | 9.82 | 26.0 x 8.7 | Dra |

Sc:SB(s)dm. An emission patch 5.5 SE of centre
is VII Zw 446. Possible member of M81 group.

- -

(10) Large, very much elongated and of even
brightness throughout; rather fine-grained in
texture, a bit like a portion of the Zodiacal
light.
($8\frac{1}{2}$) Massive object of very low surface brightness; there appears a slight increase in the
central luminosity, and the overall appearance
is uneven; 5 stars of 8 - 9 mag lie from the
E round to the NW side.

| 607 | NGC 4244 | 12 16.3 | +37 57 | 10.20 | 18.0 x 2.9 | CVn |

Sb. Radio source. Contains a very bright, small
nucleus or a superimposed star. Probably member
of the CVn I cloud.

- -

($16\frac{1}{2}$) An extremely long, narrow ray which is
brighter towards a non-stellar centre, this

WS	Cat	RA	Dec	m	AD	Con

(NGC 4244 continued).

part being a little p the visible centre; x160 it completely stretches across the field of view, and at this power the centre is seen to be wider than the extensions.

(8) Very bright streak, a good 10' long, which seems brighter to the W; no real bright centre.

608	NGC 4251	12 16.9	+28 19	10.2	1.9 x 0.8	Com

Sa. Contains a weak, outer envelope. Member of the Coma I cloud.

- -

(12) x80 a small, bright object less than 1' in and elongated.

(6) Bright centre in small nebulosity.

609	NGC 4258	12 17.7	+47 27	8.38	24.0 x 9.6	CVn
	M 106					

Sb. Radio source. Peculiar nucleus. H I arms cut almost radially through the disk in opposite directions, possibly due to ejection from the nucleus. Member of CVn I cloud.

- -

(30) Extremely bright and very large; the whole galaxy appears like a broad integral sign, with weak enhancements in arm features on opposing sides; about 4 or 5 patches are visible in the brighter arm located on the S side; the nuclear region appears slightly elongated and is sharply cut-off on the S side; as if affected by dust; a conspicuous diffuse knot lies about 30" N of centre.

(16½) Shows a small, bright central core and wide extensions; the f edge of the N extension is bright, and there is a bright streak on the p

WS	Cat	RA	Dec	m	AD	Con

(NGC 4258 continued)
edge of the S extension, which also displays
dark patches.

($8\frac{1}{2}$) The nucleus appears irregular in shape,
possibly rather triangular at HP; the extension
to the N is brighter with a faint arc of
nebulosity NW of the nucleus.

(8) The nuclear area is mottled, and a dark
area, parallel to the minor axis, is N of centre.

| 610 | NGC 4274 | 12 18.6 | +29 45 | 10.48 | 8.7 x 3.5 | Com |

SBa. The bar is seen almost end-on while the
outer arms form an outer ring. Member of the
Coma I cloud.

- -

(10) Elongated almost E-W; the nuclear area is
oval and part of the region p this definitely
appears brighter; the outer regions are diffuse
with ill-defined borders.

(6) Diffuse nucleus in oval nebulosity.

| 611 | NGC 4278 | 12 18.9 | +29 26 | 10.43 | 6.3 x 6.1 | Com |

E. PKS 1217+29. Contains many globular clusters.
Member of the Coma I cloud.

- -

(10) Bright, elliptical object with an intense,
non-stellar core; similar to M87.

| 612 | NGC 4290 | 12 19.6 | +58 14 | 12.7 | 1.5 x 0.7 | UMa |

SBb. SB(rs)ab.

- -

(10) A small nebulous patch of even brightness.

WS	Cat	RA	Dec	m	AD	Con
613	NGC 4314	12 21.3	+30 02	10,8	2.2 x 1.0	Com

SB pec. HS nucleus. Smooth, outer arms form a
pseudo outer ring.

- -

(10) Oblique with a pronounced stellar nucleus
and varying degrees of brightness.
(6) Fairly bright nucleus in oval nebulosity;
PA 140° - 320°; a 9 mag star is 15$'$ N.f.

WS	Cat	RA	Dec	m	AD	Con
614	NGC 4319	12 20.6	+75 45	13.0	3.1 x 2.5	Dra

SBb. The QSO Mkn 205 lies 42$''$ S.

- -

(16$\frac{1}{2}$) Oval nebulosity with a brighter, non-
stellar centre; Mkn 205 shows as a faint stellar
object close to the S.p. edge of 4319.

WS	Cat	RA	Dec	m	AD	Con
615	NGC 4346	12 22.2	+47 08	11.6	1.6 x 0.8	CVn

SBa.

- -

(10) Very small, fairly bright patch of light
with no definite shape; centre slightly brighter.

WS	Cat	RA	Dec	m	AD	Con
616	NGC 4395	12 24.5	+33 41	11.4	12.0 x 10.0	CVn

Sc:SA(s)n pec. NGC 4399, 4400 and 4401 are part
of it. Probably member of the CVn I cloud.

- -

(16$\frac{1}{2}$) A faint object, being only slightly above
the sky brightness; x160 a brighter centre seen.

WS	Cat	RA	Dec	m	AD	Con
617	NGC 4414	12 25.2	+31 22	9.7	3.0 x 1.5	Com

Sc. Contains a diffuse nucleus. SN: 1974 - 13^{m}.0.
Member of the Coma I cloud.

- -

(2$\frac{1}{4}$) Quite bright with a very bright centre and
two suspected bright areas N.f. and S.p. centre.

WS	Cat	RA	Dec	m	AD	Con
618	NGC 4419	12 25.7	+15 11	11.4	2.3 x 0.7	Com

Sa/Sc. AN nucleus. A strong, dark lane and
smooth arms appear on photographs.

- -

(8) PA 120° - 300°; oval in shape with a
brighter centre.

619	NGC 4448	I2 27.0	+28 46	II.4	3.0 x I.0	Com

Sb.

- -

($8\frac{1}{2}$) Faint object with no sign of a definite
nucleus but slight central brightening.

620	3C 273	12 26.6	+02 19	12.5-13.0		Vir

QSO. Low redshift object consisting of two
optical components, an almost stellar one
about $0.5''$ diam and an optical jet. Separation
$19.5''$. Radio source.

- -

(10) Indistinguishable from a star and visible
with direct vision.

621	NGC 4449	12 27.0	+44 14	9.68	10.1 x 8.7	CVn

Irr I. Radio source. Contains 81 known H II
regions. Member of the CVn I cloud.

- -

(36) A spectacular object; no sign of spiral
structure and thus obviously irregular; in good
seeing it appears resolved into many faint
knots, some appearing stellar; the overall form
is rectangular; a faint wisp juts off the SW
end and a weak dark patch lies due E of centre;
a knotty, weak enhancement runs along its length,
including the nucleus and a bright, round diffuse

WS	Cat	RA	Dec	m	AD	Con

(NGC 4449 continued).

knot; the most interesting region is one of high resolution due N of centre, where several stellar points are visible; these could be unresolved OB associations, or very bright stars.

(18) Elongated in PA 45°; structurally, it has a twinkling, starlike nucleus surrounded by a fainter, diffuse centre with two other quite bright regions each side, all being surrounded by a large, faint glow; a dark 'nick' was seen S.f. the nucleus.

(12½) Irregularly-shaped rectangle with a conspicuous nucleus; two very faint knots are visible, the brightest close SW of the nucleus.

(8½) Rectangular in shape with the NE end of the minor axis being possibly a little wider; there appear to be some brighter regions on the SE section of the major axis.

(8) Brighter centre but not stellar; not quite spindle-shaped but blunter; the N end seems to be brighter.

(2¼) Bright nucleus which is not round; the S.p. end is rather rounded and rays seem to extend N.f. the centre; the periphery is mottled.

622	NGC 4450	12 27.3	+17 14	10.11	8.8 x 6.0	Com

Sb. Contains a pseudo outer ring.

- -

(8½) PA 30° - 210°; shows an intense stellar nucleus which lies slightly N of the central bright area; a 9 mag star lies 4' to the SW.

WS	Cat	RA	Dec	m	AD	Con
623	NGC 4485	12 29.3	+41 51	12.02	3.3 x 3.1	CVn
	VV 30	Irr. Distorted.				

- -

(36) Very bright and extended with a rectangular box-shape; a very small, faint knot is close SW.
(16) Close N.f. NGC 4490; bright, elongated at right angles to NGC 4490 with a much brighter middle.
(8) Pretty faint and small and either round or elongated; brighter centre.

624	NGC 4490	12 29.4	+41 47	9.81	8.9 x 4.7	CVn
	VV 30	Sc. 3C 272. Distorted. Both this and NGC 4485				
	Arp 269	are probable members of the CVn II cloud.				

- -

(36) Shaped like a broad integral sign and is weakly enhanced along the N side, especially on the E half; the NW end is curved towards NGC 4485; in the centre a small, two-armed spiral pattern is suspected, apparently winding from a diffuse, non-circular central region; there is no nucleus within this area; the two arms are very short and fade rapidly into the surrounding nebulosity; the S-shape of the galaxy appears not to be related to this spiral structure; a faint, detached nebular streak lies on the N side.
(16) Very bright, large and much brighter to the middle where there is an intense core; the surrounding diffuse halo has a relatively straight edge on the f side; some mottling.
(8) Very bright elongated centre in the outer nebulosity; much larger with averted vision.

WS	Cat	RA	Dec	m	AD	Con
625	NGC 4494	12 29.8	+26 03	10.7	1.2 x 1.0	Com

E1/2.

- -

(12) Moderately bright nucleus in outer
nebulosity; about 2.5 in diameter.
(2¼) Appears round with a much brighter
nucleus; if there is any elongation it may
be in a N.f., S.p. direction.

626	NGC 4527	12 32.9	+02 48	10.51	7.5 x 3.5	Vir

Sb. A star may be superimposed on the nucleus.
Contains complex dark lanes. SN: 1917, 15^m.5.

- -

(12) 2.0 x 1.5; slightly irregular with no
nucleus.

627	NGC 4565	12 35.1	+26 08	9.56	20.0 x 3.6	Com

Sb. Radio source. Member of Coma I cloud.

- -

(30) Closely resembles its photographic
appearance; the planar dust lane is clearly
visible, splitting the central bulge into
two unequal hemispheres of light; the nucleus
is conspicuous on one side of the dust lane,
the latter being most obvious in the bulge.
(16½) A stellar nucleus in an oval lens
which develops into long extensions; the dark
lane is visible through the centre and x346
shows a light streak N of the lane at centre.
(8½) A bright line is seen across the centre
plus traces of the absorption lane.
(6) Large, diffuse nucleus; the extensions
are fine lines; no absorption seen.

WS	Cat	RA	Dec	m	AD	Con
628	NGC 4605	12 38.9	+61 45	9.6	3.0 x 1.0	UMa

Sc pec. Patches of dark material are present in a complex nuclear region.

- -

(16½) Elongated N.p., S.f.; no nucleus is to be seen, the centre being extended; the S edge of the major axis appears to be convex, the S edge being much straighter; the f extension narrows more than the p one; x176 dark mottling is seen along the entire major axis, being very evident in the p part; x351 the dark patches resemble those in M82 while a bright streak is on the f extension.

(8½) Bright with some mottling evident; the minor axis appears of even width for most of its length.

(6) Extended with condensations.

629	NGC 4618	12 40.3	+41 18	10.83	6.0 x 5.6	CVn
	VV 73					
	Arp 23					

Sc. A very massive spiral arm emerges from the E, curves S and then NW. Probably a member of the CVn II cloud.

- -

(30) A one-armed barred spiral, the bar being bright and very diffuse; off the E end of the bar a conspicuous diffuse arm emerges to the W and winds W; three knots are suspected in the arm, only one being definite; the overall character of this object is one of low surface brightness.

(8½) Roundish image with no central brightening; x102 the S edge appears a little brighter.

WS	Cat	RA	Dec	m	AD	Con
630	NGC 4625	12 40.5	+41 33	12.45	3.5 x 2.5	CVn
	IC 3765	Sc. Probably a member of the CVn II cloud.				

- -

(10) Shows an indefinite shape and no bright core; easily visible with direct vision.
($8\frac{1}{2}$) A small, misty round spot which gradually brightens towards the centre; at HP the nuclear region is almost lost; very faint overall.

631	NGC 4627	12 40.8	+32 43	12.53	3.7 x 3.4	CVn
		E. The outer parts are distorted by NGC 4631.				

- -

(30) Bright, small, diffuse; elliptical in shape with no nucleus.
($16\frac{1}{2}$) Faint, circular; x160 brighter in the centre with diffuse edges; x333 slightly extended.

632	NGC 4631	12 40.9	+32 41	9.29	19.0 x 4.4	CVn
	Arp 281	SB/IB/Sc. PKS 1239+32. Shows strong absorption at the centre. Connected to NGC 4656 by an H I bridge.				

- -

(30) Very majestic; it is littered with knots, patches and mottlings all along its length, and is very diffuse in its light distribution; no sign of a nucleus, but on the SE side is an arm-like feature that ends in a faint knot and appears to jut out of the plane of the galaxy; one knot is probably about 14 mag; signs of dust near centre.
($16\frac{1}{2}$) Bright centre in bright nebulosity; x222 a bright, non-stellar knot p the nucleus.
($8\frac{1}{2}$) Mottled inner regions with a condensation p the centre; the W end is thinner and the E end angled in PA 40° - 220°.

WS	Cat	RA	Dec	m	AD	Con
633	NGC 4651	12 42.5	+16 32	10.78	6.1 x 4.5	Com
	VV 56					
	Arp 189					

Sc. Radio source in the tail is apparently not connected. The $19^m.0$ QSO 3C 275.1 lies 1$'$ S.

- -

(10) Fairly large and bright with a very slightly brighter centre with a stellar nucleus; a little extended with ill-defined edges; x148 it appears slightly mottled.

634	NGC 4656	12 42.7	+32 19	10.50	14.5 x 4.1	CVn
	4657					

SB(s)m. Possible member of the CVn II cloud.

- -

(30) Very bright, large and much extended with a twist at one end; the brightest part is a diffuse, slightly extended glow on the SW end, a star also being attached; the galaxy then extends as a broad, diffuse glow to the NE which fades along its length until it reaches the first of 3 conspicuous knots; at this point the light distribution curves E and ends at the 3rd of the knots.

(16) Shows a conspicuous bright patch in the middle of 4656 and another where it merges into 4657; the whole object has a grainy texture.

(8) An object which needs good conditions, where it appears as a thin streak with a slightly brighter centre.

635	NGC 4665	12 43.9	+03 12	11.1	1.2 x 0.8	Vir
	4664					

SB0. Shows traces of smooth arms leading into a pseudo outer ring.

- -

(12) 1$'$ in diameter, quite bright and slightly irregular.

WS	Cat	RA	Dec	m	AD	Con
636	NGC 4666	12 43.9	−00 19	12.0	4.5 x 1.4	Vir

Sc. SN: 1965 - 14^{m}0 .

- -

(10) A tiny stellar nucleus in an edge-on spiral;
the extensions are of quite large size; no sign
of the companion NGC 4668.

637	NGC 4670	12 44.0	+27 16	12.7	0.8 x 0.5	Com
	Arp 163					
	Haro 9					

S0?. Two stubby extensions emerge from the main
body, both curving slightly at the ends.

- -

(16½) Stellar nucleus surrounded by slightly
elongated, diffuse nebulosity; p side brighter.
(8½) At HP a faint glow; centre brighter.

638	NGC 4676	12 44.9	+30 52	14.1	1.9 x 0.8	Com
	IC 819					
	IC 820					
	VV 224					
	Arp 242					

S0 + SB0 pec. "The Mice". Tidal effects are in
evidence, with a straight tail to the N and a
fainter, curved one to the S.

- -

(107) A strange pair, the brighter component is
like a mouse or tadpole with a long tail; the
head is quite diffuse and shows no nucleus while
the tail is straight and long; the second component is smaller and slightly extended and shows
weak enhancements, including a stellar nucleus.
(16½) x84 not bright but is elongated N.p., S.f.;
x176 it consists of two parts, the S one being
small, bright and almost stellar; N of this is a
dark area followed by an elongated, thin wedge
of nebulosity to the N; the S end is apparently
the nucleus and there is little nebulosity S of
it; x422 the dark area is quite prominent and

WS	Cat	RA	Dec	m	AD	Con

(NGC 4676 continued).

the N extension narrows as it recedes.

| 640 | NGC 4710 | 12 48.3 | +15 18 | 12.0 | 3.5 x 0.5 | Com |

Sa. Nucleus partly hidden by a dark lane.

- -

(36) A beautiful ray with uneven light distribution; a broad, diffuse nuclear bulge is flanked
on opposite sides by dips in the brightness; the
weaker light intensity in these regions suggests
the presence of dust; the brightest extensions
on either side of the bulge are pointed and a
little patchy; no nucleus seen.

(16) Elongated S.p., N.f.; dark areas lie on
each side of the centre perpendicular to the
major axis; bright knots flank these.

| 641 | NGC 4725 | 12 49.2 | +25 41 | 9.46 | 12.1 x 10.0 | Com |

SBb: SAB(r)b. One arm forms an incomplete,
pseudo outer ring. SN: 1940 - $12^m.8$, 1969 - $15^m.0$.
Member of the Coma I cloud.

- -

(30) x300 it is very bright and large; a long
bar with bright concentration with two curved
sections at the ends forming parts of the ring
which is very weak away from the ends of the
bar; the appearance is that of a ship's anchor;
an extremely faint knot is visible, apparently
in one of the arms, which were not seen.

(18) Small and bright with occasional three-
lobed appearance; a star lies just N of the
small, bright nucleus.

WS	Cat	RA	Dec	m	AD	Con

(NGC 4725 continued).

(6) Diffuse, with a small, bright nucleus.

---

642   NGC 4762   12 51.7   +11 22   11.0   3.7 x 0.4   Vir

Sa.

- -

(16½) Long extensions are seen with an elongated nucleus; x222 the N extension is mottled with a dark area halfway between the nucleus and the tip, the S extension is of uniform brightness.
(8½) Non-stellar centre in uniform nebulosity.

---

643   NGC 4775   12 52.4   -06 29   11.6   1.7 x 1.7   Vir

S.

- -

(16½) Irregularly round, like a puffy cloud; x349 a brighter centre seen plus a bright spot on the N edge; the S edge is poorly defined.

---

644   NGC 4793   12 53.4   +29 05   11.8   1.6 x 0.7   Com

Sc. PKS 1252+29. 5C4.022. Contains 3 weak outer arms, one extending to a dwarf satellite.

- -

(16½) Elongated N.f., S.p.; the centre is seen to be brighter and the N extension wider and brighter than the S.
(8½) Quite bright object with a brighter area in the NE end; 8 mag star close to the N.

---

645   NGC 4826   12 55.5   +21 49   6.6   8.0 x 5.0   Com

    M   64   Sb. PKS 1254+21. "Black-eye" galaxy. Possibly a member of the CVn I cloud.

- -

(60) Oval nebulosity extended N.p., S.f.; the

WS	Cat	RA	Dec	m	AD	Con

(NGC 4826 contined).

dark absorption patch at the centre appears to make the nucleus offset to the W.

(30) Very bright, large and oval; the "black-eye" is not totally dark and appears fairly broad and slightly curved; the nucleus is conspicuous and lies exactly on one edge of the dust lane, the latter being darkest on the E side; some patchiness near the lane on this side is suspected.

(16) A much brighter middle ends in a stellar nucleus; the absorption is very evident at all powers.

(8) Very bright and conspicuous with a clear outline; the nuclear region is small but not stellar and the whole object glows strongly; the absorption is not distinguished with certainty.

646	NGC 4861	12 57.9	+35 00	12.7	2.0 x 1.0	CVn
	Arp 266					
	Mkn 59					

Irr + E? The brightest component is at the S end. Mottled, fainter material extends N.

- -

(36) Pretty faint, large, extended and diffuse; the low surface brightness does not make it very conspicuous; it possesses a bright knot on the S end which is barely distinguishable from a star; the remainder is a diffuse, elongated glow which is patchy and brightest at the centre.

647	NGC 4868	12 56.8	+37 34	12.9	1.6 x 1.5	CVn

SA.
- -

(16) Round with slightly brighter middle; a faint star lies on the edge.

WS	Cat	RA	Dec	m	AD	Con
648	NGC 4900	12 59.5	+02 38	11.3	1.7 x 1.7	Vir

S pec.

- -

(36) Like a planetary nebula, appearing as a
symmetric, oval glow with dark spaces in the
interior; the edges are fairly sharp, and a
ring-like enhancement, broken in one place, is
suspected near the edge; also suspected is an
extremely weak bar; a bright nucleus is at the
centre and a pretty bright star on one end.
(6) Faint with no nucleus; star attached at 40°.

649	NGC 5005	13 09.8	+37 11	9.89	8.1 x 4.7	CVn

Sb/Sc. PKS 1308+37. Contains several knotty
arms with dark lanes.

- -

(16$\frac{1}{2}$) Bright and elongated with an extended
nucleus; x333 the f extension is brighter.
(10) Oblique with bright core and stellar nucleus.
(8) Rather faint and diffuse; quite bright in the
middle with a slightly non-stellar nucleus.

650	NGC 5033	13 12.3	+36 44	10.18	12.3 x 5.8	CVn

Sc. PKS 1311+36. 2 arms wind in opposite
directions. Contains a large superassociation.
SN: 1950 - 18^{m}.2.

- -

(36) Bright, very large and extended; the concentration at the centre is off-set and the W
side of this region gives a strong suspicion of
being cut-off by dust; a dust lane or knot is
suspected just S of the nuclear region; spiral
structure appears in two places, both being

WS	Cat	RA	Dec	m	AD	Con

(NGC 5033 continued).

very faint and completely disconnected from
the central section; one of the spiral features
includes an extremely faint knot.

(10) Small, compact bright centre in an outer
envelope elongated E-W.

(8) Looks almost round at first sight but soon
shows as being elongated; faint outer regions.

651	NGC 5055	13 14.7	+42 10	10.1	10.0 x 5.0	CVn
	M 63					

Sb. SN: 1971 - $11^m.5$. Member of the M101 group.

- -

($16\frac{1}{2}$) Very bright and large with a small, bright
nucleus surrounded by a nebulous glow which
fades off at the edges.

(8) A rather pale, glowing oval with a brighter
solid-looking nucleus; it stands MP well but no
detail can be seen; an 8 mag star is close NW.

652	NGC 5128	13 23.8	-42 53	6.98	31.0 x 25.0	Cen
	Arp 153					

E pec. Radio source.

- -

($16\frac{1}{2}$) Very large and pretty bright; a circular
shaped glow of nebulosity with the S half being
brighter; a wide, dark division crosses the
centre, a star being in the N.p. end of the
dark division while another is seen in the N
part of the S half.

($12\frac{1}{2}$) A lovely divided nebula; the dark lane
seemed triangular in shape and a spike of light
shows in the S part of the dark region; a very
faint halo surrounds the object.

WS	Cat	RA	Dec	m	AD	Con
653	NGC 5194	13 28.9	+47 19	8.35	14.2 x 9.5	CVn
	5195	13 29.0	+47 24	9.49	8.9 x 7.4	

M   51   Sc + Irr. 4C47.36.1. NGC 5195 appears to be

VV   1   devoid of H I. SN:(NGC 5195) 1945 - $14^{m}.0$.

Arp 85

- -

(30) The spiral pattern is clear and bright
with almost a three-dimensional effect; nearly
two dozen knots and enhancements are visible
and the connecting arm is easily visible,
brightening considerably near the connection
point; NGC 5195 is shaped something like an
earlobe with a strong dust patch SW of its
nucleus and a sharp E edge; the combination
of the linking arm and the absorption make it
appear spiral.

($16\frac{1}{2}$) A magnificent sight, being obviously
spiral; two arms are seen, one emerging from
the nuclear component of NGC 5194 in a S.f.
direction and then turning N, it then runs
almost straight for a while, where tiny points
of light are intermittently seen, then turns
W and ends near the p part of the galaxy; the
other arm is more uniform in brightness and
winds through 180° to fade into the sky f the
galaxy; NGC 5195 is bright and looks like
half a disk; it is brighter on the straight
edge and has a stellar nucleus.

(10) The larger object is very slightly oval
with a bright, well-defined nucleus; outside
this is a large, faint glow with a section of
a spiral arm in the S.f. section; irregularities
in the structure are also suspected; NGC 5195

WS	Cat	RA	Dec	m	AD	Con

(NGC 5194-5 continued).

appears irregular with faint outer areas.
(8) Appears as two glowing patches almost in
contact, both with very small, star-like
centres; a faint trace of the connecting arm
is visible on the E side and some of the
brighter knots can at times be made out; does
not stand magnification well.

| 654 | NGC 5198 | 13 29.2 | +46 48 | 12.9 | 0.7 x 0.6 | CVn |

E.

- -

$(16\frac{1}{2})$ Brighter centre in circular nebulosity;
three stars lie close to the N.
(10) Very faint and almost stellar at LP; at
higher powers a small nucleus is seen, and it
appears slightly oval in PA 80°.

655	NGC 5221	13 33.7	+13 57	14.5	2.0 x 0.7	Vir
	VV 315
	Arp 288

Sb. Plumes of material extend NW and SE.

- -

(16) Elongated oval about 1'.0 x 0'.5; of low
surface brightness but easy to see; PA 50°.

656	NGC 5222	13 33.7	+13 52	14.0	1.6 x 1.2	Vir
	VV 315
	Arp 288

E. NGC 5226 is a disrupted spiral almost in
contact to the E.

- -

(16) Quite bright and suddenly much brighter
to the middle; round and about 1'.0 in size;
NGC 5226 is very small and round with no signs
of central brightening.

WS	Cat	RA	Dec	m	AD	Con
657	NGC 5236	13 34.2	-29 37	10.1	8.0 x 7.0	Hya
	M 83					

Sc. PKS 1334-29. IR source. AN nucleus. Over
79 H II regions. An incipient bar lies in the
centre. SN: 1923 - $14^{m}.0$, 1950 - $14^{m}.5$, 1957 -
$15^{m}.0$, 1968 - $11^{m}.9$.

- -

(10) Large and bright with a much brighter,
very condensed core which is not quite stellar;
it appears slightly elliptical with two definitely brighter extensions going NW and SE
from the nucleus and involved in the larger,
diffuse outer envelope; definite mottling is
seen throughout the envelope and with averted
vision the tips of the bright extensions are
curved slightly and quite short; two faint
stars are at the tip of each arm.

657	NGC 5248	13 36.2	+09 01	11.3	3.2 x 1.4	Boo

Sc:SAB(rs)bc. Peculiar nucleus.

- -

(30) Two arms are clearly visible as distinct
enhancements immersed within an elongated,
diffuse glow; neither arm appears directly
connected to the central bulge although they
curve towards it; the bulge appears diffuse
and contains no nucleus; there is a bright,
diffuse knot near the end of the E arm.
($16\frac{1}{2}$) Bright, stellar centre in an outer
envelope extended N.p., S.f.; x160 the area
N of the nucleus is brighter and a knot lies
near the edge of the N extension; x333 a
patch lies S of the nucleus.
(6) Faint, diffuse centre with stellar point.

WS	Cat	RA	Dec	m	AD	Con
658	NGC 5273	13 41.0	+35 46	12.7	2.7 x 2.3	CVn

SO.

- -

(14) Stellar centre with a small area of fainter surrounding material; the edges are fuzzy.

| 659 | NGC 5297 | 13 45.3 | +44 00 | 12.0 | 5.6 x 0.9 | CVn |

Sc.

- -

(16½) A faint ray elongated N.p., S.f. with a slightly brighter centre; NGC 5296, 15 mag, is seen as a faint, nebulous spot 5' p.
(14) A thin spindle with a 9 mag star attached to the N edge; overall brightness with the centre larger by a small degree.

| 660 | NGC 5371 | 13 54.6 | +40 35 | 11.7 | 4.0 x 2.8 | CVn |

SBb. SB(rs)bc.

- -

(36) Initially appears as a large, elongated diffuse glow but subtle features appear on careful inspection; two spiral arms wind from near, but not connected to, the ends of a weak, cigar-shaped bar; the S arm is more conspicuous and includes two knots, one large and diffuse; between the S arm and the bar a faint arc which ends in a diffuse knot is suspected, and seems to be part of a closed ring encircling the bar. all these features are faint in the glow of the underlying disk.
(16½) Circular with a stellar nucleus; resembles a nebulous star at LP; a 9 mag star close f.
(10) Oval with a faint, stellar core.

WS	Cat	RA	Dec	m	AD	Con
661	NGC 5457	14 01.4	+54 35	9.6	10.0 x 8.0	UMa
	M 101					

Sc. NGC 5449, 5450, 5451, 5453, 5455, 5458, 5461 and 5462 are knots in the spiral arms.

- -

(30) Extremely large but not very bright; it is a complicated object to disentagle in the 30-inch; the arms are difficult to piece together and appear disconnected in many places and it took careful study to make some sense out of the spiral pattern; a total of 20 knots and enhancements are scattered within and outside the visible arms; some of these are very bright; NGC 5447, 5451, 5455 and 5458 appear faint, NGC 5453 is at the tip of fan-shaped luminosity extending S, NGC 5449 shows as a close, faint pair of knots. NGC 5462 is the brightest knot and NGC 5450 shows three condensations and is mottled; a very small, non-stellar core is at the centre within a small, diffuse region.

($16\frac{1}{2}$) Very large and diffuse extends over most of the field; a relatively bright central region, bright stellar nucleus and knots in spiral arms are visible, all with ease.

(8) A faint, fairly large misty patch which is not quite circular; a very small, bright nucleus shows in the nebulous glow; best conditions are needed to make the most of this object, but none of the spiral features are visible.

(6) Large featureless blur with possible signs of some condensations.

WS	Cat	RA	Dec	m	AD	Con
662	NGC 5474	14 04.2	+53 47	10.91	7.4 x 6.8	UMa
	VV 344	Sc. Distorted. Member of the M101 group.				

$(16\frac{1}{2})$ Irregular in shape with a bright, round
area in the N end; x349 a large, curving dark
region separates the bright and faint parts.
(8) Faint and featureless; PA 170°.

663	NGC 5533	14 15.1	+35 27	12.9	2.0 x 1.8	Boo
		Sb.				

(16) Quite bright and elongated in PA 120°; it
is brighter in the middle and about 1.5 x 0.5.
(10) Faint, small slightly brighter centre.

664	NGC 5600	14 22.6	+14 45	12.4	1.0 x 0.7	Boo
		S pec.				

$(8\frac{1}{2})$ x69 visible as a tiny but prominent spot;
x111 a very faint, stellar nucleus suspected.

665	NGC 5665	14 31.2	+08 11	12.7	1.0 x0 .8	Boo
	Arp 49	S pec. The inner regions are distorted with a				
		number of condensations and dark areas.				

$(8\frac{1}{2})$ x77 it appears rather faint and elongated
in PA 120° - 300°; higher powers reveal no more
but a slightly brighter nuclear region.

666	NGC 5676	14 31.9	+49 34	11.2	3.0 x 1.5	Boo
		Sc. Contains 4 superassociations. IC 1029,				
		is at $14^{h}30^{m}.7 +50^{\circ}07'$.				

(16) Bright, quite large and a little elongated;
a diffuse halo surrounds a bright middle and an
intense core.

WS	Cat	RA	Dec	m	AD	Con
667	NGC 5678	14 31.3	+58 01	11.2	2.6 x 1.0	Dra

SB. Distorted.

- -

(36) The features are extremely subtle; a faint
stellar nucleus is surrounded by a broad,
diffuse region of moderate surface brightness;
an extremely faint short curve is suspected
just outside this region, plus an extremely
faint knot; on the opposite side of the galaxy
is a very diffuse extension, thought to include
an extremely faint, barely recognizable arm
which nearly extends straight for some distance;
the nucleus is off-centre in the underlying glow.
(16½) Shows a well-developed centre with
extensions N-S; x222 a stellar nucleus is seen.

WS	Cat	RA	Dec	m	AD	Con
668	NGC 5746	14 43.7	+01 55	10.63	9.0 x 2.4	Vir

Sb.

- -

(36) A long spindle with a sharp edge on the E
side; the nuclear bulge includes a faint nucleus,
so the galaxy is not exactly edge-on; no light
is detected from the underside of the dust lane
which causes the sharp E edge.
(18) Elongated, with a brighter middle and a
tapering S.f. end.
(6) Faint oval with no nucleus.

WS	Cat	RA	Dec	m	AD	Con
669	NGC 5820	14 57.9	+53 59	12.8	0.7 x 0.3	Boo
	Arp 136					

E/S0. Faint material extends from the SE end.

- -

(16½) Elongated E-W; there is a bright centre
with extensions, these being brighter at their
respective ends.

WS	Cat	RA	Dec	m	AD	Con
670	NGC 5846	15 05.2	+01 42	10.5	1.0 x 1.0	Vir

E. NGC 5846A is a high-density, compact dwarf.

- -

(16) Round and quite bright with a stellar core;
the companion is small and faint with a very
small, brighter centre.

(12) Oval nebulosity with a bright core.

(8) Rather faint at first but improves at higher
 power, which makes it look larger although
more diffuse; bright, non-stellar nucleus.

WS	Cat	RA	Dec	m	AD	Con
671	NGC 5850	15 05.9	+01 38	12.9	2.6 x 2.1	Vir

SB. Member of the NGC 5850 group.

- -

(36) Considerably bright, large and extended;
the bar is evident, but no other detail other
than a small nuclear region with small nucleus.
an extremely faint star is attached near the E
end of the bar.

(12) An oval, featureless blur.

WS	Cat	RA	Dec	m	AD	Con
672	NGC 5866	15 05.8	+55 51	11.5	6.5 x 3.0	Boo
	M 102	SO				

(36) A classical lenticular galaxy with pointed
ends; along the major axis is a conspicuous
dust lane, remarkable for its extreme narrow-
ness; this is only visible across the bright,
central parts of the galaxy; no nucleus visible.

(16½) Very bright spindle with elongated arms
N.p., S.f.; the arms protrude from an oval
shaped envelope with a non-stellar nucleus; the
dark band cuts across the N extension about

WS	Cat	RA	Dec	m	AD	Con

(NGC 5866 continued).
halfway between the tip and central area; at
x422 a very faint star p the end of the N arm.
(8) A bright ellipse at LP; at HP the ends
appear more pointed and the inner, central part
is very bright.

WS	Cat	RA	Dec	m	AD	Con
673	NGC 5879	15 09.1	+57 05	12.1	3.3 x 1.3	Dra

Sb. SN: 1954 - $14^{m}.9$.

- -

(16) Elongated and slightly brighter towards
the middle; quite bright.
(6) Small and faint with a brighter centre.

WS	Cat	RA	Dec	m	AD	Con
674	NGC 5907	15 15.2	+56 24	10.41	15.7 x 2.0	Dra

Sc. NGC 5906 is part of it. SN: 1940 - $14^{m}.3$.
Possible member of the M101 group.

- -

(16) Bright and very elongated with a brighter
middle; no sign of the absorption lane.

WS	Cat	RA	Dec	m	AD	Con
675	NGC 5929	15 25.2	+41 46	14.0	1.1 x 1.0	CrB
	5930			13.0	2.2 x 0.9	

Arp   90   E/S0 + Sa. A curved plume appears to link both
I Zw 12   objects. Extensive outer nebulosity.

- -

(16) NGC 5930 is bright and much brighter in
the middle; round in shape; NGC 5929 is small
and attached to the S.p. edge of the former.

WS	Cat	RA	Dec	m	AD	Con
676	NGC 6052	16 04.0	+20 38	14.1	0.9 x 0.56	Her
	6064					

Two in contact. Distorted.

- -

VV   86   (60) Faint object about 20" in diameter.

WS	Cat	RA	Dec	m	AD	Con

(NGC 6052 continued).

	Arp 209	(10) A small, irregularly-shaped faint patch
	Mkn 297	of light; it lies a little N of the position
		shown in Atlas Coeli.

| 677 | NGC 6181 | 16 31.3 | +19 53 | 11.9 | 2.0 x 0.7 | Her |

Sc. SN: 1926 - 14^m.8.

- -

(36) Pretty bright, small and oval in shape with a bright nucleus; a wisp is suspected emerging from the E side; several stars are superimposed.

(16½) Bright central lens around a stellar nucleus; outer parts slightly elongated.

| 678 | NGC 6217 | 16 33.8 | +78 15 | 11.5 | 1.8 x 1.2 | UMi |
| | Arp   185 | Sb:SAB(s)bc. Peculiar nucleus. |

- -

(16½) A little extended N.p., S.f.; stellar nucleus in weak nebulosity.

| 679 | NGC 6207 | 16 42.2 | +36 53 | 11.3 | 2.0 x 0.7 | Her |

Sb. Lies NE of M13.

- -

(18) Quite large and bright in PA 45°; the nebulosity is fainter S of a stellar nucleus, although a bright patch lies there; a bright arc is seen N of the nucleus and the whole object showed evidence of condensations.

(12) Fairly uniform in brightness; elongated.

(8) Faint with a sudden brightening in the centre to a nucleus; no other detail seen.

WS	Cat	RA	Dec	m	AD	Con
680	NGC 6384	16 31.2	+07 05	10.5	3.0 x 3.0	Oph

Sb:SAB(r)bc. SN: 1971 - $12^m.8$.

- -

($16\frac{1}{2}$) The centre is bright and extended and
the outer nebulosity appears as arcs of light;
two stars involved to the N.

| 681 | NGC 6503 | 17 49.7 | +70 09 | 10.24 | 11.2 x 4.0 | Dra |

Sc. Possible member of the M101 group.

- -

(16) Bright with almost uniform brightness at
LP; higher power shows glimpses of bright
patches along the major axis.
($8\frac{1}{2}$) High surface brightness object with well-
defined edges; brighter along the centre of
the major axis.

| 682 | NGC 6643 | 18 20.5 | +74 34 | 11.09 | 5.1 x 2.7 | Dra |

Sb. Contains 3 superassociations.

- -

($16\frac{1}{2}$) Elongated N,f., S.p.; the extensions do
not narrow at the ends and the p one is wider
and brighter; the f extension is more defined
with a dark streak suspected along the f side.
($8\frac{1}{2}$) Fairly bright oval with two stars of
about 11.5 mag on the W edge; the edges are
well-defined with traces of a nucleus.

| 683 | NGC 6764 | 19 07.0 | +50 52 | 14.0 | 2.1 x 1.0 | Cyg. |

SB.

- -

(82) Obviously a barred spiral, but the arm
structure is difficult to see; the bar is

WS	Cat	RA	Dec	m	AD	Con

(NGC 6764 continued).

narrow and straight and crosses a small
nuclear region with a conspicuous stellar
nucleus; at opposite ends of the bar the light
distribution curves, but not sharply, and is
weakly enhanced; beyond the latter extremely
faint and narrow spiral arms are suspected;
a conspicuous companion lies to the SE and
appears very bright, small, round and with a
bright nucleus.

| 684 | NGC 6822 | 19 43.5 | -14 49 | 11.0 | 20.0 x 10.0 | Sgr |

Irr I. Contains 16 known H II regions, the
brightest being IC 1308 and IC 4895. Member
of the Local Group.

- -

($8\frac{1}{2}$) Very difficult due to its low altitude
and the effects of galactic absorption; x51
it appears as a barely discernable nebulous
patch which is extended N-S; x102 still very
faint but seems comprised of three distinct
but connected regions; no indications of the
two IC nebulae which, although not extremely
faint, are quite small.

| 685 | NGC 6946 | 20 34.3 | +60 04 | 8.96 | 14.4 x 12.6 | Cyg |
| | Arp 29 | | | | | |

Sc:SAB(rs)cd. 4C 59.31. Very rich in
molecular clouds.

- -

(30) Very large and faintish with branching
arms; a virtually stellar nucleus is at the
centre of a weak, elongated structure from

WS	Cat	RA	Dec	m	AD	Con

(NGC 6946 continued).

which a long, diffuse arm emerges off the E
end; at the end of this arm is a conspicuous
knot with a stellar core; this arm branches
into a second one which is seen as a faint
arc; a third arm is suspected winding W from
the centre and this also has a knot near its
end with a stellar core.

($16\frac{1}{2}$) Quite faint and very large, looking
rather like an irregular planetary nebula;
it appears somewhat rectangular in shape and
a little brighter towards the f edge.

(8) Very faint and formless with no nucleus
apparent but two nebulous knots seem to lie
to the W.

686	BL Lac	22 00.8	+42 01	12.0 - 15.5		Lac

BL Lac. E galaxy with an active nucleus. The
magnitude figures above refer to maximum and
minimum light. A chart of the region, with
comparison magnitudes, will be found in the
list of additional objects.

- -

(18) Stellar on all powers.

687	NGC 7217	22 06.7	+31 14	10.20	7.4 x 6.1	Peg

Sb.

- -

($16\frac{1}{2}$) Nucleus almost stellar and very bright;
the outer regions appear as a small, nebulous
glow; a faint star is on the N edge.

(10) Almost round; gradually bright centre.

WS	Cat	RA	Dec	m	AD	Con
688	NGC 7331	22 35.9	+34 18	9.56	13.5 x 7.0	Peg

Sb. PKS 2232+34. Brightest in a group.

- - - - - - - - - - - - - - - - - - - -

(36) Nearly but not quite edge-on; the light
distribution is extended with a sharp edge
on the W side; about 15" - 20" W of the edge
is an extremely faint, narrow streak, this
must be an effect of dust; a conspicuous
nucleus is centred in a bright bulge.

(16½) Extended with a bright, extended nucleus;
x160 there is a faint star or nebulous knot
near the end of the S.f. extension; the area
between this and the centre is dark.

(8½) x51 a long spindle in PA 165°; there is
gradual central brightening to a very faint
stellar nucleus; x102 the f edge is much more
diffuse than the p edge.

(6) Fairly bright spindle with much brighter
centre and well-defined nucleus; the edges
pass imperceptably into the sky.

WS	Cat	RA	Dec	m	AD	Con
689	NGC 7335	22 36.1	+34 19	14.5	1.1 x 0.6	Peg

S.

- - - - - - - - - - - - - - - - - - - -

(36) Pretty bright, small, round, diffuse.
(16½) Elongated with S part wider and brighter.
(8½) Appears very faint and slightly elongated; a point source initially.

WS	Cat	RA	Dec	m	AD	Con
690	NGC 7448	22 58.8	+15 51	11.2	2.0 x 0.8	Peg
	Arp 13					

Sc. Contains 3 superassociations.

- - - - - - - - - - - - - - - - - - - -

(8½) Elongated NW-SE; centre brighter but not
to a nucleus; bright star lies close E.

WS	Cat	RA	Dec	m	AD	Con
691	NGC 7463	22 59.3	+15 42	13.0	3.0 x 0.5	Peg.

S.

- -

(16) Elongated E-W; quite bright with brighter centre and diffuse edges.

| 692 | NGC 7464 | 22 59.3 | +15 42 | 14.0 | 0.3 x 0.3 | Peg |

S.

- -

(16) Small and round with a brighter middle; attached to the f end of NGC 7463.

| 693 | NGC 7465 | 22 59.5 | +15 41 | 13.0 | 1.0 x 0.7 | Peg |
| | Mkn 313 | | | | | |

SB. Unconfirmed SN in 1950.

- -

(16) Small, round with brighter centre.

| 694 | NGC 7469 | 23 03.0 | +08 44 | 13.0 | 1.6 x 1.1 | Peg. |
| | Arp 298 | | | | | |

SBa. Class 1 Seyfert. Nucleus a radio source and optically variable. IC 5283, $14^m.8$, lies 1.3 NE.

- -

(16) Small, faint and round nebulosity of almost uniform surface brightness; dominated by a bright stellar nucleus.
($8\frac{1}{2}$) Appears at first as a tiny star with the nebulosity becoming visible after a time.

| 695 | IC 5285 | 23 04.4 | +22 40 | 14.4 | 1.7 x 1.3 | Peg |

S. Surrounded by a faint, outer ring.

- -

($8\frac{1}{2}$) Extremely faint and only detectable at LP; an 11 mag star lies very close due S.

WS	Cat	RA	Dec	m	AD	Con
696	NGC 7479	23 04.7	+12 11	11.6	3.0 x 2.5	Peg

SBc:SB(s)bc.

- -

(36) A fine asymmetric barred spiral; the
bar is bright and crosses a small bulge with
a stellar core; the N half of the bar is
about 1' long and diffuse; a weak spiral arm
emerges at a right angle from this half and
can be traced for about 150° around; on the
S half the bar curves gradually into a
brilliant arc which winds about 90°; there
is slight patchiness in the S half of the
bar at the point where it curves W.

(16½) Quite bright and elongated N.f., S.p.;
at HP the nucleus appears stellar and the
S extension is suspected to curve towards a
bright star p; nebulosity also seems to be
present p a faint star p the nucleus.

(12½) The main bulk is very conspicuous
with a bright centre; the NE part shows as a
sort of light feather.

(8½) Elongated blur of overall luminosity at
LP; x102 structural variations seen but these
are very indefinite.

697	NGC 7603	23 17.7	+00 07	14.4	1.4 x 0.9	Peg
	Arp 92					

S. Seyfert.

- -

(60) Sharp, compact nucleus in a large, faint
oval of nebulosity.

WS	Cat	RA	Dec	m	AD	Con
698	NGC 7640	23 20.9	+40 42	11.0	13.5 x 3.6	And
	VV 280	SBc:SB(s)c. Contains no definite nucleus.				

- -

(30) Bright, very large and extended; it is shaped like a large integral sign; a small, diffuse nuclear bulge shows patchy surroundings; the ends of the galaxy are curved in opposite directions and three or four knots are visible in the outer parts, all of these being extremely faint; the most conspicuous is off the S end and appears unconnected to the rest of the galaxy.

(16) Elongated, bright and brighter to the middle; in a rich field.

(8½) Rather wispy nebulosity which appears slightly irregular in brightness; there is a possibility of the S end being wider; quite faint for a highly inclined object.

699	NGC 7678	23 27.2	+22 17	12.9	1.4 x 1.1	Peg
	Arp 28	SBc. A very large, high surface brightness spiral arm lies S of the centre.				

- -

(30) Pretty faint, small and of low surface brightness; a conspicuous, stellar core is immersed within a round, diffuse glow; from one side emerges a very short arc of luminosity with two patches along its length; it looks like a small, "ring-tail" spiral.

(8½) Lies in a close triangle of stars; it appears elliptical with a brighter centre and possibly a more definite SW edge.

WS	Cat	RA	Dec	m	AD	Con
700	NGC 7973	23 25.5	+23 20			**Peg**

S.

- -

(8½) Just visible at LP and MP as a very
faint, elongated blur aligned E-W; possibly
a slightly brighter region is associated,
but this is very uncertain with the small
aperture used.

A Catalogue of Galaxies.

Drawings of 156 Galaxy Fields.

158

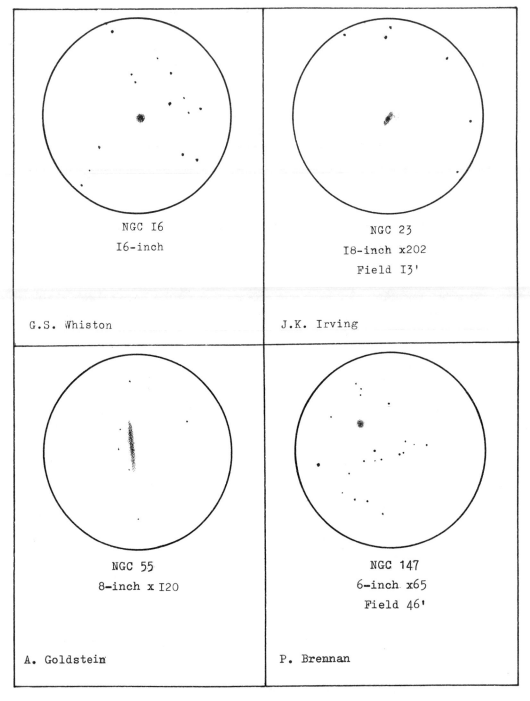

NGC 16
16-inch

G.S. Whiston

NGC 23
18-inch x202
Field 13'

J.K. Irving

NGC 55
8-inch x 120

A. Goldstein

NGC 147
6-inch x65
Field 46'

P. Brennan

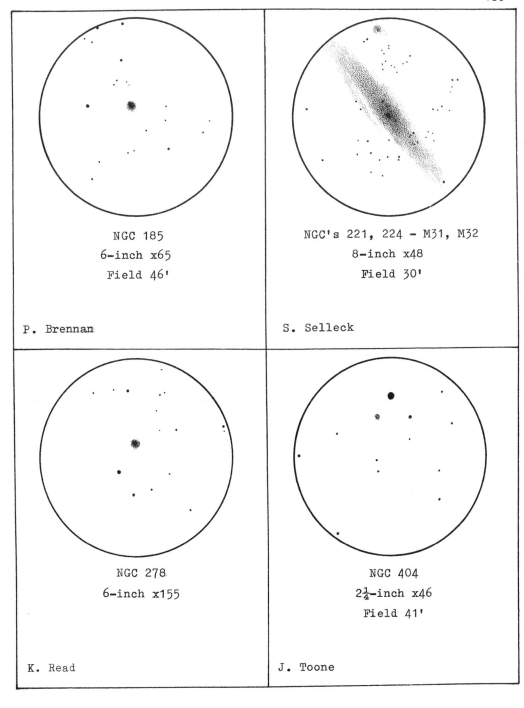

NGC 185
6-inch x65
Field 46'

P. Brennan

NGC's 221, 224 - M31, M32
8-inch x48
Field 30'

S. Selleck

NGC 278
6-inch x155

K. Read

NGC 404
$2\frac{1}{4}$-inch x46
Field 41'

J. Toone

160

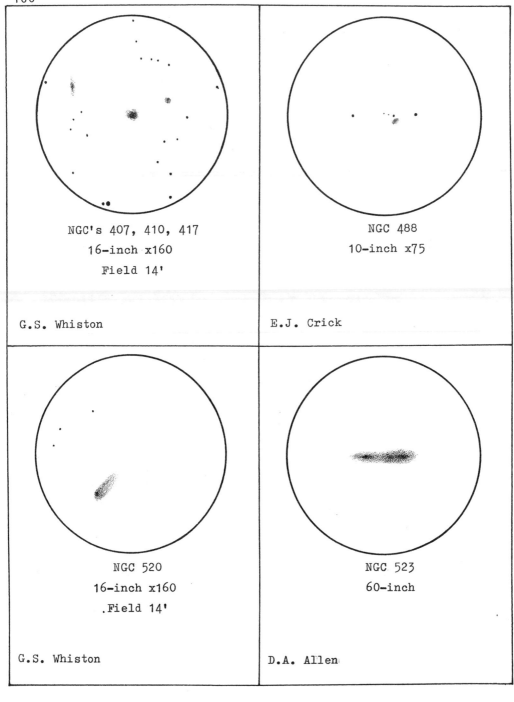

NGC's 407, 410, 417
16-inch x160
Field 14'

G.S. Whiston

NGC 488
10-inch x75

E.J. Crick

NGC 520
16-inch x160
.Field 14'

G.S. Whiston

NGC 523
60-inch

D.A. Allen

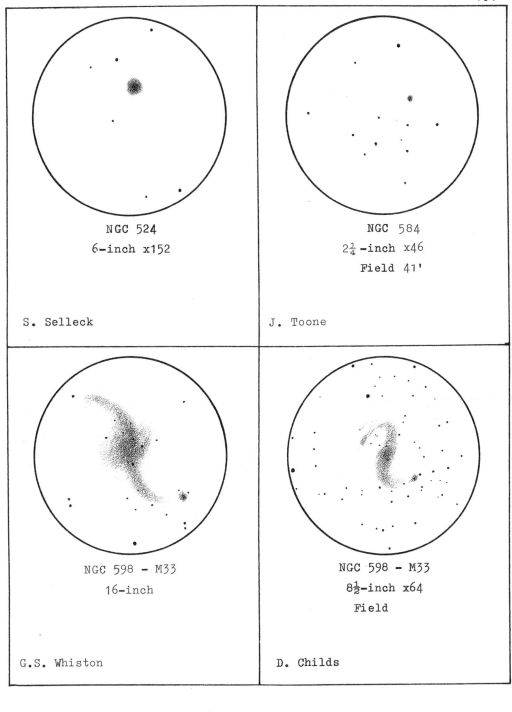

NGC 524
6-inch x152

S. Selleck

NGC 584
$2\frac{1}{4}$-inch x46
Field 41'

J. Toone

NGC 598 — M33
16-inch

G.S. Whiston

NGC 598 — M33
$8\frac{1}{2}$-inch x64
Field

D. Childs

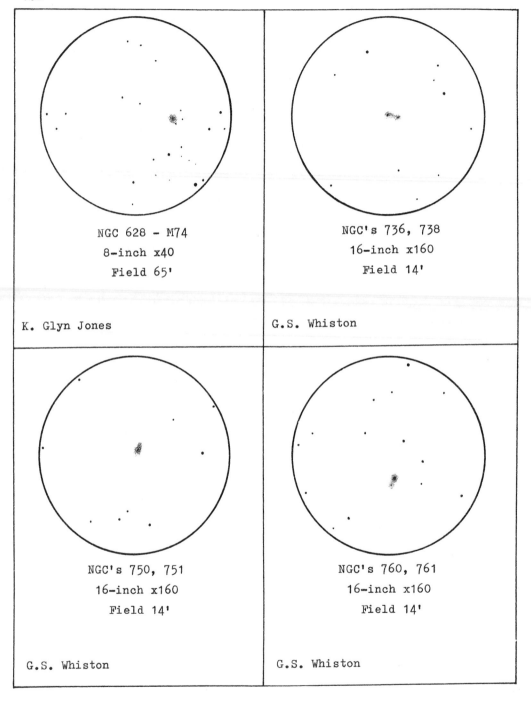

NGC 628 - M74
8-inch x40
Field 65'

K. Glyn Jones

NGC's 736, 738
16-inch x160
Field 14'

G.S. Whiston

NGC's 750, 751
16-inch x160
Field 14'

G.S. Whiston

NGC's 760, 761
16-inch x160
Field 14'

G.S. Whiston

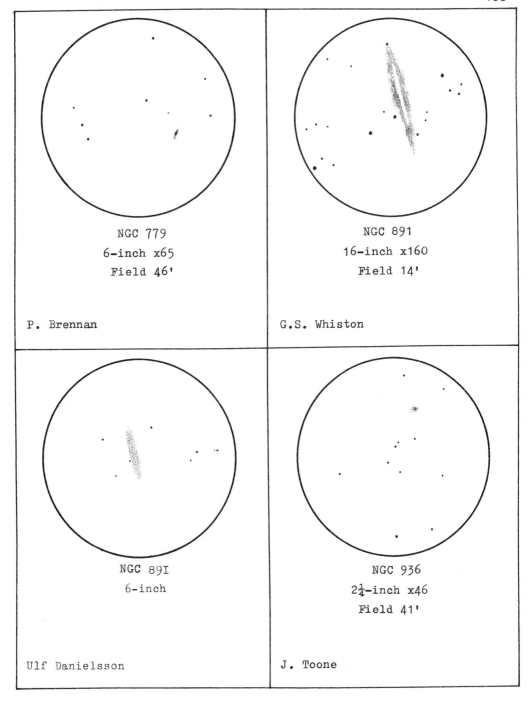

NGC 779
6-inch x65
Field 46'

P. Brennan

NGC 891
16-inch x160
Field 14'

G.S. Whiston

NGC 89I
6-inch

Ulf Danielsson

NGC 936
2¼-inch x46
Field 41'

J. Toone

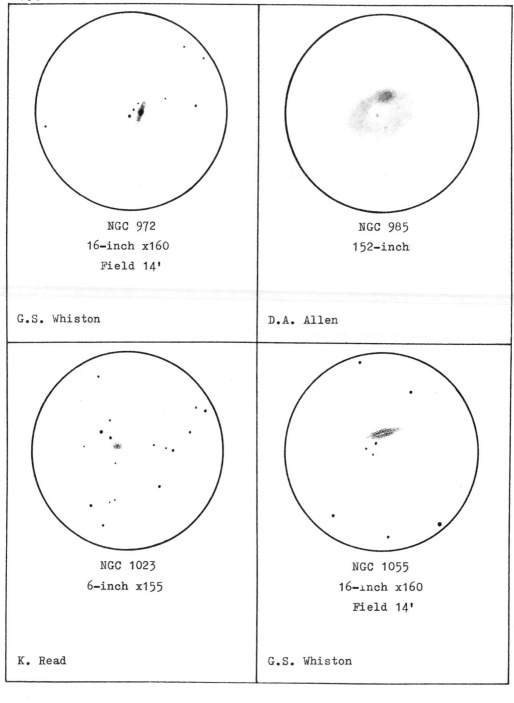

NGC 972

16-inch x160

Field 14'

G.S. Whiston

NGC 985

152-inch

D.A. Allen

NGC 1023

6-inch x155

K. Read

NGC 1055

16-inch x160

Field 14'

G.S. Whiston

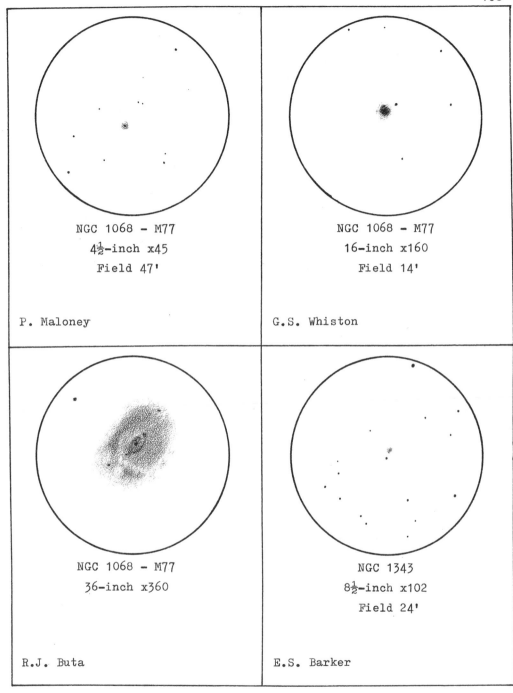

NGC 1068 - M77
4½-inch x45
Field 47'

P. Maloney

NGC 1068 - M77
16-inch x160
Field 14'

G.S. Whiston

NGC 1068 - M77
36-inch x360

R.J. Buta

NGC 1343
8½-inch x102
Field 24'

E.S. Barker

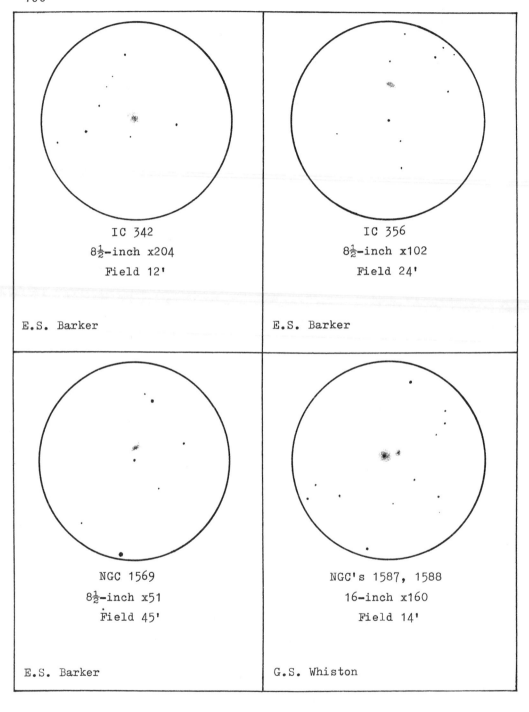

IC 342

8½-inch x204

Field 12'

E.S. Barker

IC 356

8½-inch x102

Field 24'

E.S. Barker

NGC 1569

8½-inch x51

Field 45'

E.S. Barker

NGC's 1587, 1588

16-inch x160

Field 14'

G.S. Whiston

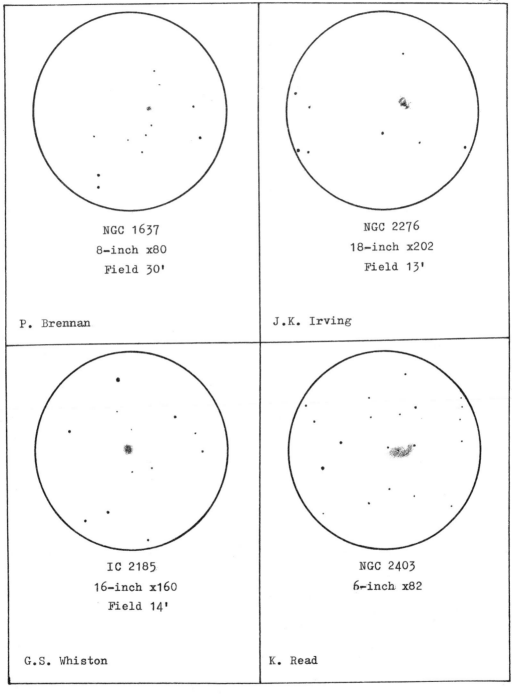

NGC 1637
8-inch x80
Field 30'

P. Brennan

NGC 2276
18-inch x202
Field 13'

J.K. Irving

IC 2185
16-inch x160
Field 14'

G.S. Whiston

NGC 2403
6-inch x82

K. Read

168

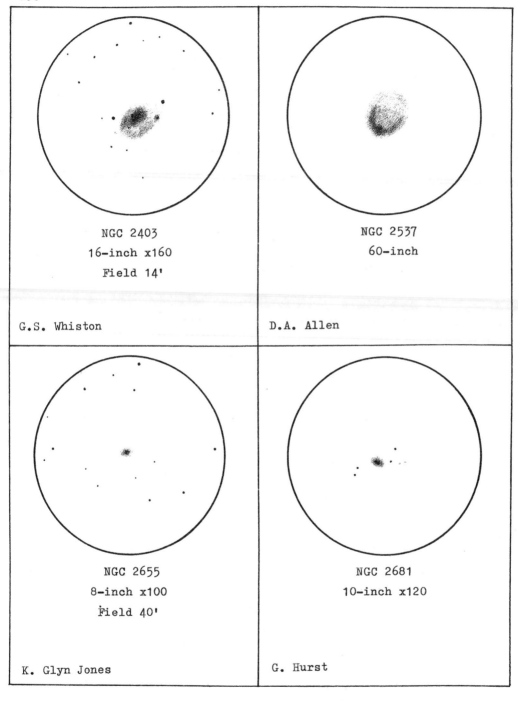

NGC 2403
16-inch x160
Field 14'

G.S. Whiston

NGC 2537
60-inch

D.A. Allen

NGC 2655
8-inch x100
Field 40'

K. Glyn Jones

NGC 2681
10-inch x120

G. Hurst

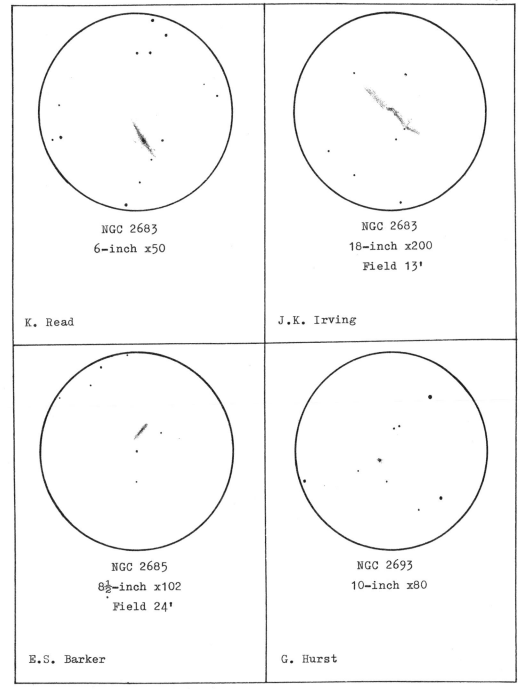

NGC 2683
6-inch x50

K. Read

NGC 2683
18-inch x200
Field 13'

J.K. Irving

NGC 2685
8½-inch x102
Field 24'

E.S. Barker

NGC 2693
10-inch x80

G. Hurst

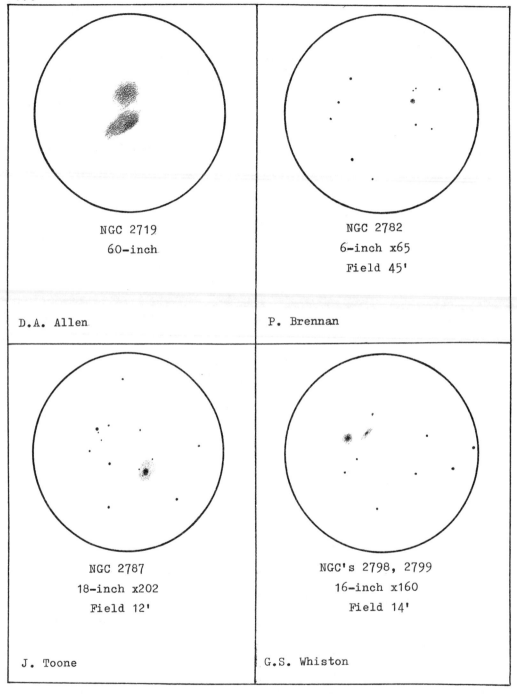

NGC 2719
60-inch

D.A. Allen

NGC 2782
6-inch x65
Field 45'

P. Brennan

NGC 2787
18-inch x202
Field 12'

J. Toone

NGC's 2798, 2799
16-inch x160
Field 14'

G.S. Whiston

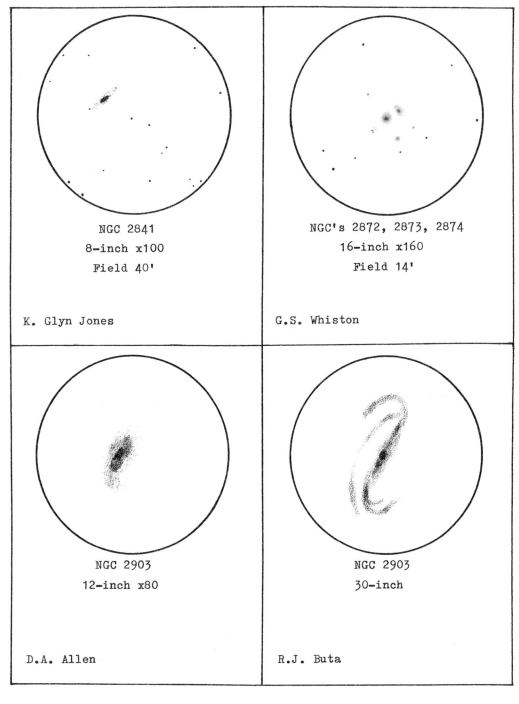

NGC 2841

8-inch x100

Field 40'

K. Glyn Jones

NGC's 2872, 2873, 2874

16-inch x160

Field 14'

G.S. Whiston

NGC 2903

12-inch x80

D.A. Allen

NGC 2903

30-inch

R.J. Buta

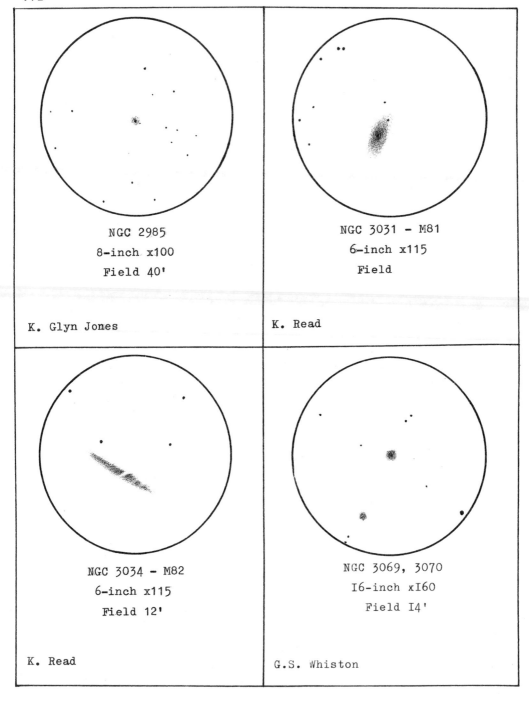

NGC 2985
8-inch x100
Field 40'

K. Glyn Jones

NGC 3031 - M81
6-inch x115
Field

K. Read

NGC 3034 - M82
6-inch x115
Field 12'

K. Read

NGC 3069, 3070
I6-inch xI60
Field I4'

G.S. Whiston

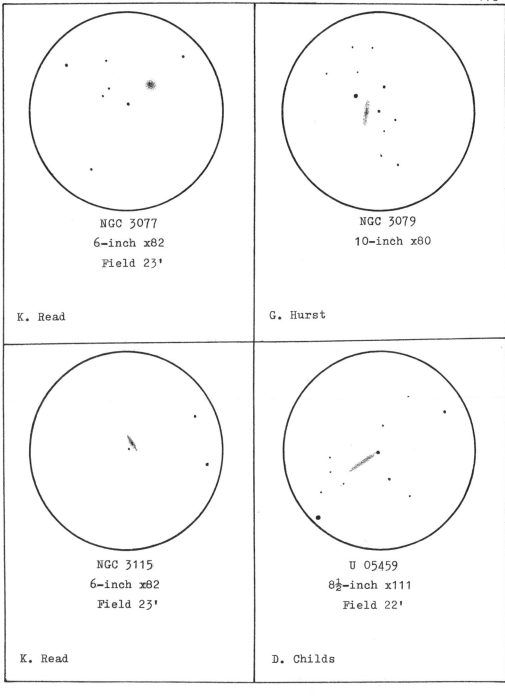

NGC 3077
6-inch x82
Field 23'

K. Read

NGC 3079
10-inch x80

G. Hurst

NGC 3115
6-inch x82
Field 23'

K. Read

U 05459
8½-inch x111
Field 22'

D. Childs

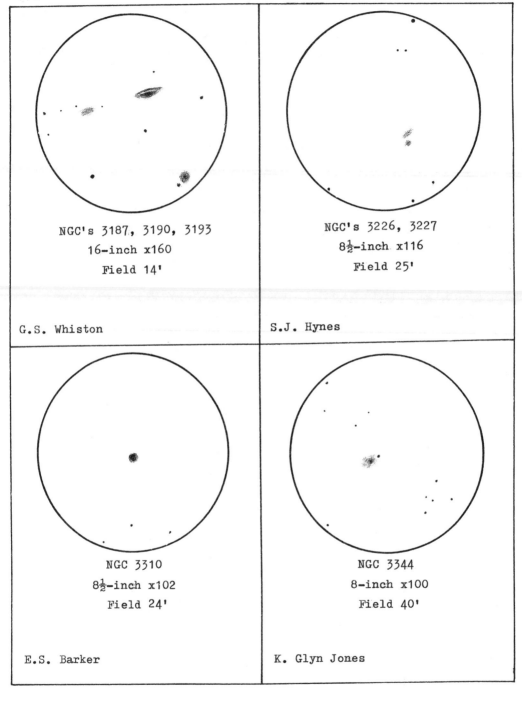

NGC's 3187, 3190, 3193
16-inch x160
Field 14'

G.S. Whiston

NGC's 3226, 3227
8½-inch x116
Field 25'

S.J. Hynes

NGC 3310
8½-inch x102
Field 24'

E.S. Barker

NGC 3344
8-inch x100
Field 40'

K. Glyn Jones

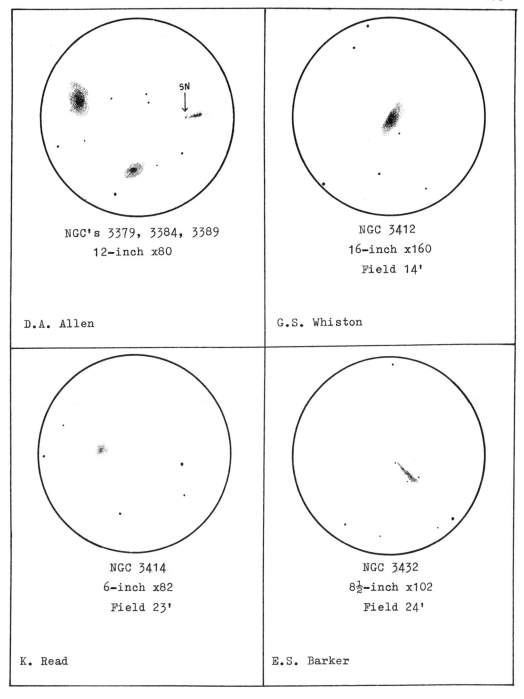

NGC's 3379, 3384, 3389
12-inch x80

D.A. Allen

NGC 3412
16-inch x160
Field 14'

G.S. Whiston

NGC 3414
6-inch x82
Field 23'

K. Read

NGC 3432
8½-inch x102
Field 24'

E.S. Barker

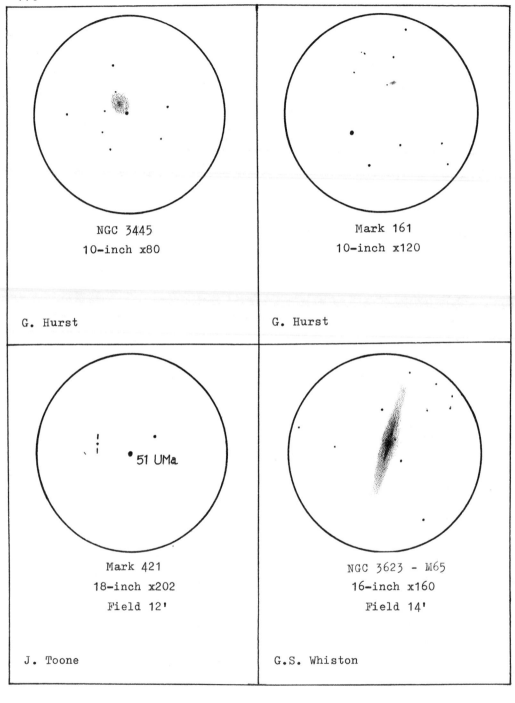

NGC 3445

10-inch x80

G. Hurst

Mark 161

10-inch x120

G. Hurst

51 UMa

Mark 421

18-inch x202

Field 12'

J. Toone

NGC 3623 - M65

16-inch x160

Field 14'

G.S. Whiston

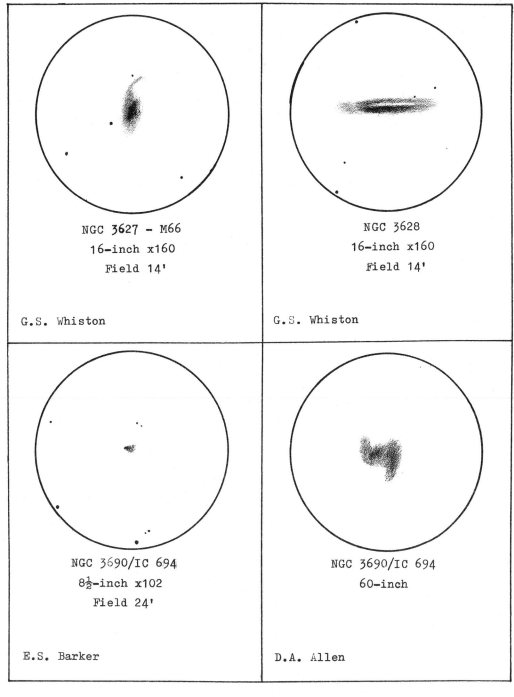

NGC 3627 - M66
16-inch x160
Field 14'

G.S. Whiston

NGC 3628
16-inch x160
Field 14'

G.S. Whiston

NGC 3690/IC 694
8½-inch x102
Field 24'

E.S. Barker

NGC 3690/IC 694
60-inch

D.A. Allen

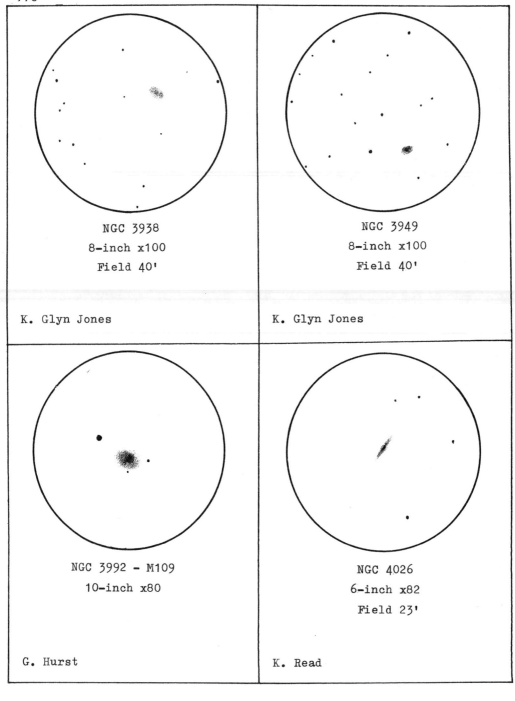

NGC 3938
8-inch x100
Field 40'

K. Glyn Jones

NGC 3949
8-inch x100
Field 40'

K. Glyn Jones

NGC 3992 - M109
10-inch x80

G. Hurst

NGC 4026
6-inch x82
Field 23'

K. Read

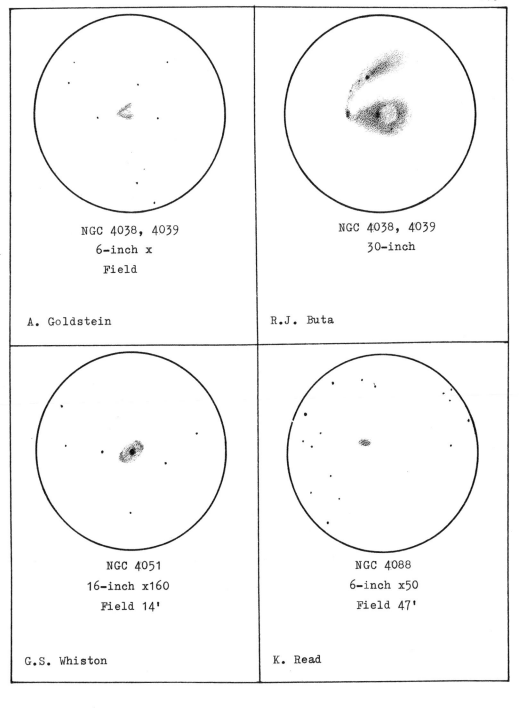

NGC 4038, 4039

6-inch x

Field

A. Goldstein

NGC 4038, 4039

30-inch

R.J. Buta

NGC 4051

16-inch x160

Field 14'

G.S. Whiston

NGC 4088

6-inch x50

Field 47'

K. Read

180

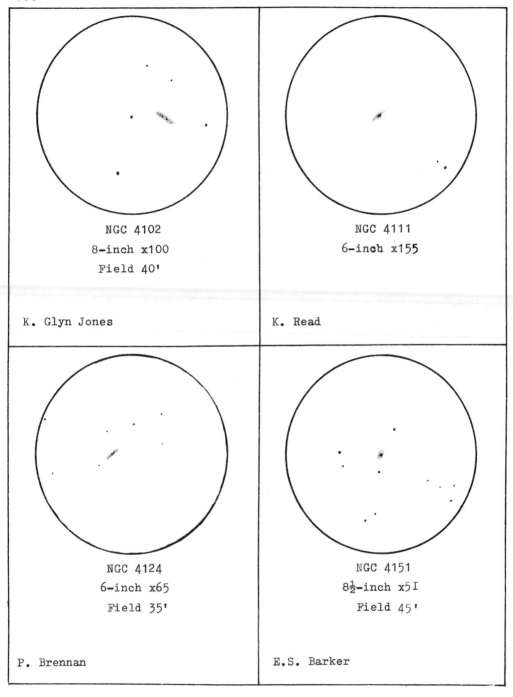

NGC 4102
8-inch x100
Field 40'

K. Glyn Jones

NGC 4111
6-inch x155

K. Read

NGC 4124
6-inch x65
Field 35'

P. Brennan

NGC 4151
8½-inch x5I
Field 45'

E.S. Barker

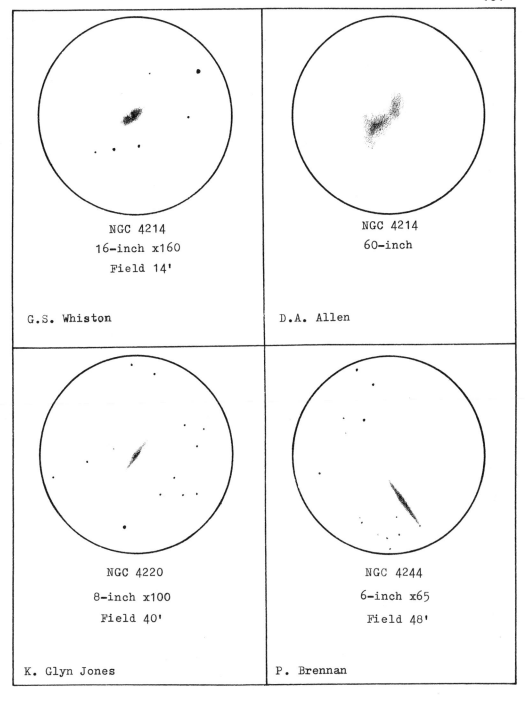

NGC 4214
16-inch x160
Field 14'

G.S. Whiston

NGC 4214
60-inch

D.A. Allen

NGC 4220
8-inch x100
Field 40'

K. Glyn Jones

NGC 4244
6-inch x65
Field 48'

P. Brennan

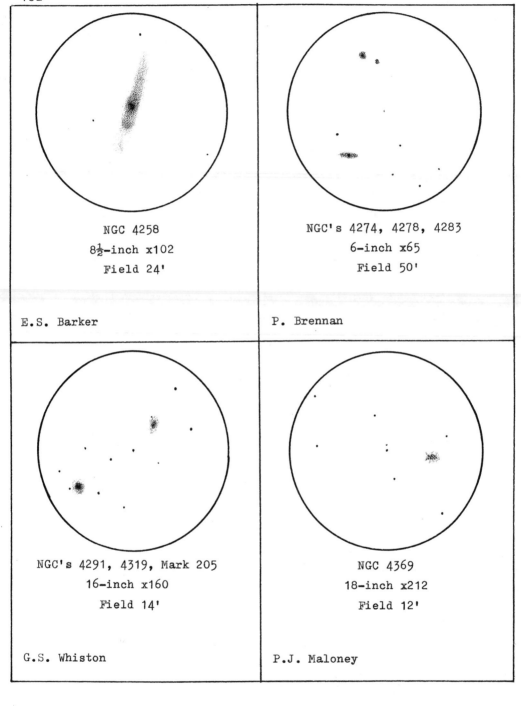

NGC 4258

8½-inch x102

Field 24'

E.S. Barker

NGC's 4274, 4278, 4283

6-inch x65

Field 50'

P. Brennan

NGC's 4291, 4319, Mark 205

16-inch x160

Field 14'

G.S. Whiston

NGC 4369

18-inch x212

Field 12'

P.J. Maloney

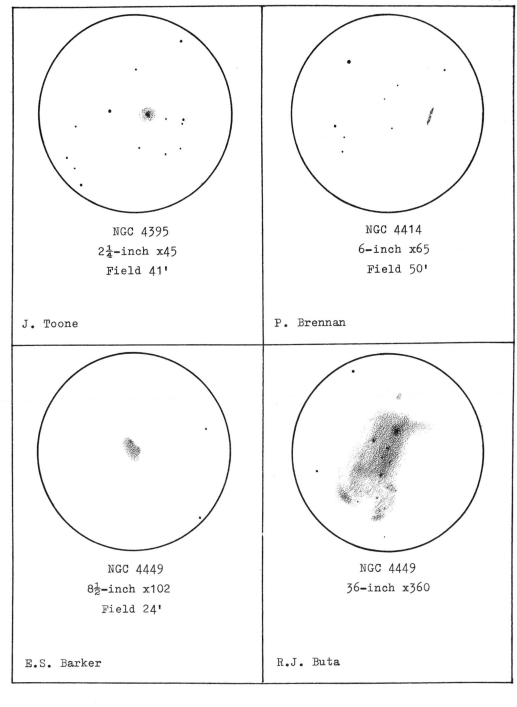

NGC 4395
2¼-inch x45
Field 41'

J. Toone

NGC 4414
6-inch x65
Field 50'

P. Brennan

NGC 4449
8½-inch x102
Field 24'

E.S. Barker

NGC 4449
36-inch x360

R.J. Buta

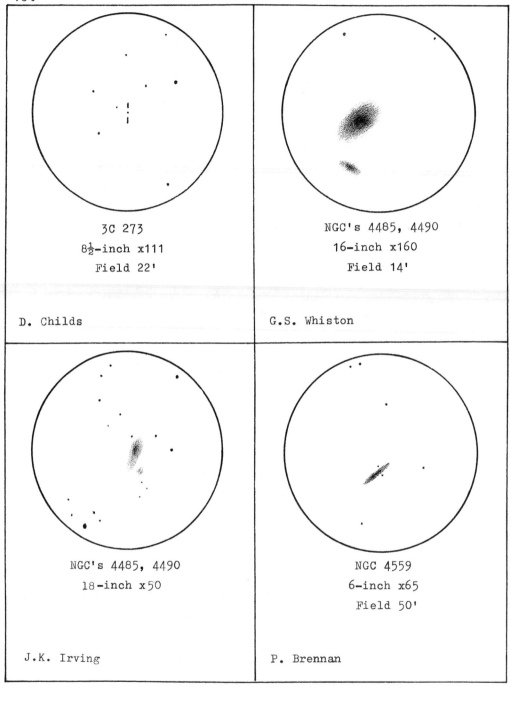

3C 273

8½-inch x111

Field 22'

D. Childs

NGC's 4485, 4490

16-inch x160

Field 14'

G.S. Whiston

NGC's 4485, 4490

18-inch x50

J.K. Irving

NGC 4559

6-inch x65

Field 50'

P. Brennan

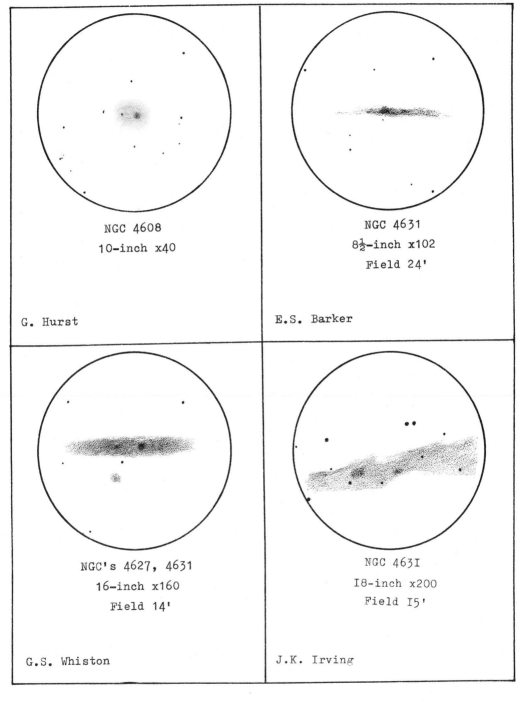

NGC 4608

10-inch x40

G. Hurst

NGC 4631

8½-inch x102

Field 24'

E.S. Barker

NGC's 4627, 4631

16-inch x160

Field 14'

G.S. Whiston

NGC 4631

18-inch x200

Field 15'

J.K. Irving

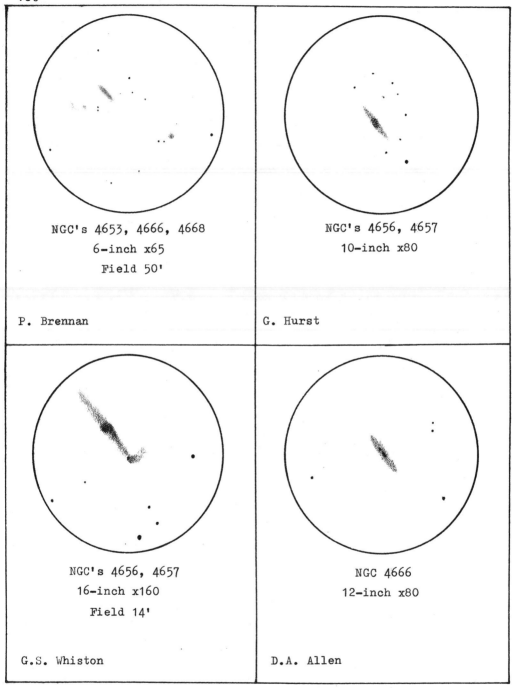

NGC's 4653, 4666, 4668
6-inch x65
Field 50'

P. Brennan

NGC's 4656, 4657
10-inch x80

G. Hurst

NGC's 4656, 4657
16-inch x160
Field 14'

G.S. Whiston

NGC 4666
12-inch x80

D.A. Allen

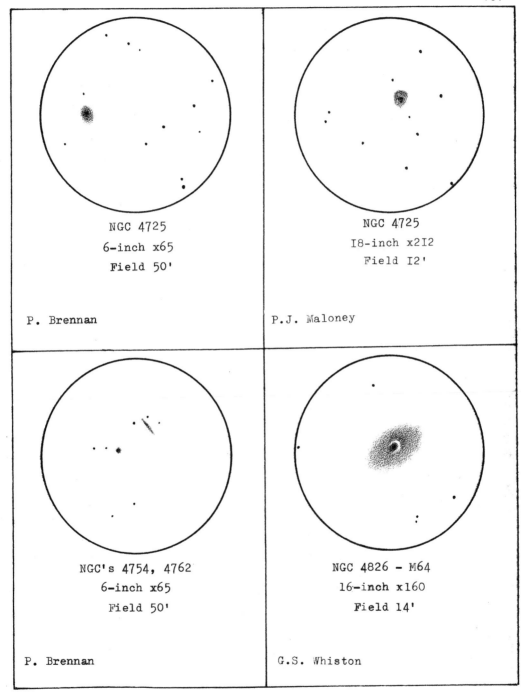

NGC 4725
6-inch x65
Field 50'

P. Brennan

NGC 4725
I8-inch x2I2
Field I2'

P.J. Maloney

NGC's 4754, 4762
6-inch x65
Field 50'

P. Brennan

NGC 4826 – M64
16-inch x160
Field 14'

G.S. Whiston

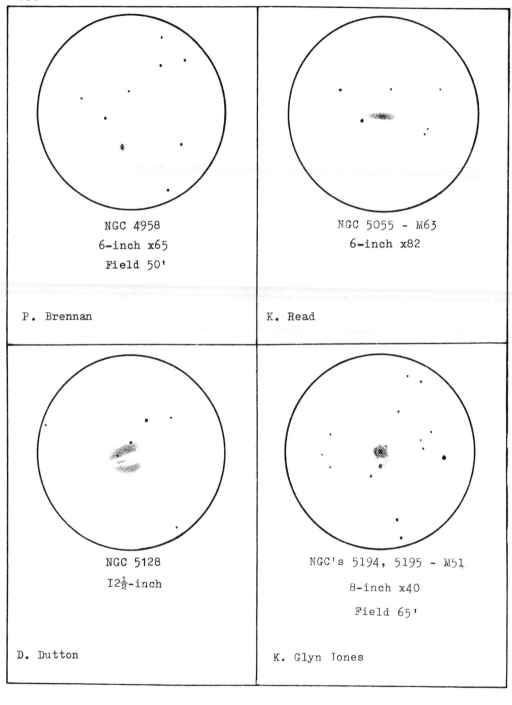

NGC 4958
6-inch x65
Field 50'

P. Brennan

NGC 5055 - M63
6-inch x82

K. Read

NGC 5128
12½-inch

D. Dutton

NGC's 5194, 5195 - M51
8-inch x40
Field 65'

K. Glyn Jones

189

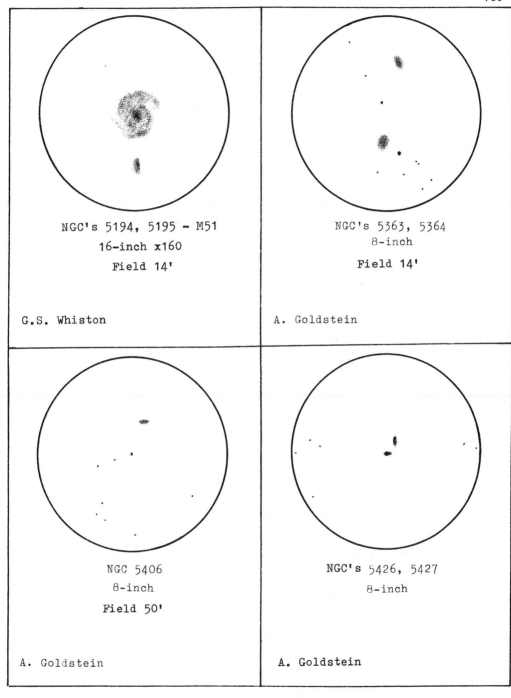

NGC's 5194, 5195 - M51
16-inch x160
Field 14'

G.S. Whiston

NGC's 5363, 5364
8-inch
Field 14'

A. Goldstein

NGC 5406
8-inch
Field 50'

A. Goldstein

NGC's 5426, 5427
8-inch

A. Goldstein

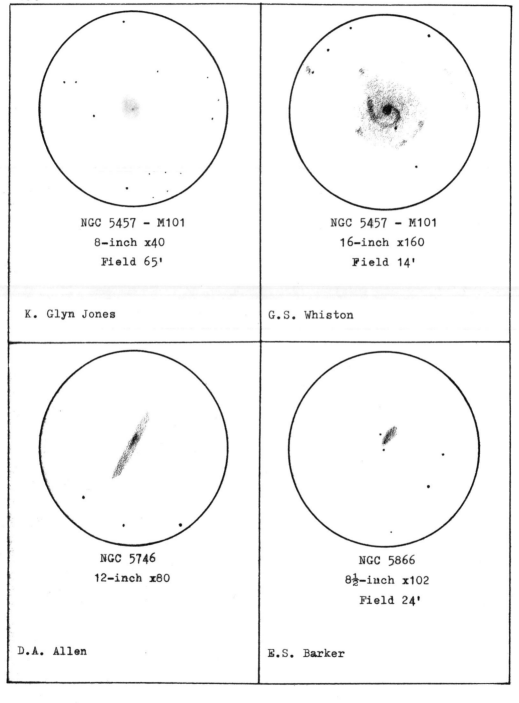

NGC 5457 - M101
8-inch x40
Field 65'

K. Glyn Jones

NGC 5457 - M101
16-inch x160
Field 14'

G.S. Whiston

NGC 5746
12-inch x80

D.A. Allen

NGC 5866
8½-inch x102
Field 24'

E.S. Barker

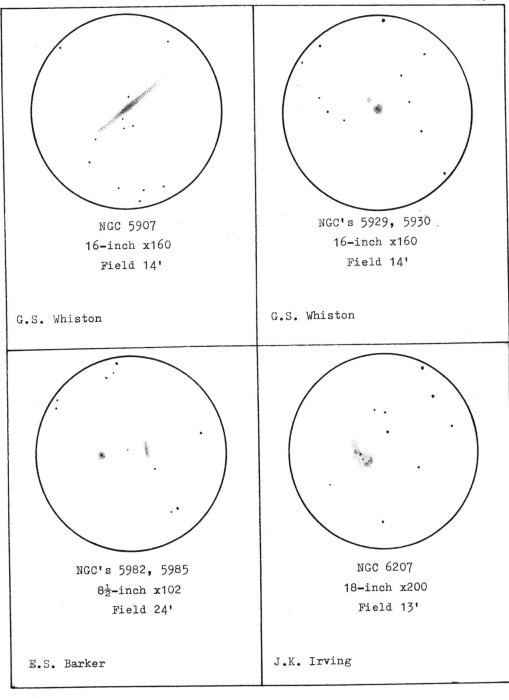

NGC 5907
16-inch x160
Field 14'

G.S. Whiston

NGC's 5929, 5930
16-inch x160
Field 14'

G.S. Whiston

NGC's 5982, 5985
8½-inch x102
Field 24'

E.S. Barker

NGC 6207
18-inch x200
Field 13'

J.K. Irving

192

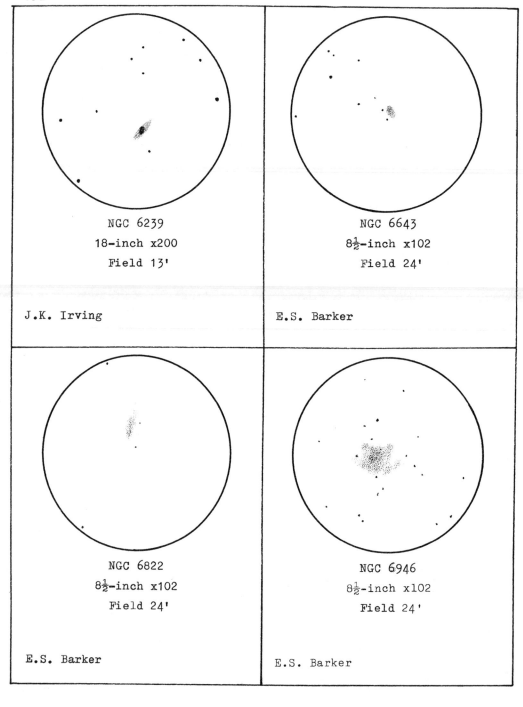

NGC 6239
18-inch x200
Field 13'

J.K. Irving

NGC 6643
8½-inch x102
Field 24'

E.S. Barker

NGC 6822
8½-inch x102
Field 24'

E.S. Barker

NGC 6946
8½-inch x102
Field 24'

E.S. Barker

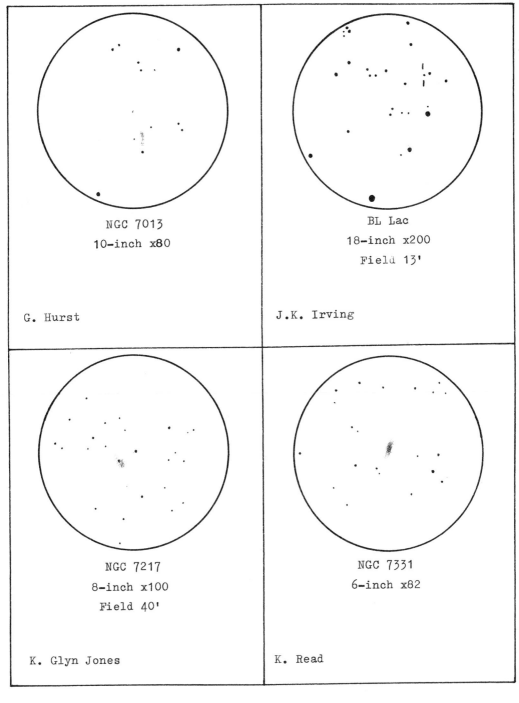

NGC 7013
10-inch x80

G. Hurst

BL Lac
18-inch x200
Field 13'

J.K. Irving

NGC 7217
8-inch x100
Field 40'

K. Glyn Jones

NGC 7331
6-inch x82

K. Read

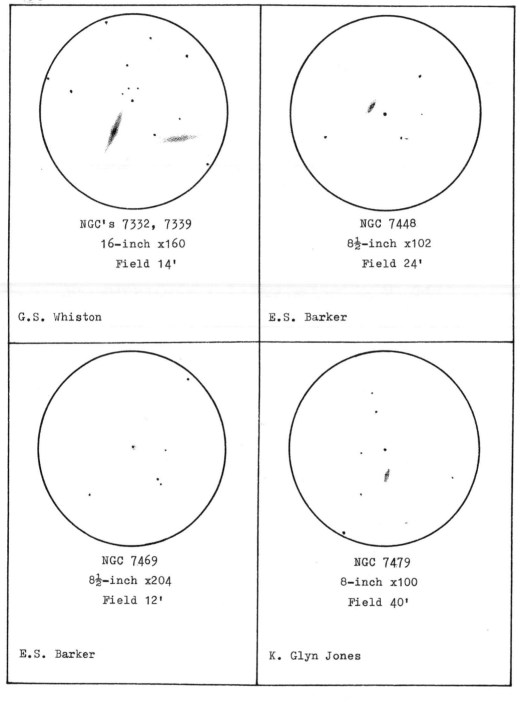

NGC's 7332, 7339
16-inch x160
Field 14'

G.S. Whiston

NGC 7448
8½-inch x102
Field 24'

E.S. Barker

NGC 7469
8½-inch x204
Field 12'

E.S. Barker

NGC 7479
8-inch x100
Field 40'

K. Glyn Jones

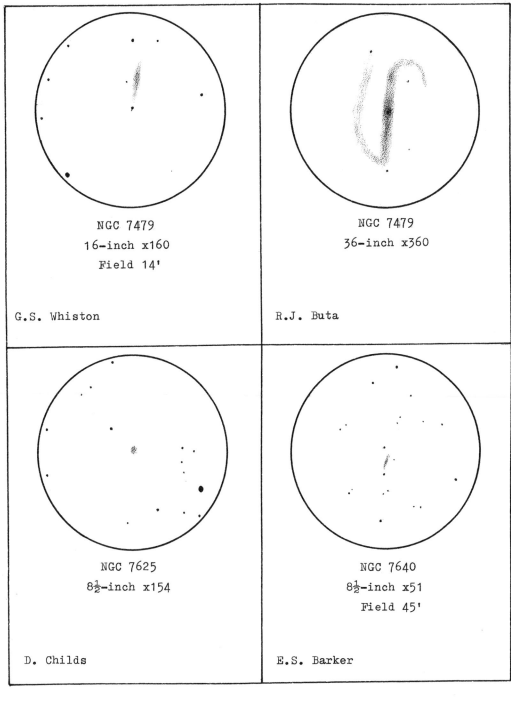

NGC 7479
16-inch x160
Field 14'

G.S. Whiston

NGC 7479
36-inch x360

R.J. Buta

NGC 7625
8½-inch x154

D. Childs

NGC 7640
8½-inch x51
Field 45'

E.S. Barker

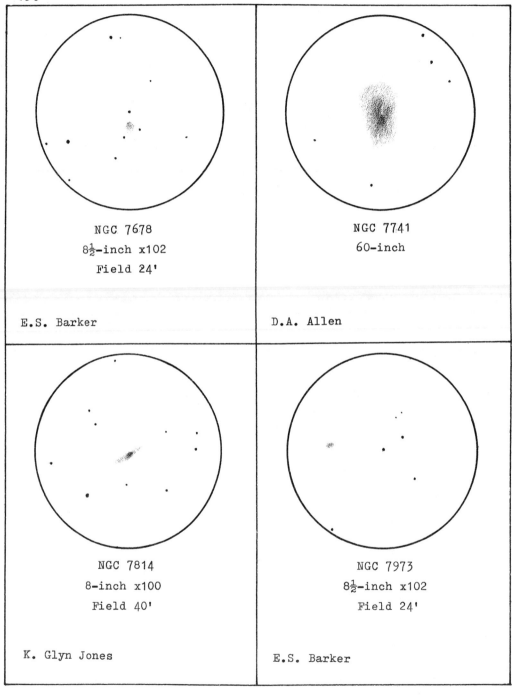

NGC 7678

8½-inch x102

Field 24'

E.S. Barker

NGC 7741

60-inch

D.A. Allen

NGC 7814

8-inch x100

Field 40'

K. Glyn Jones

NGC 7973

8½-inch x102

Field 24'

E.S. Barker

PART THREE : LIST OF ADDITIONAL OBJECTS.

In this section we have selected Interacting and Peculiar galaxies, Compact galaxies, Seyfert galaxies and a number of variable sources. Due to constrictions of space, it has not been possible to show finding charts for all these objects, and consequently they are shown only for 13 Seyferts and 7 variable systems. The Seyfert charts are taken from the red (E) prints of the Palomar Sky Survey, and each covers an area 16' x 16', except that of 3C 390.3, on which a scale is marked. Individual scales are also marked on the charts for the 7 variable sources, all of which, barring W and X Comae and AP Lib, are from photographs taken by the late Walter Pennell. The charts from the Sky Survey are reproduced courtesy of Palomar Sky Survey - National Geographic Society. Orientation for all of the charts is North up, East to the left.

List of Additional Objects.

Interacting and Peculiar Galaxies

Cat		RA	Dec	m	AD	Con
NGC	70	00 17.1	+29 56	14.5	2.0 x 1.6	And
VV	166	Sb. In a compact group.				
Arp	113					
		00 22.3	-00 39	15.4	1.3 x 0.7	Psc
		Type uncertain. Disrupted.				
		00 24.7	+25 46	14.9	1.9 x 1.3	And
		SB0 + ? Disrupted pair in contact.				
NGC	455	01 I4.7	+05 03	I4.0	2.7 x 1.0	Psc
Arp	164	Pec. Eruptive.				
		0I 56.6	+05 39	I4.6	1.7 x 0.5	Psc
		Type uncertain. Distorted with a long jet.				
NGC	1024	02 37.8	+10 44	14.0	4.8 x 1.7	Ari
Arp	333	Sb. Extremely faint spiral arms.				
		02 52.6	+14 52	I4.6	1.0 x 0.8	Ari
		Types uncertain. Double system in contact. Distorted.				
NGC	1143	02 53.9	-00 17	14.0	1.4 x 1.2	Cet
	1144			13.0		
Arp	118	E + disrupted spiral.				
		03 22.4	+00 22	15.3	1.2 x 0.7	Tau
		Types uncertain. Triple group in contact.				
		04 41.8	+00 41	I5.3	1.0 x 1.0	Ori
		Type uncertain. Compact with a superimposed star.				
		07 II.4	+73 30	13.7	2.7 x 1.0	Cam
		Pec. Jets + plume.				
NGC	2444	07 45.2	+39 05	14.0	3.0 x 2.3	Lyn
	2445	E + compact objects in a gaseous envelope.				
VV	117					
Arp	143					
NGC	2535	08 09.7	+25 17	13.5	3.6 x 2.5	Cnc
	2536	2 spirals with distorted arms.				
VV	9					
Arp	82					

List of Additional Objects.

Cat	RA	Dec	m	AD	Con
NGC 2608 Arp 12	08 33.8	+24 34	12.9	1.7 x 0.7	Cnc

SBb. Double nucleus or superimposed star.
SN: 1920 - 10.5 mag.

NGC 2648 Arp 89	08 41.3	+14 23	13.0	3.6 x 1.1	Cnc

Sa. Edge-on companion with absorption lanes lies
close to the SE. A faint plume links both.

NGC 2623 VV 79 Arp 243	08 36.9	+25 5I	14.5	2.2 x 0.7	Cnc

Triple system in contact. Strongly distorted with
long plumes, rather like NGC 4038-9.

NGC 2854 Arp 285	09 22.3	+49 19	13.8	1.7 x 0.5	UMa

SBb.

NGC 2944 VV 82 Arp 63	09 37.8	+32 25	14.5	1.1 x 0.4	LMi

Double system in contact. Disrupted.

NGC 3023	09 48.6	+00 44	13.5	3.0 x 1.5	Sex

S. Distorted.

NGC 3239 Arp 263	10 23.8	+17 17	13.5	5.0 x 4.0	Leo

Pec. Faint plumes and knots. A star is superimposed
on the SE edge.

IC 609	10 24.3	-02 06	14.4	1.6 x 0.7	Sex

SBb. Distorted.

NGC 3303	10 33.7	+18 16	14.5	2.5 x 2.0	Leo

Double system with plumes.

NGC 3509 VV 75	11 03.1	+04 58	14.0	2.0 x 0.9	Leo

S pec. Loop.

Mayall's Object VV 32 Arp 148	11 03.6	+40 52	15.0	0.3 x 0.2	UMa

2 objects in contact, appearing to be an edge-on
and a ring-like spirsl.

	11 06.0	+18 34	14.7	1.9 x 1.i	Leo

Type uncertain. Disrupted with plumes.

	11 06.8	+53 46	14.1	0.9 x 0.8	UMa

Pec + jet.

List of Additional Objects.

Cat		RA	Dec	m	AD	Con
IC	677	11 12.6	+12 27	13.6	0.8 x 0.45	Leo

Sb. Distorted.

NGC	3656	11 22.2	+53 59	13.4	1.7 x 1.7	UMa
VV	22
Arp	155

Pec. Loop to the S with a very faint outer ring-like
structure. Fan-shaped absorption across the centre.

| | | 11 26.1 | +79 07 | 14.7 | 1.3 x 0.8 | Cam |

Pec. Eruptive or containing a jet.

| IC | 701 | 11 29.5 | +20 36 | 14.7 | 1.1 x 0.3 | Leo |

Pec. Streamers.

| NGC | 3799 | 11 38.9 | +15 28 | 14.4 | 0.7 x 0.4 | Leo |
| VV | 350 |

S. NGC 3800, 13.1 mag, is in apparent contact close
NW, and has a high surface brightness centre.

| NGC | 3808 | 11 39.5 | +22 35 | 14.1 | 2.5 x 0.8 | Leo |

Types uncertain. Double, distorted system. 2 bridges.

| | | 11 41.0 | +00 29 | 13.7 | 0.4 x 0.4 | Vir |

Pec. Jets + plume.

| | | 11 50.0 | +00 29 | 13.7 | 0.5 x 0.4 | Vir |

Pec. Jet + plume.

NGC	3994	11 56.3	+32 25	13.7	1.0 x 0.5	UMa
VV	249
Arp	313

S. Contains strings of knots like H II regions which
trail along the SE edge.

| NGC | 3995 | 11 56.5 | +32 26 | 12.9 | 2.2 x 0.6 | UMa |

S. VV and Arp as for NGC 3994.

| NGC | 4016 | 11 57.2 | +27 41 | 13.5 | 1.1 x 0.5 | Com |
| Arp | 305 |

SBc/Irr.

IC	883	13 19.4	+34 16	14.8	0.5 x 0.25	CVn
Arp	193
I Zw	55

Jets extend from the SE and SW edges.

| NGC | 5614 | 12 23.1 | +34 58 | 12.9 | 1.0 x 0.8 | Boo |
| | 5615 |

Sa + comp. A plume extends from the companion,
NGC 5615, which is on the NW edge of NGC 5614's
spiral arms.

List of Additional Objects.

Cat		RA	Dec	m	AD	Con
IC	4461	14 33.9	+26 45	14.3	1.0 x 0.9	Boo
	4462	Double system with a bridge.				
		14 59.2	+35 39	14.2	0.9 x 0.9	Boo
		Types uncertain. Jets.				
NGC	7585	23 16.7	-04 48	12.8	1.0 x 0.7	Aqr
Arp	223	S0 pec. A faint, outer arc extends from the N through to the E.				
NGC	7783	23 52.9	+00 16	14.1	1.6 x 0.5	Peg
VV	208	Double system in contact.				
Arp	323.					

Zwicky Compact Galaxies

		RA	Dec	m	AD	Con
III Zw	3	00 14.1	+24 21	14.5	11	And
		Nucleus 3" diameter.				
IV Zw	20	00 46.6	+22 14	14.9	16	And
		Faint plume extends 30" E.				
II Zw	1	01 20.8	-01 10	15.1	15	Cet
III Zw	43	02 02.5	+04 00	14.3	9	Psc
		Nucleus 5" x 3".				
III Zw	53	03 19.4	+15 51	15.4		Ari
		Double system 7.5 apart.				
V Zw	372	04 12.4	+29 06	15.0	90 x 30	Tau
		Nucleus 10" diameter.				
II Zw	33	05 09.7	-02 43	14.0	26 x 13	Ori
		High surface brightness.				
I Zw	20	08 45.0	+45 53	14.9	60	UMa
		Nucleus 18" diameter.				
I Zw	22	08 57.8	+52 23	14.9	13	Uma
I Zw	23	10 19.9	+28 03	15.2	10, 13	LMi
		2 objects separated by 13".				

List of Additional Objects.

Cat	RA	Dec	m	AD	Con
1l Zw 53	11 37.6	+45 44	15.3	13	UMa
I Zw 40	12 23,9	+14 53	13.5	12	Com
	2 objects.			12 x 7	
I Zw 83	14 20.9	+45 50	15.5	10	Boo
II Zw 70	14 49.9	+35 39	14.5	19	Boo
II Zw 71	2 objects both with plumes.			13	
VV 324a,b.					
I Zw 96	14 58.7	+42 07	14.8	21 x 13	Boo
I Zw 117	15 35.0	+43 35	15.3	12	Boo
	MCG 7-32-34, a brighter elliptical is 70" NE.				
I Zw 122	15 36.4	+55 20	15.2	13	CrB
I Zw 125	15 46.8	+37 16	15.2	17	CrB
I Zw 128	15 55.8	+41 57	14.3	10	Dra
	Close to I4 mag galaxy MCG 7-33-16				
I Zw 133	16 08.3	+41 49	15.5	40 x 15	Dra
	Core is I3" diameter.				
I Zw 15l	16 26.8	39 28	15.4	16 x 12	Her
I Zw 165	16 47.6	+48 44	14.6	10	Dra
I Zw 205	18 25.7	+39 19	15.0	30 x 10	Lyr
	The nucleus is I0" diameter.				
II Zw 136	21 31.2	+10 03	14.6	25 x 10	Peg
II Zw 187	23 02.8	+22 29	14.7	8	Peg
I Zw 153	23 20.8	+25 23	15.0		Peg
	Double system 8" apart.				

List of Additional Objects.

Seyfert Galaxies.

Cat		RA	Dec	m	AD	Con
Mkn	335	00 03.8	+19 55	14.0	15	Peg
		Stellar in appearance.				
NGC	262	00 46.1	+31 42	15.5	24	And
Mkn	348	Spherical + outer envelope.				
Mkn	352	00 57.1	+31 33	15.0	15 x 12	Psc
		Spheroid with diffuse edges.				
NGC	449	01 13.1	+32 50	15.5	27 x 16	Psc
Mkn	1					
Mkn	372	02 46.5	+19 05	15.5	20 x 14	Ari
Mkn	3	06 10.1	+71 03	15.0	35 x 23	Cam
IC	450	06 45.5	+74 29	15.0	20	Cam
Mkn	6	Displays a faint outer envelope.				
Mkn	374	06 55.7	+54 17	15.5	7	Lyn
		A 16.5 mag system is in interaction.				
Mkn	10	07 43.2	+61 03	14.5	20	Cam
		Pec. spiral with stellar centre.				
Mkn	382	07 52.0	+39 19	15.5	12 x 7	Lyn
NGC 2691		08 51.5	+39 44	14.5	24 x 18	Lyn
3C 390.3		18 45.6	+79 43	13.8	20	Dra
		Variable, at times reaching a minimum of 16.2 mag.				
Mkn	315	23 01.5	+22 21	15.0	15	Peg.
II Zw 187		Compact.				

(Finding charts for the above 13 objects are shown overleaf).

List of Additional Objects.

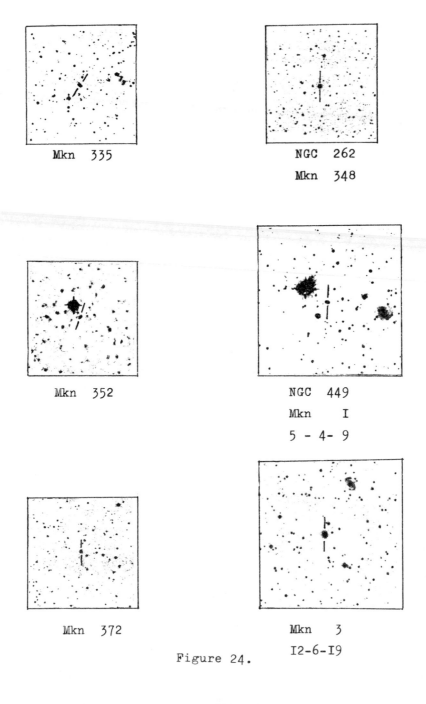

Mkn   335

NGC   262
Mkn   348

Mkn   352

NGC   449
Mkn   I
5 - 4- 9

Mkn   372

Mkn   3
I2-6-I9

Figure 24.

List of Additional Objects.

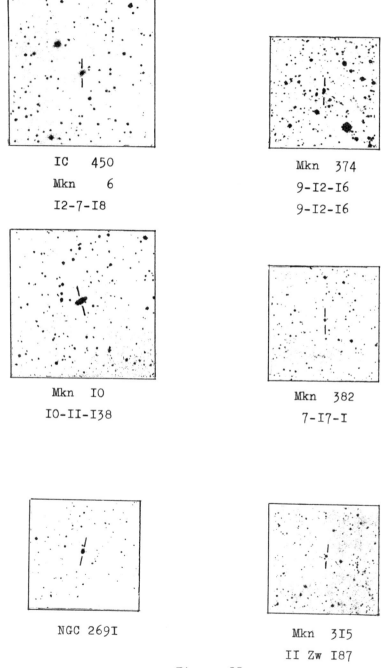

IC   450
Mkn   6
I2-7-I8

Mkn   374
9-I2-I6
9-I2-I6

Mkn   IO
IO-II-I38

Mkn   382
7-I7-I

NGC 269I

Mkn   3I5
II Zw I87

Figure 25.

List of Additional Objects.

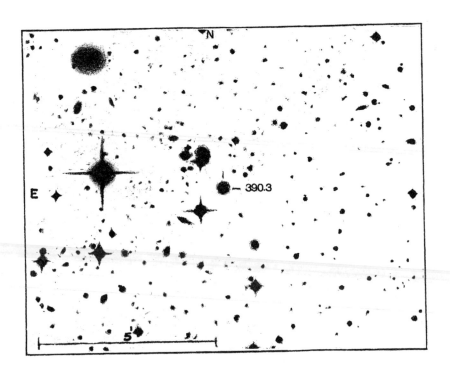

Figure 26. 3C 390.3. Reproduced by
courtesy of M.V. Penston, Royal
Greenwich Observatory.

List of Additional Objects

Variable Extragalactic Sources.

In this section we give details of seven variable sources. These consist of one QSO, three Seyfert galaxies and three BL Lac objects. Positions, types and maxima and minima are shown below, while finding charts and comparison sequences appear in the pages following.

Cat	RA	Dec	m^{max}	m^{min}	Con
BW Tau	04 31.8	+05 18	13.7	14.6	Tau
3C 120	Seyfert.				
PKS 0430+05					
OJ 287	08 53.4	+20 12	12.0	15.0	Cnc
	BL Lac.				
W Com	12 20.3	+28 22	11.5	16.5	Com
ON 231	Seyfert.				
X Com	12 57.9	+28 04	16.1	17.2	Com
	Seyfert. Although this reaches a low magnitude at maximum, owners of large telescopes may wish to attempt to catch its upper limit either visually or photographically.				
AP Lib	15 16.3	-24 16	14.5	16.0	Lib
PKS 1514-24	BL Lac.				
3C 371	18 07.0	+69 49	13.1	15.9	Dra
	N-galaxy.				
BL Lac	22 01.6	+42 10	12.0	15.5	Lac
	BL Lac.				

208

List of Additional Objects.

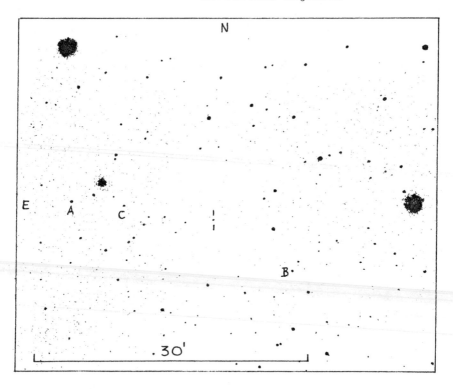

Figure 27. Finding chart for BW Tau (3C 120). The
comparison sequences of stars A, B and C are shown
below.

Comparison Stars for BW Tau.

Star.		m_{pv}
A	-	13.6
B	-	14.3
C	-	15.0

List of Additional Objects.

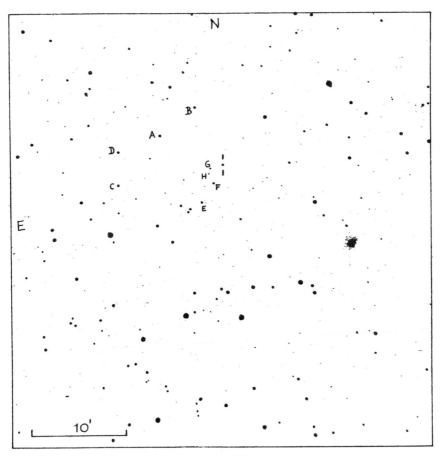

Figure 28. Finding chart for OJ 287. The comparison
sequence of stars A to H is shown below.

Comparison Stars for OJ 287.

Star		m_{pv}	Star		m_{pv}
A	–	12.9	E	–	14.0
B	–	13.2	F	–	14.2
C	–	13.3	G	–	14.6
D	–	13.6	H	–	14.9

List of Additional Objects

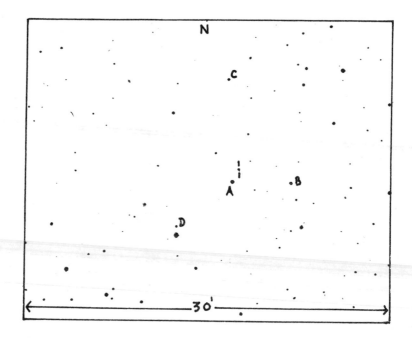

Figure 29. Finding chart for W Com. The
comparison sequence of stars A to D is
shown below.

Comparison Stars for W Com.

Star	m_{pg}
A	12.67
B	13.68
C	14.47
D	15.30

List of Additional Objects

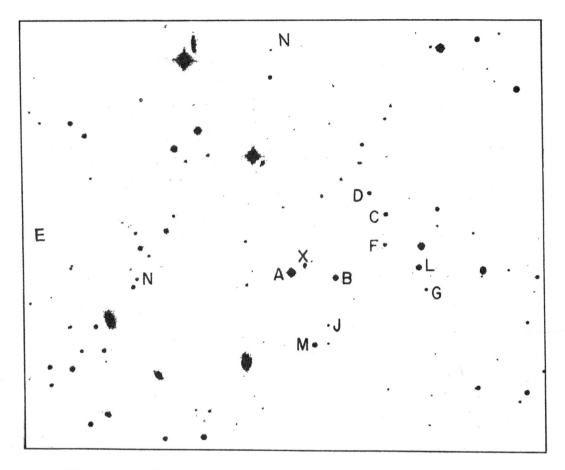

Figure 30. Finding chart for X Com. The comparison sequence of stars A to N is shown below. Photograph taken by
J. Hoessel with the Palomar 48-inch Schmidt. Reproduced
by courtesy of R.F. Green, Steward Observatory.

Star		m_{pv}	Star		m_{pv}	Star		m_{pv}
A	-	11.84	F	-	15.64	M	-	14.16
B	-	14.24	G	-	17.62	N	-	17.59
C	-	16.14	J	-	17.71			
D	-	15.74	L	-	13.02			

List of Additional Objects

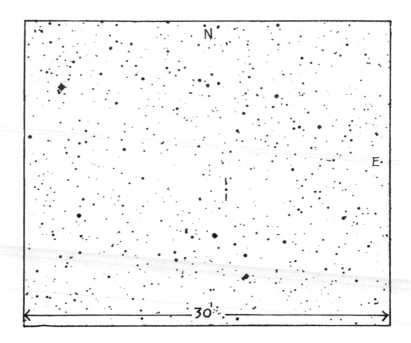

Finding chart for AP Lib. No sequence is
available for this object.

List of Additional Objects.

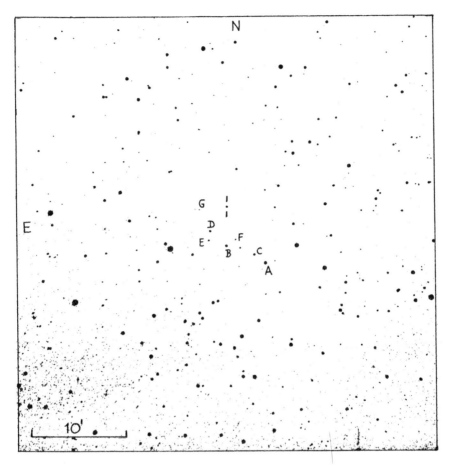

Figure 32. Finding chart for 3C 371. The comparison sequence of stars A to G is below.

Comparison Stars for 3C 371.

Star.		m_{pv}			
A	–	13.5	E	–	15.1.
B	–	14.3	F	–	15.7
C	–	14.8	G	–	16.0
D	–	15.0			

List of Additional Objects.

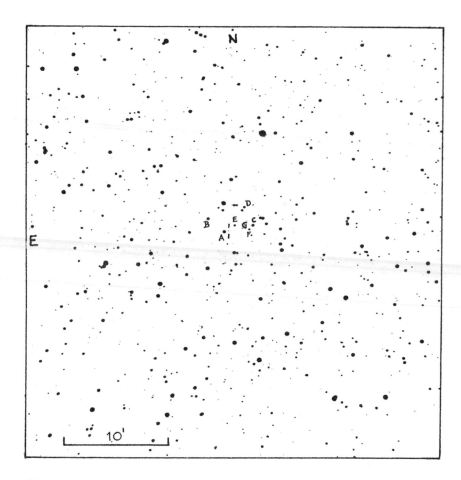

Figure 33. Finding chart for BL Lac. The comparison
sequence of stars A to G is below

Comparison Stars for BL Lac.

Star		m_{pv}	Star		m_{pv}
A	-	12.90	E	-	14.28
B	-	13.26	F	-	14.42
C	-	13.43	G	-	15.48
D	-	14.10			

215

APPENDIX 1.

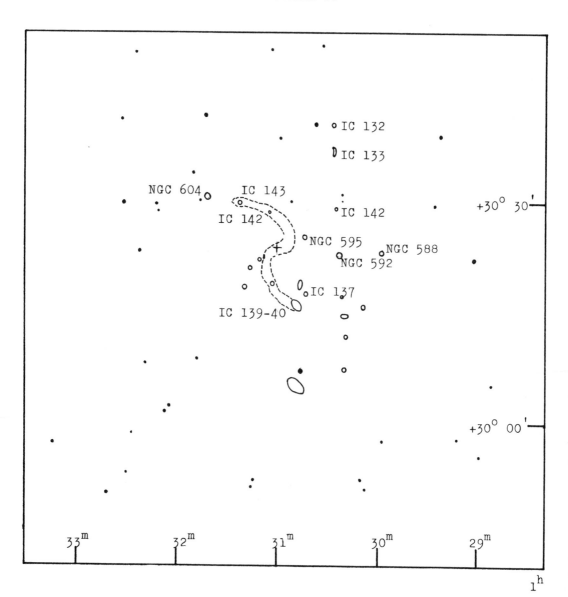

Figure 34. Positions of emission regions in
M33. From a chart by Ronald J. Buta, McDonald
Observatory, University of Texas. Coordinates
are for 1950.

APPENDIX 2.

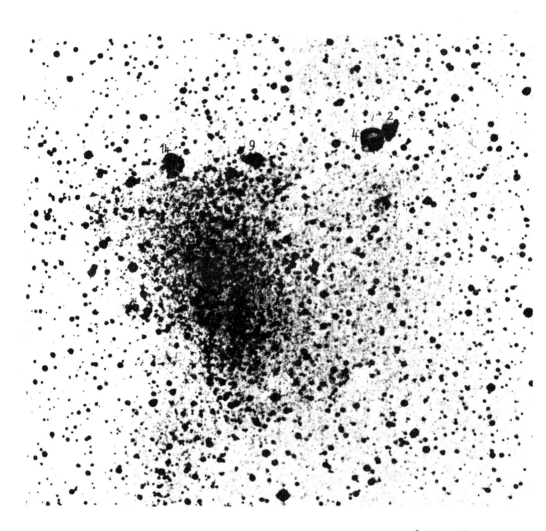

Figure 35. Four brightest H II regions in NGC 6822. The
numbers on the chart correspond to the following Hubble
designations: (2) = Hubble I; (4) = Hubble III; (9) =
Hubble V; (14) = Hubble X.

APPENDIX 3.
THE DISTANCES OF GALAXIES.

   The first distances to external galaxies were derived by Hubble in the
early 1920's, when Cepheid variables in M31 and M33 were used to obtain
figures of about 340 kpc. Due to observations by Baade with the 100-inch reflector on Mt. Wilson some twenty years later, it was found that the Cepheids
consist of two types, I and II, and that use of the former to obtain distances of M31 increased the distance figure considerably. As well as Cepheids,
other types of stars can be used to obtain distances, these being RR Lyrae's,
long-period variables, giant stars in globular clusters and novae and supernovae. In addition there are H II regions and, leaving individual objects,
such parameters as surface brightness, radial velocities, spectral features
and sizes.

   In extragalactic distance determination the first stepping stone beyond
the Galaxy itself is the Local Group of galaxies. Here individual stars can
be compared with identical objects in the Galaxy, for which accurate absolute
magnitudes are known. The difference between the apparent magnitude and the
absolute magnitude (m-M) is the distance modulus; distance figures obtained
by this method are known as luminosity distances. By this method stars in
such Local Group galaxies as the Magellanic Clouds, M31, IC 1613 and the
dwarf systems in Leo, Draco and Ursa Minor have been observed and distances
derived, the stars used being classical Cepheids and RR Lyrae's.

   Cepheids, however, can be used up to distances of about 4Mpc (m-M = 28),
which takes in galaxies outside of the Local Group, although still fairly
near. In all these cases correction must be made for the effects of any absorption in the observed galaxies or along the line of sight to them. RR
Lyrae stars, not being very luminous intrinsically, are observable out to
slightly lower distances than Cepheids in other galaxies, the limit being
of the order of m-M = 22 mag.

   Finally we can take novae, which can be used as distance indicators out
to 10 Mpc. It is only for M31, however, that accurate work on novae has been
carried out, principally by Arp, Rosino and Schmidt-Kaler. Comparison of the
M31 distance moduli obtained by classical Cepheids and novae shows good
agreement. While similar results are extant for novae in the Magellanic
Clouds, the certainty of the work on the Clouds novae is not absolute. Due
to their high intrinsic luminosities, novae can be used as distance indicators for objects in the M81 and M101 groups, where their apparent
magnitudes would be between 17 and 18 mag.

   Beyond the Local Group other methods of deriving distances are required;
these include the 3rd brightest cluster galaxy, the diameters of H II
regions, supernovae, galaxy diameters and finally radial velocities.
The H II region diameter method has been used out to about 10 Mpc, as it
appears that angular diameters of these emission regions are remarkably
similar for galaxies of a given type. An advantage is that no corrections
need be made for absorption but there must be complete resolution in order
to obviate seeing effects, and therefore Hα filters used in conjunction with
large telescopes are essential.

220

Supernovae would appear to be extremely useful in distance derivation, as direct comparison with galactic supernovae can be achieved, and no intermediate steps are necessary. The problem here is the lack of very accurate data on known galactic supernovae, including the outburst of 1572, for which the most accurate information is available.

In concluding this brief coverage of extragalactic distances we come to the red shift, whereby the degree to which spectral lines are moved to the red end of a spectrum is directly related to distance. H II region diameters, luminosity classifications, mass-to-light ratios, galaxy diameters and other methods have been used to arrive at a figure for this effect, known as the Hubble constant. Currently the figure used is 50 km s^{-1} Mpc, although figures widely different from this have been used in the past. The further the galaxy the greater the redshift, until at extreme distances, such as those evinced by QSO's, spectral lines normally located in the ultraviolet are shifted into optical regions of the spectra, as shown below in Figure 36. At large redshifts the normal formula for recession of the galaxies is no longer viable, and a new equation, accounting for relativistic effects, is used.

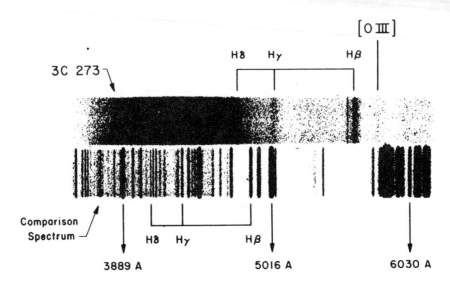

Figure 36. Spectrum of the QSO 3C 273 showing the Balmer hydrogen lines with a redshift z = 0.158. The comparison spectrum is of hydrogen, helium and neon. (Reprinted courtesy of Maarten Schmidt, Hale Observatories).

APPENDIX 4.

NON-VELOCITY REDSHIFTS.

The redshift exhibited by the spectra of galaxies is, as we have seen, taken to indicate distance, high redshift objects being considered to be at extreme distances, with QSO's being extreme examples. For some years, however, it has been felt by some researchers that this redshift-distance relation is not applicable in all cases, and a great deal of work on this subject has been undertaken by Arp and others.

As a result of these observations, evidence has been produced to show that a link seems to show between the companions of large galaxies and QSO's, and furthermore that field QSO's, unrelated to other galaxies, are not the norm. Arp feels that the probability of any line-of-sight effect with galaxies and QSO's is remote, and therefore that we are dealing with physical processes, and that the bright galaxies act as catalysts and eject the QSO's. It is postulated that as a result of this the ejected QSO will display a high redshift and that as evolutionary processes in the object take place the redshift will decrease until, after a long period of time, the observed redshift will be a true distance-related feature of the object.

Observations which seem to indicate such processes have been made, and collations of this work show that the high redshift QSO's are situated closest to the bright, parent galaxies while the low redshift QSO's appear at larger angular diameters from the latter, Bringing into the picture the BL Lac objects, the sequence of events is thought to be as follows. Initially the parent galaxy ejects an object which is seen as a BL Lac-type system;ffrom here the object evolves into a high redshift QSO of high luminosity and finally into a low redshift QSO of low luminosity. Examples of close associations between bright galaxies and QSO's are NGC 7413 and 3C 455, IC 1746 and PHL 1226 and NGC 3079 and Mkn 132.

Not all cases of anomalous redshifts are concerned with galaxy/ QSO pairings, however. Probably the prime example of this is to be found in Stephan's Quintet, where the redshift of one of the group, NGC 7320, is considerably lower than the redshifts of the remainder of the group. An interesting group of objects in this context is to be found in the neighbourhood of the Seyfert galaxy NGC 4151. These include NGC 4156, a small elliptical system, a dwarf-like galaxy (MCG 7-25-46), a luminosity class I spiral and, probably of most interest, an absorption-line galaxy displaying a bright filament on the end of which is three emission-line objects of almost stellar appearance. This association, with the respective redshifts indicated, is shown overleaf in Figure 39. Arp has pointed out that the region of NGC 4151 appears rich in objects of peculiar morphology and anomalous redshifts, and that such an amalgam of unusual systems is far from ubiquitous in the sky.

Appendix 4.

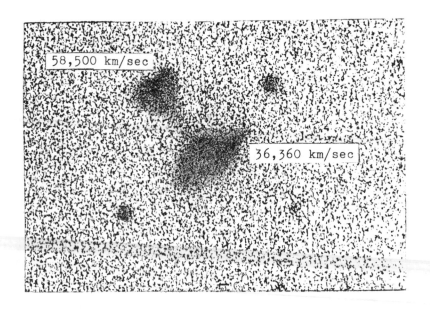

Figure 37. Photograph of Nonequilibrium Number 3.
Reproduced courtesy of Halton Arp.

The amount of material published which is concerned with this topic
is considerable, and we have no space here to even broadly cover all
of its aspects. For those wishing to delve more deeply into the subject
a review up to 1976 can be found in Arp, 1976, I.A.U. Colloquium No. 37,
while for a comprehensive up-to-date survey there is Arp, 1980 in
Proceedings 9th Texas Symp. Relativistic Astrophysics (Ann. NY Acad.
Sci., 336, 1-599). For an interesting discussion on the pros and cons
of the subject there is The Redshift Controversy, Benjamin, 1973.

APPENDIX 5.

Illustrated below and overleaf are 12 galaxies from Arp's Atlas of Peculiar Galaxies. All the examples shown are of objects which appear in the preceding catalogue, thereby allowing comparisons. They are shown in RA order and not as they appear in the original publication. The photographs are reprinted courtesy of Halton Arp and The Astrophysical Journal, published by the University of Chicago Press; © 1966 The American Astronomical Society.

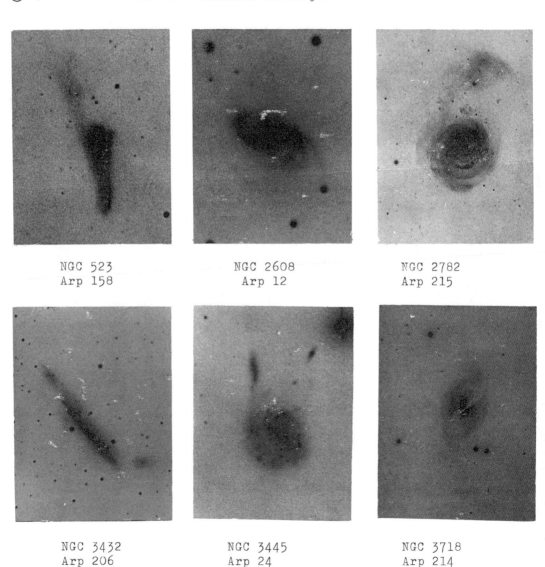

NGC 523
Arp 158

NGC 2608
Arp 12

NGC 2782
Arp 215

NGC 3432
Arp 206

NGC 3445
Arp 24

NGC 3718
Arp 214

Figure 38

Appendix 5.

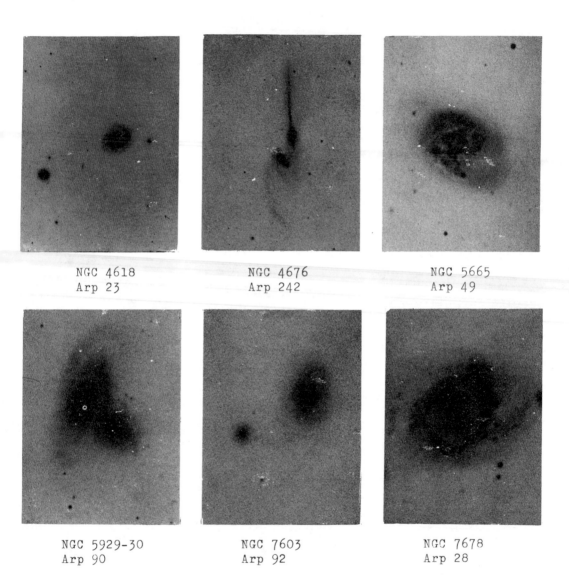

NGC 4618   NGC 4676   NGC 5665
Arp 23   Arp 242   Arp 49

NGC 5929-30   NGC 7603   NGC 7678
Arp 90   Arp 92   Arp 28

Figure 39

APPENDIX 6.

Illustrated on the following five pages are drawings of six galaxies made by Ronald J. Buta using the 36 and 30-inch reflectors of the McDonald Observatory, University of Texas. All of the objects depicted appear in the present catalogue and drawings of them with smaller apertures have also been shown. Due to the amount of detail shown in these drawings, they have been reproduced to the exact scale of the originals, although this will be reduced by 10% during the printing process. Details of the telescopes and magnifications used are shown for each drawing.

Appendix 6.

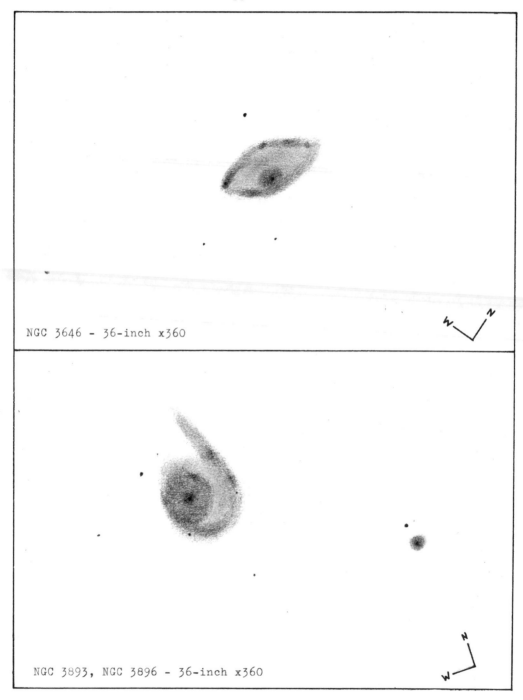

NGC 3646 - 36-inch x360

NGC 3893, NGC 3896 - 36-inch x360

Appendix 6.

NGC 3034, M82 - 36-inch x360

Appendix 6.

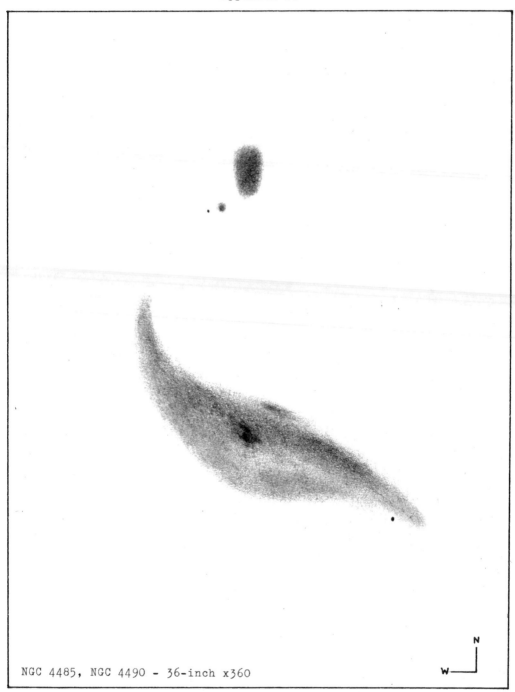

NGC 4485, NGC 4490 - 36-inch x360

N

W

Appendix 6.

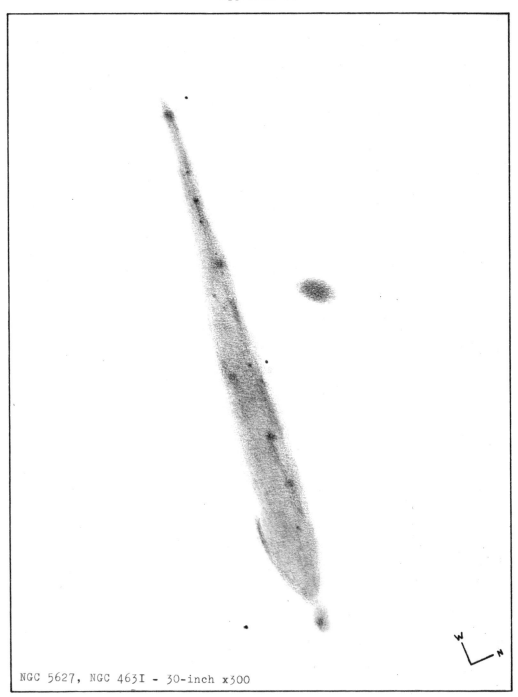

NGC 5627, NGC 463I - 30-inch x300

230

Appendix 6.

NGC 5I28 - 36-inch

N

W

APPENDIX 7.

FAINT SYSTEMS NEAR NGC GALAXIES.

The following 4I faint galaxies have been observed by Malcolm Thompson using the $15\frac{1}{2}$-inch reflector of Westmont College Observatory, Santa Barbara, California. No detail is apparent in these objects, but as some observers with suitable telescopes may wish to attempt observations, we show these objects below. Their positions relative to the nearby NGC galaxies have been measured by Thomson on the O (blue) prints of the Palomar Sky Survey. Column 'A' gives the NGC galaxies; 'B' their RA and Dec; 'C' their magnitudes; 'D' the designation of the faint galaxies; 'E' their magnitudes; 'F' their offsets from the NGC galaxies in RA; 'G' their offsets in Dec. In the designations of the faint systems, CGCG = Catalogue of Galaxies & Clusters of Galaxies; U = Uppsala Catalogue of Galaxies and MCG = Morphological Catalogue of Galaxies.

A	B	C	D	E	F	G
20	$00^h06^m.8$ +33 03	$14^m.0$	U00065	$13^m.8$	1 24" p	15' S
262	46.1 31 40	14.0	U 499 (Notes)		8 f	Same Dec
507	01 20.9 33 00	12.8	MCG 5-4-48	16.0	18 f	4' N
1346	03 27.7 05 43	15.0	MCG-1-9-41	16.0	6 p	I' S
1573	04 29.0 73 10	14.0	MCG 12-5-6	15.0	1 12 p	2' N
1573			MCG 12-5-7	15.0	48 p	3' S
2521	08 04.8 57 55	14.0	MCG 10-12-80	14.0	36 f	Same Dec
2719	57.0 35 56	14.0	MCG 6-20-18	14.5	Same RA	30" S
2785	09 12.0 41 06	14.0	MCG 7-19-39	14.0	30 p	2' S
2798	14.2 42 11	13.0	MCG 7-19-54	14.0	6 p	5' S
2832	16.6 33 57	13.5	MCG 6-21-24	15.0	1 00 f	1' S
2863	21.2 10 12	13.0	Uncatalogued		12 p	Same Dec
2880	25.7 62 42	12.6	Anon CGCG	15.I	Same RA	3' N
3079	58.5 55 56	11.10	MCG 9-17-9	15.0	40 p	2' N
3079			MCG 9-17-27	12.0	6 24 f	$2°36S$
3168	10 13.0 60 29	14.7	MCG 10-15-54	14.0	30 f	3' N
3209	17.8 25 45	13.9	MCG 4-25-4	15.2	20 f	1' N
3214	19.8 57 18	14.0	MCG 10-15-70	15.0	36 p	1' S
3219	19.7 38 49	14.3	MCG 7-21-49	14.7	11 p	1' N
3219			MCG 7-21-47	14.7	30 p	4' S
3245	24.5 28 52	11.8	Anon CGCG	15.4	18 p	8' N

Appendix 7.

A	B	C	D	E	F	G
3725	11 31.0 +62 10	$14^{m}.0$	MCG 10-17-3	$14^{m}.0$	12" p	4' S
3738	33.1 54 48	12.0	MCG 9-19-125	15.0	48 p	8' N
3888	45.0 56 15	12.7	MCG 9-19-191	16,0	18 f	2' N
4108	12 04.5 67 26	13.1	Anon CGCG		1' 6 f	14' N
4211	12.9 28 27	14.4	MCG 5-29-46	15.5	36 f	2' N
4741	48.7 47 58	13.2	MCG 8-23-97	16.0	18 p	15' N
4834	54.2 52 33	15.0	MCG 9-21-71	16.0	2 00 f	15' N
4926	59.6 27 53	I4.1	MCG 5-31-107	15.1	12 f	2' N
4926			Uncatalogued		9 f	2' N
4926			Uncatalogued		6 p	1' S
4944	13 01.5 28 27	13,3	U408167 (Notes)		6 f	Same Dec
5975	15 37.7 21 36	14.5	MCG 4-37-21	14.5	12 f	3' N
7081	21 28.8 02 17	14.0	MCG 0-55-2	14.0	1 00 f	3' S
7223	22 08.0 40 46	12.9	Uncatalogued		3 p	40" N
7265	20.2 35 57	13.0	Anon CGCG		38 f	10' S
7265			MCG 6-49-9	14.0	18 f	1' S
7342	35.8 35 12	14.0	MCG 6-49-58	14.0	18 f	10' S
7342			MCG 6-49-56	15.0	12 f	7' S
7342			MCG 6-49-60	15.0	24 f	9' S
7342			MCG 6-49-62	16.0	30 f	10' S.

APPENDIX 8.

Photographic References.

Over the years, many photographs of galaxies have appeared in books
and journals, and a few examples of such sources are presented below.
For an overall view of most of the sky there are the Palomar Sky
Survey prints, although differing degrees of detail are blotted out
in some cases, due to overexposure. For interacting and peculiar
galaxies there are the respective atlases of Vorontsov-Velyaminov and
Arp, to which reference is given in the text.

Roberts, I.   1912, Mon. Not. Roy. Astr. Soc.
                                72, 408. (NGC 278).

Randers, G.   1940, Ap. J., 92, 236.
                                (NGC 488).

Johnson, H.M.   1961, Ap. J., 133, 314.
                                (NGC 524).

Zwicky, F.   1964, Astr. J., 69, 759.
Karpowicz, M.   (NGC 3992).

Burbidge, E.M. & G.R.   1965, Ap. J., 142, 649.
Prendergast, K.M.   (NGC 972).

Kiang. T.   1967, Ap. J. Lett., 150, L31.
                                (NGC 3353 + Haro galaxies).

Simkin, S.M.   1967, Astr. J., 72, 1032.
                                (NGC 2683).

Vorontsov-Velyaminov, B.A. 1967, in Modern Astrophysics. Gauthier-
                                (New morphological types).   Villars.

Ables, H.D.   1971, Pub. United States Naval Obs.
                                Vol. XX, Part IV.
                                (NGC 1569, NGC 6946, IC 342, IC 356,
                                IC 1613, A 1009).

Penny, A.J.   1972, Observatory, 93, 27.
Fairall, A.P.   (NGC 1343).

Lynds, B.T. et al.   1973, Ap. J., 182, 659.
                                (NGC 4314).

Appendix 8.

Shostak, G.S.

1973, Astron. & Astrophys, 24, 411.
(NGC 4236).

Sandage, A.

1975, Stars & Stellar Systems, Chicago.
Vol. 9. (NGC's 157, 628, 925,
1072, 1300, 1302, 2366, 2811,
2841, 3185, 3504, 3623, 3810,
3898, 4088, 4293, 4395, 4643,
4569, 5055, 5204, 5236, 5248,
5273, 5457, 6643, 6814, 6951,
7741, 7743, IC 2574, Ho II).

Kormendy, J.

1977, Ap. J., 214, 359.
(Red compact galaxies).

Wehinger, P.A.
Wyckoff, S.

1977, Mon. Not. Roy. Astr. Soc.,
181, 211.
(13 Markarian Seyferts).

Arp, H.C.

1980, Ap. J., 239, 469.
(NGC 53, NGC 7603, AM 059-4024,
AM 2054-2210).
1980, Ap. J., 240, 415.
(NGC 2859 + companions).

APPENDIX 9.

BIBLIOGRAPHY.

Classification.

Wolf, M.	1908, Publ. Ap. Inst. Konig Heidelberg, Vol. 3, No. 5.
Hubble. E.	1936. The Realm of the Nebulae. Yale.
Seyfert, C.	1943, Ap.J. 97,28.
Bergh, S. van den.	1960, Pub. David Dunlap Obs. Vol II, No. 6.
Vorontsov-Velyaminov, B.A. Krasnogorskaya, A.	1962, Morphological Catalogue Moscow of Galaxies, Vol. 1.
Bergh, S. van den.	1966, Astr.J., 71, 922-926.
Zwicky, Z.	1966, Ap.J., 143, 192.
Lequeux, P.	Structure and Evolution of Gordon & Galaxies. Breach.
Oke, J.B. Gunn, J.E.	1974 Ap.J., 189, L5 - L8.
Ulrich, M.H., et al.	1975, Ap.J., 198, 261-266.
Page, T.	1975, in Stars & Stellar Systems Chicago. Systems, Vol. 9. (Ed. A. Sandage, M. Sandage, J. Kristian).
Sandage, A.	Ibid.
Shane, C.D.	Ibid.
Kunth, D. Sargent, W.L.W.	1978, ESO Preprint No. 30.

Distribution.

Materne, J.	1974, Astron. & Ap., 33, 451-454.
Peterson, B.A.	1974, in IAU Symp. 58. Reidel. (Ed. J.R. Shakeshaft).

236

Appendix 9.

Vaucouleurs, G. de.   1975, in Stars & Stellar Systems   Chicago.
                      Vol. 9. (Ed. A. Sandage,
                      M. Sandage, J. Kristian).

Schuster, S.   1976, Astron. & Ap., 49, 129.
West, R.M.

Cesarsky, D.A., et al. 1977, Astron. & Ap., 61, L31-33.

Lanstsen, S.L., et al. 1977, Astron. & Ap., 54, 639.

Tammann, G.A.   1978, IAU Symp.77.   Reidel.
Kraan, R.   (Ed. E.M. Berkhuijsen, R. Wielebinski).

Tully, R.B.   Ibid.
Fisher, J.R.

Thuan, T.X.   1979, Ap.J.Lett., LII.
Martin, G.E.

Formation and Evolution.

Lequeux, P.   1969, Structure & Evolution   Gordon &
                      of Galaxies.   Breach.

Strom, S.E.   1978, in IAU Symp.77.   Reidel.
Strom, K.M.

Tinsley, B.M.   Ibid.   Reidel.

Tinsley, B.M.   1979, Preprint of Talk to Royal Soc.

Visser, H.C.D.   1978, in IAU Symp.77.   Reidel.

Gaseous and Stellar Content.

Roberts, M.S.   1970, in IAU Symp. 44   Reidel.
                      (Ed. D.S. Evans).

Spinrad, H.   1975, in Stars & Stellar Systems, Chicago.
Peimbert, M.   Vol. 9. (Ed. A. Sandage,
                      M. Sandage, J. Kristian).

Knapp, S.R., et al.   1978, Ap.J., 222, 800-814

Whiteoak, J.B.   1978, in IAU Symp. 77.   Reidel.

Appendix 9.

Hulst, J.M. van der.   1979, Astron. & Ap., 71, 131-140.

Ibid.   1979, Astron. & Ap., 75, 97-111.

Nuclei.

Morgan, W.W.   1958, P.A.S.P., 70, 364.

Morgan, W.W.   1959, P.A.S.P., 71, 394.

Sersic, J.L.   1965, P.A.S.P., 77, 287.
Pastoriza,

Ambartsumian, B.   1966, Trans. IAU, 12B, 578.

Sandage, A.   1971, in Nuclei of Galaxies,   N. Holland
                          (Ed. D.J.K. O'Connell).   Pub. Co.

Thomassian,   1972, Ap.J. Lett. 178, L47.

                          1978, P.A.S.P., 90, 241-243.

Seyfert Galaxies, QSO's and Related Objects.

Morgan, W.W.   1970, in IAU Symp. 44.   Reidel
                          (Ed. D.S Evans).

Schwarzschild, M.   1971, Bull. Am. Astr. Soc., 3, 243.

Oke, J.B.   1974, Ap.J., 189, L5-L8.
Gunn, J.E.

Ulrich, M.H., et al.   1975, Ap.J., I89, 261-266.

Weedman, D.W.   1976, Q.J. Roy. Astr. Soc., 17, 227.

Kellerman, K.I., et al.   1977, Ap.J., 211, 658-668.

Condon, J.J.   1978, Ap.J., 221, 456.
Dressel, L.L.

Rees, M.J.   1978, Observatory, 98, 210-223.

Hazard, C.   1979, in Active Galactic Nuclei   Cambridge
                          (Ed. C. Hazard & S. Mitton).   U.P.

Osterbrock, D.   Ibid.

Appendix 9.

Graham, J.A.   1979, Ap.J., 232, 60-73.

Zotov,   1979, Ap.J., 229, L5.
Tapin,

Interacting and Peculiar Galaxies.

Vorontsov-   1959, Atlas of Interacting   Moscow
Velyaminov, B.A.   Galaxies.

Arp, H.C.   1966, Ap.J. Supp., 123, 1-20.

Lynds, R.   1974, Ap.J., 194, 569-585.
Toomre, A.

Thompson, L.A.   1977, PASP, 89,
Gregory, S.A.

Fosbury, R.A.E.   1977, M. Not. Roy. Astr. Soc.,
Hawarden, T.G.   178, 473-487.

Vorontsov-   1977, Astron. & Ap. Supp. 28,
Velyaminov, B.A.   1-118.

Toomre, A.   1978, in IAU Symp. 77.   Reidel

Schweizer, F.   Ibid.

Toomre, A.   1980, Private communication.

Observation of Galaxies.

Stebbins, J.   1952, Ap.J., 284.
Whitford, A.E.

Petit, E.   1954, Ap.J., 120, 413.

Holmberg, E.   1958, Medd. Lunds Astr. Obs.
                        Ser. 2., No. 136.

Ables, H.D.   1971, Pub. U.S. Naval Obs.,
                        2nd Ser., XX - Part I.